Concentrate

D1152777

Bonus study and revision support available **free,** online

online resource centre
www.oxfordtextbooks.co.uk/orc/concentrate/

Take your learning further:

➤ Multiple-choice questions

➤ Outline exam answers

➤ Revision technique advice

➤ Flashcards of key cases

➤ An interactive glossary

... and much more

New to this Edition

- Coverage of new case law, including *Fitzwilliam v Richall Holdings Services Ltd* [2013], *89 Holland Park (Management) Ltd v Hicks* [2013], and *Wilkinson v Kerdene Ltd* [2013]
- Expanded coverage of s144 Legal Aid, Sentencing and Punishment of Offenders Act 2012, and proprietary estoppel
- Discussion of proposed reforms to easements as recommended in The Law Commission Report No. 327
- Updated figures and Revision tips throughout

Land Law
Concentrate

4th edition

Victoria Sayles

Associate Principal Lecturer, BPP
University College of Professional Studies

OXFORD
UNIVERSITY PRESS

OXFORD
UNIVERSITY PRESS

Great Clarendon Street, Oxford, OX2 6DP,
United Kingdom

Oxford University Press is a department of the University of Oxford.
It furthers the University's objective of excellence in research, scholarship,
and education by publishing worldwide. Oxford is a registered trade mark of
Oxford University Press in the UK and in certain other countries

First edition 2009
Second edition 2011
Third edition 2013
Impression: 1

Published in the United States of America by Oxford University Press
198 Madison Avenue, New York, NY 10016, United States of America

British Library Cataloguing in Publication Data
Data available

Library of Congress Control Number: 2014940644

ISBN 978-0-19-870381-5

Printed in Great Britain by
Ashford Colour Press Ltd, Gosport, Hampshire

Contents

Table of cases

Table of cases

✳✳✳✳✳✳✳✳✳✳

Table of cases

✱✱✱✱✱✱✱✱✱✱

Table of cases

✱✱✱✱✱✱✱✱✱✱✱

Table of legislation

Table of legislation

****

Table of legislation

Table of legislation

✳✳✳✳✳✳✳✳✳✳

UK Secondary Legislation

European legislation

International legislation

#1

Introduction:
proprietary rights

The examination

Issues discussed in this chapter may be examined as self-contained topics, specifically those relating to the definition of land. Typical problem questions may involve:

- assessing how far a person's rights over a piece of land extend, where, for example, there has been an invasion of airspace or removal of vegetation;
- assessing whether a purchaser can insist upon the return of numerous items removed from a property between exchange of contracts and completion of sale (ie whether the items removed were fixtures or chattels);
- assessing who has superior rights over items found on land.

(Note that these issues may also form part of another question. Take guidance from your own course as to where these issues may appear in a question.)

Depending upon the nature of your course, you may be required to explore the concepts of proprietary and personal rights and their distinguishing characteristics. Otherwise, much of the information contained in this chapter may be treated as foundation material: not specifically examinable by itself, but information which you must understand in order to comprehend how land law works.

Key facts

- Proprietary rights govern your ability to use and enjoy both land you physically possess and land physically possessed by others.

- Proprietary rights are rights in the land itself which makes them capable of enduring changes of ownership to the land.

- Whilst technically all land is owned by the Crown, holding an **estate** in land, and in particular a freehold estate that gives you rights to possess, enjoy, and use the land forever, is tantamount to actual ownership.

- Holding an estate in land gives you rights to possess, enjoy, and use the land beyond just the physical surface area of that land.

- Apart from an estate in land, the other type of proprietary right that exists is an interest in land.

- Whilst an estate gives you a slice of time during which you are entitled to use and enjoy land you physically possess, an interest gives you rights to use and enjoy land physically possessed by another.

- Proprietary rights can be either legal or equitable in status.

Chapter overview

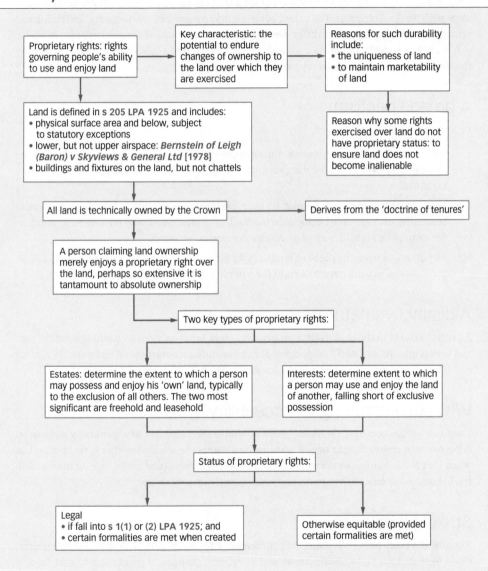

Introduction: proprietary rights

Property law concerns the regulation and management of people's enjoyment and relationships with particular things. The extent of the ability to enjoy and use property, and rights and remedies stemming from this, differ depending upon the nature of the property in question.

Where the property in question is land, rights governing people's ability to use and enjoy the land are known as **proprietary rights**.

A broad spectrum

Proprietary rights can:

- vary from being very extensive, for example the ability to use and possess land to the exclusion of everyone else (tantamount to ownership), to quite narrow, for example a right to fish;
- relate to what you can, or cannot, do over land that you physically possess, for example the ability to carry on a business on the land, or to land physically possessed by another, for example a right of way or an ability to restrict building;
- be numerous over one piece of land: a right for a person to physically possess it; a right for a person to walk over it; a right for a person to restrict building on it etc.

A distinctive nature

As seen as rights in the land itself, a proprietary right is not only enforceable against the person who originally granted it to you, but also, in certain circumstances, enforceable against any other person who may come to the land over which that right is exercised.

Why such enduring enforceability?

Land is a unique commodity: no one piece of land is the same. It's also generally expensive. A person who enjoys a right over a piece of land wants the assurance that it will not be lost when that land changes ownership. Without such assurance, land could lose its marketability, become economically stagnant and consequently lose its value.

Striking a balance

Equally, if a piece of land became overburdened by too many proprietary rights being exercised over it, such rights being capable of surviving changes of ownership to that land, it may become an unattractive investment. Consequently, some rights, although exercised in relation to land, are not given proprietary status. Licences are an example. They remain, for most, **personal rights**, enforceable only against the person who granted it to you and not against the land itself.

✅ **Looking for extra marks?**

A proprietary right is considered to be a right *in rem*. It is enforceable against the property itself ie the land. Where a holder of a proprietary right is denied that right, he is entitled to seek action to recover the actual land/use of the land, rather than be limited to recovering its value or damages to compensate loss of use. Personal rights are rights *in personam*. They are enforceable not against the actual property but against the person who granted the right in the first place. If revoked, even if wrongly so, the holder of the personal right may be entitled to damages but cannot insist upon recovering possession or use of the property itself. It is this fundamental difference which explains potential durability of proprietary rights which personal rights do not enjoy.

Revision tip

Some licences have been found to be enforceable against third parties and thus appear to have proprietary status. This is considered in more detail in chapter 11. Be prepared to make this link if required to examine the characteristics of proprietary, as opposed to, personal rights.

'Ownership' of 'land'

- Technically, all land is owned by the Crown (see 'The history behind land ownership: the doctrine of tenures' as to how this came about).

- The most you could have over a piece of land is a proprietary right to physically possess, use, enjoy, and deal with the land to the exclusion of anyone else, known as an estate.

- There are two key types of estate: the freehold and the leasehold (see 'Estates or interests' and chapters 5 and 6).

- The broadest is the freehold (the reasons for which are outlined later in this section). A person holding a freehold estate is, in practical terms, seen as the owner of the land. Their rights and relationship to the land that they physically possess are indistinguishable from that of an absolute owner.

- Where someone holds a freehold estate, giving them rights to possess and enjoy the land tantamount to absolute ownership, the extent of those rights depends upon how land is defined.

- A statutory definition has been given to 'land' in **Law of Property Act 1925, s 205(1)(ix)**. This is further clarified in case law.

In summary, where a person has a right to possess and enjoy a piece of land by virtue of holding a freehold estate, tantamount to making him the owner of the land, his rights extend to:

- the physical surface area of the land;

- the lower airspace above the physical surface area necessary for his ordinary use and enjoyment of that land. Any invasion of this lower airspace is *prima facie* actionable as a trespass: *Anchor Brewhouse Developments v Berkley House (Docklands Developments) Ltd* (1987), with a remedy of an injunction where damages would not be adequate. This is qualified by statute, for example the Civil Aviation Act 1982, which allows for aircraft to pass over land at a reasonable height, without amounting to an actionable trespass. A landowner has no claim to trespass where there is interference with his *upper* airspace, ie that airspace not necessary for his ordinary use and enjoyment of the land: *Bernstein of Leigh (Baron) v Skyviews & General Ltd* [1978]. To allow otherwise would create absurdities and stifle the ability of the general public to take advantage of developments in science regarding airspace (for example satellites);

- the ground below the surface area, including mines and minerals, although this is qualified by various statutes, for example the Coal Industry Act 1994 which vests ownership of coal in the Coal Authority;

- buildings or parts of buildings found on the land, whether the division is vertical or horizontal;

- wild plants growing on the land. Commercially grown plants are not considered part of the land and belong to those who planted them;

- dead wild animals killed on the land, irrespective of who killed them. Living wild animals do not belong to anyone, although a landowner has a right to kill them whilst they are on his land, subject to any statutory protection they might enjoy;

- the soil over which water flows. Where two plots of land are separated by a river, each plot owner owns the soil up to the middle of the river. As regards any fish that may be found in these waters, where the water is non-tidal the owner of the land has exclusive fishing rights, subject to him having granted this right to others. Where the water is tidal, the public has the right to fish up to the point of ebb and flow of the tide;

- some items found on the land. Whether the landowner's rights extend to such items depends upon the answer to a series of questions, as outlined in Figure 1.1;

- **incorporeal hereditaments**. These are those intangible rights that benefit the land in question, for example a right of way or an ability to restrict the neighbouring landowner from building on his land;

- **fixtures** found on the land. Where a **chattel** has become attached to the land, or a building on it, it can become part of the land itself changing from being a mere chattel to a fixture. Whether this is the case will depend upon the *degree of annexation* the object has to the land, or building on it, and the *purpose of its annexation*: *Holland v Hodgson* (1872). The label that parties give to the object is not conclusive of its status: *Melluish v BMI (No 3) Ltd* [1996].

  - The degree of annexation test: the greater the degree of annexation, the more likely the object is a fixture. Absence of any annexation at all would generally be decisive in making the object a chattel, unless the object is one that, by reason of its own weight, does not require any annexation: *Elitestone Ltd v Morris* [1997]. However, this test must now be used in conjunction with the *purpose of annexation* test, which today is the dominant test out of the two: *Hamp v Bygrave* (1983).

– The purpose of annexation test: consider the purpose for which the object has been annexed to the land. If annexation is merely to enjoy the object as a chattel, it will remain a chattel: *Leigh v Taylor* [1902]. If it is to make an improvement to the property itself, the chattel will become a fixture: *D'Eyncourt v Gregory* (1866). The purpose of annexation must be judged objectively (*Dean v Andrews* [1986]), although subjective intentions of the person who annexed the object may be persuasive.

✅ *Looking for extra marks?*

In the case of *Botham v TSB Bank plc* [1997] it became clear that in making a decision as to whether an object is a fixture, and thus part of the land, a court takes into account a number of factors in addition to the degree and purpose of annexation tests, including:

- whether the object is part of the overall design of the building;
- the moveability of the object: where moved regularly, more likely a chattel;
- the lifespan of the object: where limited, more likely a chattel;
- the damage caused to the land, or building, when moved: where great, more likely a fixture;
- the type of person who installed/attached the object to the land: where a builder, more likely a fixture; where a contractor, more likely a chattel.

The significance of determining the status of an object often arises upon the sale of land where fixtures are deemed to convey with the land: **s 62 LPA 1925**. A purchaser is entitled to receive anything that is a fixture at 'exchange of contracts' (or perhaps earlier where land is inspected: *Taylor v Hamer* [2003]), subject to any contrary agreement.

Revision tip

An examiner would want to see good use of case law to enhance your arguments as to whether an item is a fixture or a chattel. Draw appropriate comparisons and use the legal reasoning to demonstrate you understand the factors that influence a court.

Ownership of items found on the land

Figure 1.1 The ownership of items found on the land

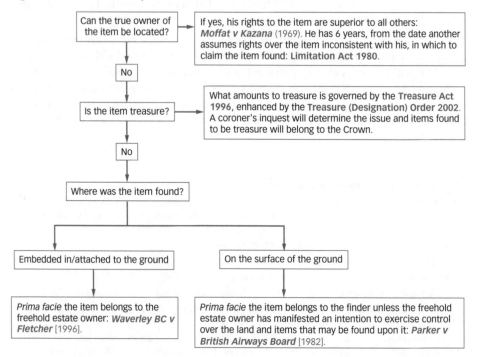

The history behind land ownership: the doctrine of tenures

The fact that, technically, all land is owned by the Crown stems from the Norman Conquest in 1066 when the King, William the Conqueror, declared himself as owner of all the land in England. A system of landholding developed whereby the King would allow people to use and occupy his land in return for the performance of certain services. Ownership of the land was never actually transferred to such persons. Such holders of the land were known as tenants and they in turn would allow others to use and occupy their land in return for services to them. This was known as *subinfeudation*. A feudal system of land ownership thus arose. The nature of the services provided by the tenant to his immediate lord differed depending upon the nature of the **tenure** in question: see Table 1.1.

Table 1.1 The doctrine of tenures

Free tenure	Unfree tenure
Characteristic – services provided to the immediate lord were fixed and certain	Characteristic – services provided to the immediate lord were not fixed as to their nature and duration
Types • Chivalry • Socage • Spiritual	Types • Villeinage • Customary

Since 1926, there has been only one form of tenure: *free and common socage* or *freehold* as it is now known. The tenure exists in name only. The freehold tenant need not provide an immediate lord with services. Indeed, almost all freehold tenants hold the land directly from the Crown, the feudal pyramid of landholding having disappeared. The Crown still technically owns the land. Someone who claims ownership of land through having a freehold actually merely enjoys a proprietary right over the land that is so extensive it is tantamount to actual ownership.

Proprietary rights under the microscope

There are two key ways in which proprietary rights may be classified:

Estates or interests

An estate is a more extensive proprietary right than an interest. The freehold estate and the leasehold estate are the two most important. Whilst discussed further in their relevant chapters (chapters 5 and 6 respectively), the following key points about estates can be made here:

- holding an estate in a piece of land gives you a 'slice of time' during which you are entitled to possess and enjoy that land.
- the 'slice of time' given to you is determined by the type of estate that you hold:
  - with a freehold estate (known technically as the fee simple absolute in possession), the slice of time is perpetual. It will only come to an end if the estate holder dies with no heirs (when the estate reverts to the Crown *bona vacantia*. This is the most obvious indication today that land is still owned by the Crown). This is why someone who holds a legal freehold estate sees themselves as tantamount to the actual owner of the land.
  - With a leasehold estate (known technically as term of years absolute), the slice of time is fixed and the estate will come to an end when the time expires. It is therefore

the smaller of the two estates. (It is further inferior to a freehold estate since the leasehold estate holder will be subject to more restrictions as to what he can and cannot do over the land than a freehold estate holder.)

The system of holding land by virtue of an estate can create a hierarchy of estates over one piece of land. For example, one piece of land could be subject to a freehold estate and one or more leasehold estates. By dealing with land in these 'slices of time' it is possible for people to use land to make money; carving estates out of their own and selling them to others to raise capital. (The precise status of an estate, where others exist in the same piece of land, is dealt with in detail in chapter 5.)

Whilst an estate determines the extent to which you can possess and enjoy your 'own' land, an **interest** concerns rights you have over the land of another. Although interests may take on a possessory character, possession will be restricted so that the estate holder of the land can still use and enjoy the land for himself. It is for this reason that interests are more limited in what they allow the holder to do than estates. However, they are no less important in the role they play in governing people's relationship to land.

Legal or equitable

All proprietary rights will have either legal or equitable status. The types of proprietary right that can be legal, where certain formalities have been met, are found in a closed list in s 1 LPA 1925. Where such formalities are not met, the right may only exist in equity, but this again will be dependent upon satisfaction of certain formalities, all of which is discussed in more detail in chapter 2. (An example of a right that can have legal or equitable status is an easement. The conditions that determine its status are explained in chapter 12.)

Despite being limited to those found in the s 1 LPA 1925 list, legal rights are not insignificant. Those that are listed commonly arise over land and they include the most extensive of the two types of proprietary rights: freehold and leasehold estates.

Other types of proprietary rights can only ever exist in equity, since their recognition as proprietary rights stemmed from equity's intervention in resolving the inadequacies of common law when dealing with disputes over land. A classic example, and one discussed in more detail in chapter 13, is the restrictive covenant.

Revision Tip

The status of a proprietary right as either legal or equitable is discussed in more detail in chapter 2 and again in relation to specific rights in the relevant chapters. Be sure you understand how status is determined.

 Key cases

Case	Facts	Principle
Bernstein of Leigh (Baron) v Skyviews & General Ltd [1978] QB 479	Flying a plane over land in order to take aerial photographs did not amount to a trespass of that land.	An owner of an estate in land has rights that extend only as far as the *lower* airspace above the physical surface area of the land necessary for the ordinary use and enjoyment of that land.
Botham v TSB Bank plc [1997] 73 P&CRD 1	The plaintiff owned a flat which was mortgaged. When he fell into arrears with the mortgage repayments, the bank sought possession and sold the property. A question arose as to whether some of the contents of the flat were fixtures, and thus part of the security for the debt.	In deciding the issue of whether an item is a fixture or chattel, look beyond the two key tests of degree and purpose of annexation (as discussed in 'Ownership' of 'land').
D'Eyncourt v Gregory (1866) LR 3 Eq 382	Despite being free-standing, marble statues of lions, garden seats, and ornaments were held to be fixtures, and thus part of the land.	Where evidence is produced that objects have been positioned so as to improve the overall architectural design of a property, those objects may become fixtures, even where there is no degree of annexation.
Elitestone Ltd v Morris [1997] 1 WLR 687	Wooden bungalows, not themselves attached to the land, rested on concrete pillars that were attached. The bungalows were deemed to be fixtures.	Even where there is no physical attachment to the land, an object could be a fixture where it is deemed to be used *in situ* and could not be removed without physical destruction.
Leigh v Taylor [1902] AC 157	Tapestries attached to a wall of a building were held to be chattels.	Although physical attachment of an object to the land might suggest that object has become a fixture, this may not be the case where such attachment is purely so that the object can be enjoyed.
Parker v British Airways Board [1982] QB 1004	The plaintiff, a passenger at Heathrow airport, found a gold bracelet on the floor of the executive lounge. He handed it in to an employee of the defendant requesting it be returned to him should no-one claim the item. No-one claimed the bracelet but the defendant sold it and retained the proceeds. It was held that the plaintiff was entitled to damages.	The rights of the finder of an object found on the surface of the ground can only be displaced by the owner of the land where the object was found if the latter manifested an intention to control the land and items found on it.

Case	Facts	Principle
Waverley BC v Fletcher [1996] QB 334	The defendant, lawfully in a public park, unlawfully used a metal detector to detect a gold brooch buried in the ground. It was held that the council's rights to the brooch were superior to the finder's.	Where an object is found in or attached to land, the owner of that land has better title to that object than the finder.

 Exam questions

Problem question

Tim purchased the freehold estate of a property known as Nector House two weeks ago. Upon moving into the property he noticed that a water fountain had been removed from the garden and a stained glass window had been removed from the dining room and replaced with normal glass. Two days ago, a postman picked up a valuable emerald necklace from under a bush as he walked up the garden path to the door of Nector House. The true owner of the necklace cannot be found and the postman has told Tim he is keeping it for himself. Tim has also discovered that branches from his neighbour's willow tree hang over his land.

Advise Tim whether:

1. he can insist upon the return of the water fountain and the stained glass window;

2. he can require the postman to return the emerald necklace to him; and

3. he can cut off the overhanging branches from his neighbour's willow tree and use them to make a basket.

See the Outline Answers section in the end matter for help with this question.

Essay question

'*Cuius est solum eius est usque ad coelum et ad inferos*': he who owns land owns everything up to the sky and down to the centre of the earth.

To what extent is this Latin phrase misleading today?

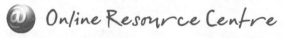 Online Resource Centre

To see an outline answer to this question log onto www.oxfordtextbooks.co.uk/orc/concentrate/

#2

The distinction between legal and equitable interests

The material covered in this chapter is unlikely to appear in a self-contained problem question. Rather it is pervasive material that forms the foundation upon which land law is built. Your understanding of this material is therefore essential to your overall understanding of land law. You will see that much of the material on formalities, and the creation of legal and equitable interests in land, is repeated elsewhere in this book. Chapters devoted to specific interests repeat rules outlined in this chapter and expand upon these where necessary. The enforcement of interests against third parties in both registered and unregistered land, discussed in chapters 3 and 4 respectively, requires a consideration of the exact status of an interest when ascertaining which rules to apply.

An essay question may focus on just the material covered in this chapter but it is more likely to be combined with principles discussed elsewhere, for example the issue of notice and its role today (link with chapters 3 and 4).

Key facts

- The intervention of equity in land law can be seen in two key areas: the development of new equitable interests in land, and the availability of equitable remedies to enforce interests in land.

- Following the intervention of equity, interests in land may now have either legal or equitable status.

- To be legal, the interest must be one listed under **s 1(2) Law of Property Act 1925** and certain formalities must be met in its creation, notably being granted by deed (**s 52 LPA 1925**). Where these formalities are not met, the interest may have equitable status instead, but only where equity can find a specifically enforceable valid contract to create the interest.

- All other interests in land can only ever be equitable (**s 1(3) LPA 1925**). To achieve equitable status, formalities in creation of the interest must be met and these formalities will differ depending upon the type of interest.

- The status of an interest in land as either legal or equitable traditionally determined the rules of enforcement of that interest against third parties: legal interests bound all third parties, whereas equitable interests would only bind third parties who were not *bona fide purchasers for value of a legal estate without notice*.

- Today enforcement of interests in land against third parties is determined less by its status as legal or equitable, and more upon concepts of registration.

- However, traditional rules of enforcement still play a minor role in unregistered land.

Chapter overview

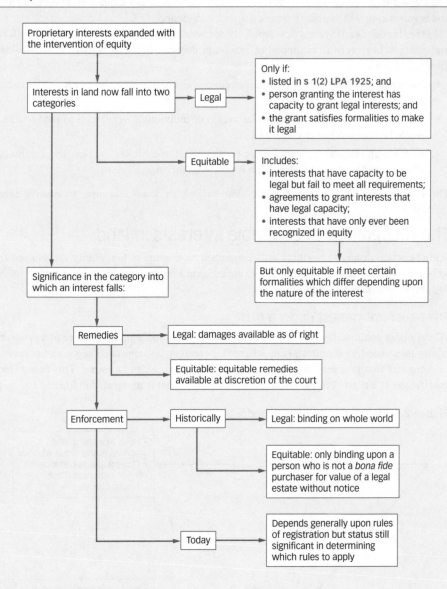

Proprietary interests expanded with the intervention of equity

Interests in land now fall into two categories

→ Legal → Only if:
- listed in s 1(2) LPA 1925; and
- person granting the interest has capacity to grant legal interests; and
- the grant satisfies formalities to make it legal

→ Equitable → Includes:
- interests that have capacity to be legal but fail to meet all requirements;
- agreements to grant interests that have legal capacity;
- interests that have only ever been recognized in equity

But only equitable if meet certain formalities which differ depending upon the nature of the interest

Significance in the category into which an interest falls:

Remedies → Legal: damages available as of right

Equitable: equitable remedies available at discretion of the court

Enforcement → Historically → Legal: binding on whole world

Equitable: only binding upon a person who is not a *bona fide* purchaser for value of a legal estate without notice

Today → Depends generally upon rules of registration but status still significant in determining which rules to apply

The intervention of equity

The impact that equity has had on the development of land law cannot be underestimated and is something that you must appreciate and understand.

As the English Legal System developed, it soon became clear that the courts of law, enforcing common law, were ill equipped at resolving disputes between holders of estates and interests in land:

- the writ procedure followed in these courts was complicated and burdened by excessive formality and thus delay;
- the common law failed to recognize rights of individuals in relation to land where it would be fair and just to do so; and
- where such proprietary rights were recognized, the common law remedy of damages often proved inadequate when such rights were infringed.

The development of the law of equity has helped, in some measure, to resolve these inadequacies.

The recognition of equitable interests in land

Whilst certain proprietary rights are recognized as existing at law, equity established the existence of some new proprietary rights based upon a desire to do justice and act on enforcing obligations of conscience.

The beneficial interest under a trust

Whilst under common law, recognition was only given to the legal title holder of a property, equity intervened, in circumstances where this common law approach was unconscionable, to recognize that property may be legally held for the benefit of another. This recognition was by way of a **trust**. The beneficial interest under a trust is illustrated in Figure 2.1.

Figure 2.1 The beneficial interest under a trust

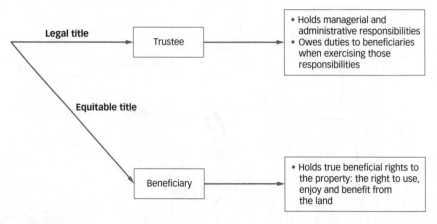

| | | • Holds managerial and administrative responsibilities |
| Legal title → | Trustee | • Owes duties to beneficiaries when exercising those responsibilities |

| Equitable title | | • Holds true beneficial rights to the property: the right to use, enjoy and benefit from the land |
| | Beneficiary | |

(The beneficial interest under a trust is discussed in more detail in chapters 9 and 10.)

Equitable right to redeem

Under common law, where the borrower (mortgagor) failed to redeem the mortgage loan (ie repay the capital plus interest and costs) on the date specified in the contract, he lost the property which served as security; ownership being transferred to the lender (mortgagee).

Considering this unfair and unjust, equity recognizes the equitable right to redeem. Borrowers can redeem the mortgage even after the legal date specified in the contract has passed. (This equitable right is discussed in more detail in chapter 14.)

Restrictive covenants

Common law does not allow for the burden of a covenant to pass to a successor in title of the land burdened by that covenant. This is because the successor is not a party to the original contract in which the covenant was created. And this is the case even in circumstances where the successor has knowledge of the covenant, prior to the purchase, and has consequently paid a reduced price for the land.

Such inadequacy at common law has led to the intervention of equity. By recognizing restrictive covenants as creating equitable interests in land (provided certain formalities are met), the burden of such covenants are potentially enforceable against successors in title to the burdened land. (These interests in land are discussed in more detail in chapter 13.)

Estate contracts

Where a person enters into a contract to grant another an estate over a piece of land, and that contract is breached by the grantor failing to transfer the estate in land to the grantee as agreed, the grantee has the common law personal remedy of damages for breach of contract.

As land is seen as unique, equity may provide an equitable remedy of specific performance.

The expectation of specific performance has meant that equity views the grantee as having an interest in the land at the time of the contract. Legal title will remain with the grantor of the contract but the equitable owner is the grantee. The equitable proprietary interest he holds is known as an estate contract.

You must remember, however, that such an equitable interest will only arise in circumstances where an order for specific performance is available. Where circumstances are such that equity would not exercise its discretion to make such an order, no equitable proprietary interest will arise.

This type of proprietary interest is discussed in more detail in both chapters 5 and 6.

Equitable remedies

As well as recognizing new proprietary rights, equity also developed new equitable remedies. This was in response to the inadequacy of the common law remedy of damages. Such inadequacy has already been seen in relation to breaches of land contracts (see 'Estate contracts').

Types

There are two principal equitable remedies:

Specific performance

An order of specific performance requires someone to do something, for example to perform a contract to transfer an estate in land.

Injunction

Whilst different types of injunctions exist, in general terms they forbid someone from doing something, for example forbidding a person from building a fence to obstruct a right of way.

Common characteristics

- Failure to comply with an order for either remedy results in being found in contempt of court.
- Where common law remedies are available as of right once the wrong has been proven, equitable remedies are awarded at the discretion of the court. The intervention of equity is conscience driven and is underlined by certain maxims, for example, he who comes to equity must come with clean hands; the person seeking the equitable remedy must not have disqualified himself from obtaining it by acting in a grossly unconscionable manner: *Coatsworth v Johnson* (1885).

Identifying the status of a proprietary interest

Revision tip

Link to chapter 1 and ensure that you understand the difference between the two key types of proprietary rights: estates and interests. The following considers interests in more detail. (Estates are considered in more detail in chapters 5 and 6.)

An interest in land can have either legal or equitable status.

Legal interests

The list

To have legal capacity, the interest must be listed under **s 1(2) LPA 1925**.

Out of the five interests in the following list, perhaps the most important today are those listed in paragraphs **(a)**, **(c)**, and **(e)**.

s 1(2)(a)   an easement, right, or privilege but only if it is equivalent in duration to one of the two legal estates in land ie it is to last forever (equivalent to a legal freehold), or it has a fixed and certain duration (equivalent to a leasehold). An easement granted for the duration of someone's life could therefore never have legal status. (Easements and *profits à prendre* are discussed in more detail in chapter 12.);

s 1(2)(b)   a rentcharge in possession issuing out of or charged on land being either perpetual or for a term of years absolute. (This is similar to rent paid in respect of a lease but here it relates to a freehold estate.);

s 1(2)(c)   a charge by way of a legal mortgage. (Mortgages are discussed in more detail in chapter 14.);

s 1(2)(d)   . . . any other similar charge on land which is not created by an instrument; and

s 1(2)(e)   rights of entry. These are rights normally reserved by a landlord to re-enter leased property and forfeit the lease where the tenant is in breach of covenant (discussed in more detail in chapter 6)

Once deemed capable of being legal, by virtue of being listed under **s 1(2) LPA 1925**, the interest will only become legal if certain formalities are satisfied.

The formalities

- The person granting the interest must have the capacity to grant legal interests in land. For example, an owner of an equitable lease would not be able to grant legal easements. You cannot grant more than you have yourself.

- The interest must, in principle, be granted by **deed**: **s 52 LPA 1925**. The requirements for a valid deed created on/after 31 July 1990 are laid down in **s 1 Law of Property (Miscellaneous Provisions) Act 1989** (deeds created before this date had to be signed, sealed, and delivered):

---

s 1 LP(MP)A 1989

The document must be:

- clear on its face that it is a deed;
- signed by the grantor;
- witnessed; and
- delivered.

Identifying the status of a proprietary interest

✱✱✱✱✱✱✱✱✱✱

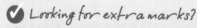 **Looking for extra marks?**

When the grantor signs there need only be one witness, but where someone signs on his behalf there must be two witnesses. The witness(es) must attest the document, which requires that they also sign the document. A deed is delivered by showing that the grantor intends to be bound by the document. His signature and the dating of the document will evidence this intention.

- There is an additional requirement of registration in some circumstances, where the interest is being created over registered land. Where:

  - an easement equivalent in duration to a legal estate is being expressly granted/reserved; or

  - a legal charge is being granted; or

  - a rentcharge or right of entry is being expressly granted/reserved,

  the disposition must be registered. The interest will not operate at law until this has been done: **s 27 Land Registration Act 2002** (see chapter 3).

Unless all the above requirements have been satisfied, the interest will not be legal. At best, it could only be equitable but this would be dependent upon meeting the requirements in equity (see 'Failed attempts to grant legal interests').

Equitable interests

These include:

Failed attempts to grant legal interests

If an interest which has legal capacity does not satisfy the legal formalities, it cannot have legal status. Equity, however, may recognize this failed attempt to grant a legal interest as a contract to create that interest. To do this there must be:

- a valid contract ie one compliant with **s 2 LP(MP)A 1989**:

---

s 2 LP(MP)A 1989

The contract must be:

- in writing;
- contain all the terms; and
- be signed by both parties.

(Subject to exemptions under s 2(5), notably contracts to create short leases.)
These formalities are discussed in more detail in chapter 5.

- The contract must be one that is capable of specific performance ie one upon which equity would exercise its discretion to grant such an order (see earlier discussion under 'Equitable remedies').

- By applying the maxim that equity views as done that which ought to be done (ie that the contract should be performed), an equitable interest arises.

Where there is no specifically enforceable valid contract, no equitable interest will arise.

> ✅ *Looking for extra marks?*
> Whilst the statement in the second bullet point is generally true, in some circumstances equity may intervene to give a person equitable rights even where no specifically enforceable contract exists. This intervention is based upon the finding of an estoppel and is discussed further in chapter 5.

Agreements to grant interests in land

Rather than actually granting someone an interest in land, the grantor may agree to do this some time in the future. Where this agreement is contained in a valid contract, capable of specific performance, equity will recognize the grantee as having an equitable interest in the land, by applying the maxim, equity views as done that which ought to be done. This can be seen, for example, in agreements to transfer a freehold estate and agreements to grant leases, both of which are discussed in more detail in chapters 5 and 6 respectively.

Interests that can only ever be equitable

Estates or interests that are not listed in either s 1(1) or s 1(2) LPA 1925 could never have legal status and could only ever be equitable (s 1(3) LPA 1925). These include life estates (discussed in chapter 5), restrictive covenants (discussed in chapter 13), and beneficial interests behind a trust (discussed in chapters 9 and 10). To achieve equitable status they would need to satisfy certain formalities, the nature of which differ depending upon the interest in question (discussed in more detail in the relevant chapters of this book). Where the formalities are not met, the right over land fails to gain proprietary status at all and remains a mere personal right between the creating parties.

Summary

In determining whether an interest is legal or equitable, remember the questions in Figure 2.2:

Figure 2.2 Is the interest legal or equitable?

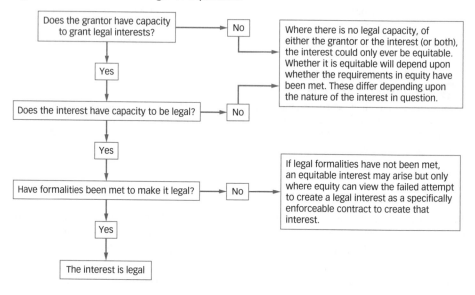

Significance of the distinction between legal and equitable interests

Revision tip

Link to material covered in chapters 3 and 4 on the enforcement of interests against third parties where the status of an interest is one of the factors in determining which rules of enforcement to apply.

Remedies

Where a legal interest is infringed, a remedy is available as of right. At common law, the remedy is damages, although equity may provide an equitable remedy where damages are seen as being inadequate.

Where an equitable interest has been infringed, only equitable remedies are available and whether such remedies are awarded will depend upon the discretion of the court (see 'Common characteristics').

Enforcement

As discussed in chapter 1, a proprietary right, in certain circumstances, may be enforceable not only against the person who granted the right, but also against any other person who may come to the land over which the right exists (the burdened land).

The question of whether a proprietary interest is binding on a third party, for example a purchaser of the burdened land, traditionally rested upon the nature of the interest:

Legal interests

These were considered binding on the whole world. Anyone who came to the burdened land would have to respect the existence of the legal interest and thus be bound by it, allowing the exercise of that right to continue.

Equitable interests

Equitable interests would only bind a person if he was **not** a *bona fide purchaser of a legal estate for value without notice*. To be such a purchaser, and thus take the land free from the equitable interest, he would need to be:

1. acting *bona fide* ie in good faith, honestly, and without any fraudulent intent; and

2. a **purchaser** ie someone acquiring the land through the act of another rather than automatically through an operation of law. (Examples of people who acquire land through an operation of law include trustees in bankruptcy (see chapter 10) and adverse possessors (see chapter 8)); and

3. a purchaser *for value* ie providing some sort of consideration for the land. (An example of someone who provides no value would be someone who was gifted the land.); and

4. a purchaser *of a legal estate*. This includes someone purchasing a legal freehold or leasehold estate but also a mortgage (s 87 LPA 1925); and

5. purchasing the land *without notice of the interest*. A purchaser will be deemed to have notice of an interest if:

   - he has **actual notice** ie actual knowledge of the existence of the interest at the time of purchase; or

   - he has **constructive notice** ie knowledge of all things he could have acquired actual notice of, had he made those enquiries and inspections which he ought reasonably to have done. What type of enquiries is a purchaser expected to make?

     - Investigate the title. This will involve looking at the title deeds back to the root of title which is set at 15 years: s 23 LPA 1969 (see chapter 4).

     - Inspect the land and make suitable enquiries of any person discovered in occupation of that land: *Hunt v Luck* [1901]. The extent of such enquiries was discussed in *Kingsnorth Trust Ltd v Tizard* [1986].

Significance of the distinction between legal and equitable interests

✳✳✳✳✳✳✳✳✳✳✳✳

....

Kingsnorth Trust Ltd v Tizard [1986] 1 WLR 783

A mortgagee's agent was held to have constructive notice of a wife's equitable interest in a property that was being mortgaged by the husband and which was in his sole name. The agent, when inspecting the property, discovered that the husband was married but separated, despite having stated on his mortgage application form that he was single. This should have led the agent to make further enquiries as to the whereabouts of the wife and any interest she may have in the property. Failure to make such enquiries, deemed reasonable, gave the agent constructive notice of the wife's equitable interest.

....

- he has **imputed notice** ie knowledge of all the things about which his agents working on the land transaction have actual or constructive notice. In *Kingsnorth Finance v Tizard* [1986], the mortgagee acquired imputed notice of its agent's constructive notice of the wife's equitable interest.

Only where the purchaser of the burdened land could establish all five components listed would he take the land free from any equitable interests that might exist over it. Once this occurred, the equitable interest lost its ability to bind any future third parties who came to that land: *Wilkes v Spooner* [1911].

✅ *Looking for extra marks?*

It has been argued that if a purchaser has notice of an interest, he is not acting in good faith and thus the requirement of good faith merely duplicates the requirement of acting without notice. However, Lord Wilberforce in the case of *Midland Bank Trust Co Ltd v Green* [1981] (discussed in chapter 4) made it clear that the two requirements are separate from one another and that one could be satisfied whilst the other is not, although it is difficult to point to circumstances where this may be the case.

Relevance of the distinction today

It soon became clear that the rules regarding the enforcement of interests in land against third parties, dependent upon whether the interest was legal or equitable, were imperfect (see 'Enforcement'). Attempts to improve upon these rules of enforcement by introducing systems of registration are discussed in more detail in the next two chapters. That is not to say that the system of enforcement outlined under 'Enforcement' has no role to play today. It does play a small part in the system of enforcement of interests that exist over unregistered land.

Revision tip

Make sure you link the previous discussion on the doctrine of notice to the role it plays in unregistered land, discussed in chapter 4.

 Key cases

Case	Facts	Principle
Coatsworth v Johnson (1885) 55 LJQB 220	Claimant sought specific performance of an agreement for a lease which was declined since the claimant was himself in breach of one of the covenants in the lease to which the agreement related.	A court will not exercise its discretion and grant specific performance in favour of a claimant who himself has acted unconscionably and not come to the court with clean hands.
Hunt v Luck [1901] 1 Ch 45	The vendor sold land occupied by his tenant. The purchaser was held to have constructive notice of the tenant's rights.	A purchaser must make enquiries as to the rights of persons who are not the vendor and who are in occupation of the land being purchased. Failure to do so fixes the purchaser with constructive notice of any rights those persons in occupation may have in the land.
Kingsnorth Trust Ltd v Tizard [1986] 1 WLR 783	Mr Tizard sought to obtain a mortgage over a house which was in his sole name. In his mortgage application form he stated he was single but when the mortgagee's surveyor went to inspect the property, his true status as married but separated became known. No enquiries were made about any rights his wife might have in the house and consequently the surveyor and mortgagee were deemed to have notice of the wife's beneficial interest in the property.	Where it is reasonable to expect a purchaser to make further enquiries about any rights a person may have in the land being purchased, failure to do so will give the purchaser notice of any such rights.
Wilkes v Spooner [1911] 2 KB 473	A purchaser of a legal estate took free from an existing equitable interest over the land as he was a *bona fide* purchaser for value of a legal estate without notice. His successor also took free from the equitable interest despite having notice of it.	Once an equitable interest has been destroyed by virtue of a transfer of the land over which it exists, to a purchaser acting in good faith with no notice of its existence, that equitable interest cannot be revived upon a subsequent transfer of the land.

 Exam question

Essay question

An interest in land may have legal or equitable status. How does one determine the status of an interest in land and what is the significance of this distinction?

 Online Resource Centre

To see an outline answer to this question log onto www.oxfordtextbooks.co.uk/orc/concentrate/

#3
Registered land

This is a topic area that may be examined in a self-contained question or as part of a question concerning another topic area. It may be combined with unregistered land or issues of adverse possession. It can also appear in questions concerning a particular interest in land, for example an easements question or a restrictive covenants question, where the interest exists over registered land and issues of enforcement against a purchaser of that land arise.

Problem questions typically focus upon rules of enforcement of interests over registered land. For example, you may be told about various types of interests that exist over a piece of registered land. (Sometimes those interests will be clearly identified; other times you may have to work out what they are for yourself.) That land will then pass to a purchaser and you will be required to work out whether those interests will be binding upon that purchaser.

Essay questions sometimes demand drawing comparisons between the registered and unregistered land systems. You may be required to consider how, if at all, the three principles underpinning registered land are met. Frequently, attention is focused upon overriding interests and in particular how they appear to undermine the perceived objectives behind the introduction of a registered land system.

Key facts

- Registered land is land where title has been registered at the Land Registry. The objective behind registered land is to create a register which accurately reflects the state of registered property, both in terms of its current owner and any third party proprietary interests affecting it. In theory, a purchaser need look no further than the register when making enquiries about a piece of registered land. (In reality, the presence of overriding interests which bind a purchaser despite appearing nowhere on the register, means that a purchaser must look beyond the register.)

- Unregistered land can be brought into the registered land system either by the owner voluntarily applying to be registered or compulsorily upon the occurrence of certain events, notably sale of the freehold, the grant of a lease of more than seven years, or the grant of a protected first legal mortgage. Failure to register title when required can lead to the loss of legal title to that land (ss 4, 6, and 7 LRA 2002).

- Once registered, subsequent disposals of the freehold, or leasehold of more than seven years in duration, must be completed by registration to confer legal title (s 27 LRA 2002).

- When registering title to land, the specific class of title registered will reflect the strength of that title; with the strongest and most common class registered being absolute title.

- In principle, third party proprietary interests will only affect a purchaser of registered land where they have been entered on the register, typically as a notice but sometimes (where a beneficial interest under a trust) as a restriction.

- However, where interests have not been correctly entered on the register they may still bind a purchaser of registered land if they meet the requirements of an overriding interest under Sch 3 para 2.

- In any case, certain interests are not required to be entered on the register at all and yet are still deemed to be binding upon a purchaser of registered land, notably overriding interests under Sch 3 paras 1 and 3.

Chapter overview

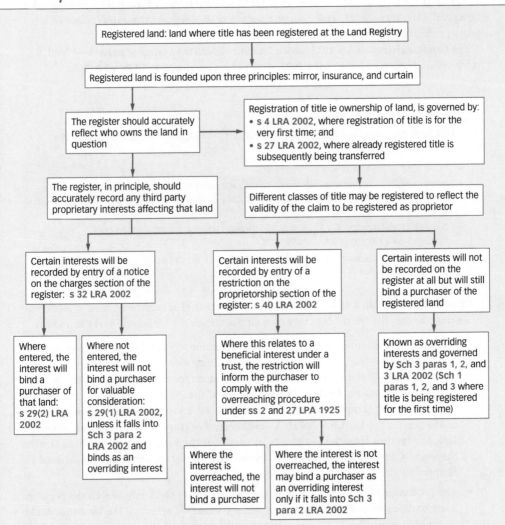

Registered land: land where title has been registered at the Land Registry

Registered land is founded upon three principles: mirror, insurance, and curtain

The register should accurately reflect who owns the land in question

Registration of title ie ownership of land, is governed by:
- s 4 LRA 2002, where registration of title is for the very first time; and
- s 27 LRA 2002, where already registered title is subsequently being transferred

The register, in principle, should accurately record any third party proprietary interests affecting that land

Different classes of title may be registered to reflect the validity of the claim to be registered as proprietor

Certain interests will be recorded by entry of a notice on the charges section of the register: s 32 LRA 2002

Certain interests will be recorded by entry of a restriction on the proprietorship section of the register: s 40 LRA 2002

Certain interests will not be recorded on the register at all but will still bind a purchaser of the registered land

Where entered, the interest will bind a purchaser of that land: s 29(2) LRA 2002

Where not entered, the interest will not bind a purchaser for valuable consideration: s 29(1) LRA 2002, unless it falls into Sch 3 para 2 LRA 2002 and binds as an overriding interest

Where this relates to a beneficial interest under a trust, the restriction will inform the purchaser to comply with the overreaching procedure under ss 2 and 27 LPA 1925

Known as overriding interests and governed by Sch 3 paras 1, 2, and 3 LRA 2002 (Sch 1 paras 1, 2, and 3 where title is being registered for the first time)

Where the interest is overreached, the interest will not bind a purchaser

Where the interest is not overreached, the interest may bind a purchaser as an overriding interest only if it falls into Sch 3 para 2 LRA 2002

Introduction

There exist today two types of land: registered and unregistered, each with its own rules concerning the transfer of land from one person to another and the enforcement of third party proprietary interests affecting the land.

The **Land Registration Act 1925**, which first introduced the system of **registered land**, was reviewed and repealed by the **LRA 2002**, which came into force on 13 October 2003.

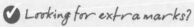 *Looking for extra marks?*

The **LRA 2002** has maintained the basic structure of registered land introduced by the **LRA 1925**. However, under the new Act:

- more titles to land must now be registered;
- more interests must now be entered on to the register to be protected, consequently reducing the number of interests that automatically bind without being entered on the register (overriding interests);
- the way in which property can be acquired through adverse possession has been fundamentally watered down (see chapter 8);
- a system has been put in place which paves the way for electronic conveyancing.

The objective intended to be met by the introduction of a registered land system was essentially to simplify the process by which land is transferred from one party to another.

- With the introduction of registered conveyancing, ownership of land (or title to land) is registered at the Land Registry on a register which effectively acts as a public record of land ownership. The state guarantees the accuracy of the register in terms of who owns the land. (This is known as the *insurance principle* and indeed the state would compensate anyone who suffered a loss due to any errors present in the register: s 103 LRA 2002.) A purchaser, therefore, need not be concerned to look any further than the register to be sure that the vendor is entitled to deal with the land. (Contrast with the need to 'prove title' in unregistered land, discussed in chapter 4.)

- The purchaser of registered land, in principle at least, need only search the register itself to discover any third party proprietary interests affecting the land that could be binding upon him. (According to the *mirror principle*, the register should be an accurate reflection not only as to who owns the land, but also any third party interests affecting it. This is somewhat tainted by the existence of **overriding interests** (technically known as 'interests which override registered dispositions'—see 'Interests which override the register') and, therefore, in practice, a purchaser of registered land must conduct further enquiries beyond just looking at the register to discover third party interests.)

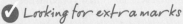

Looking for extra marks

For a further example as to how this 'mirror' principle is undermined, see *Fitzwilliam v Richall Holdings Services Ltd* [2013].

(Remember that there is a third principle behind title registration, known as the **curtain principle** whereby purchasers are not required to look behind the register. This particularly relates to trust property and the **overreaching** process (see 'Overreaching: What is it?') by which a purchaser can take land free from any beneficial trust interests.)

Revision tip

Exam questions sometimes focus upon whether the three principles behind title registration are upheld. Give thought to this when looking at the rules of registered land.

It has always been the intention that all land in England and Wales becomes registered land and, indeed since the introduction of compulsory registration in 1990 which has been further extended by the LRA 2002 (see 'Registration of title'), a majority of titles are now registered. However, there still remain titles that are not registered, which is why you need to be familiar with both systems of land.

The register

The register of title is a largely computerized, public (see s 66 LRA 2002) record maintained by the registrar at the Land Registry (s 1 LRA 2002). The register is divided into three parts:

1. *The Property Register*: this describes the land, the nature of the estate(s) registered, and any third party interests benefiting the land, for example a right of way.

2. *The Proprietorship Register*: this names the **registered proprietor**, states the title that has been registered (see 'Registration of title'), and contains any **restrictions** which limit the way in which the registered proprietor can deal with the land (see 'Interests entered as a restriction').

3. *The Charges Register*: this contains **notices** relating to any interests that burden the land, for example restrictive covenants, mortgages etc (see 'Interests entered on the register').

Registration of title

Some estates and interests are 'substantively registered' so that they acquire their own title number and file. These are:

- the freehold estate;
- the leasehold estate where there are more than seven years left to run;

- a rentcharge (the Rentcharges Act 1977 prevents the creation of new rentcharges);
- a franchise; and
- a *profit à prendre* in gross (see chapter 12) (s 2 LRA 2002).

Registration for the first time

Registration of title for the very first time can take place in the following circumstances:

- A person can voluntarily apply to the registrar to be registered as the proprietor of any one of the above interests, and financial incentives exist to encourage this: s 3 LRA 2002.
- In respect of a freehold estate, and a leasehold estate with more than seven years unexpired, certain events will trigger the need to compulsorily register title. Such events are now specified under s 4 LRA 2002 and include:
  - the transfer (for consideration, by way of a gift, in pursuance of a court order, or by personal representatives upon death) of an unregistered legal estate be it freehold (the fee simple absolute in possession: see chapter 5) or leasehold with more than seven years left to run;
  - the grant of a lease of more than seven years (for consideration, by way of a gift, or in pursuance of a court order);
  - the grant of a lease of any duration to take effect in possession after the end of a period of three months beginning with the date of the grant (known as a **reversionary lease**);

  (The occurrence of these events triggers the need to register title to the estate that has been transferred/granted.)

  - the creation of a protected first legal mortgage, defined in s 4(8) LRA 2002.

  (This event triggers the need to register the estate charged by the mortgage.)

- The duty to register title upon the occurrence of one of the above events generally falls on the transferee or, in the case of the creation of a protected first legal mortgage, generally the mortgagor: s 6 LRA 2002.
- Registration should be applied for within two months beginning with the date of the triggering event (subject to any extension granted by the registrar).
- Upon receiving an application for registration, the registrar will make various enquiries so as to determine the class of title to register (see 'Classes of title that can be registered') and there currently appears no direct means for appealing his decision.
- Persons with interests in the land who may be affected by first registration have the ability, in certain circumstances, to lodge a caution against first registration. This effectively means that when the registrar receives an application for first registration, he must notify the cautioner who then has 15 working days within which to object to the application. Where objections are made within this time frame that are not unwarranted, the matter must be referred to an adjudicator: s 71 LRA 2002.

- The consequences of failing to register title when required within the time frame are laid down in s 7 LRA 2002:
  - where the event triggering registration was the transfer of a freehold, or leasehold with more than seven years unexpired, title to the legal estate will revert to the transferor, who will hold it on bare trust for the transferee;
  - where the event triggering registration was the grant of a lease or first legal mortgage, the effect of non-registration is to treat what has happened as a contract for valuable consideration to grant that particular interest.
- Late registration will be accepted with costs being the responsibility of the person who failed to register on time.

Registration on subsequent transactions

Once title has been registered, a subsequent transfer of that registered estate and the grant of a lease of more than seven years in duration out of a registered estate, must be completed by registration, so that the transferee/grantee is registered as proprietor: s 27(2) LRA 2002.

Failure to register such transactions means that the transfer will not operate at law (s 27(1) LRA 2002), the transferor retaining legal title.

The new registered proprietor will take the estate subject only to those interests entered on the register and interests which override the register, as defined in Sch 3 (see 'Interests which override subsequent transactions of already registered land').

Classes of title that can be registered

When title is registered at the Land Registry, for the first time or following subsequent dealings with the registered estate, it is important to show the strength of that title ie the validity of the claim to be registered as proprietor. The register must accurately reflect the state of title (ownership), especially since it will compensate anyone who suffers a loss due to errors present on the register (the insurance principle—see 'Introduction'). The different classes of title that may be registered are laid down in ss 9 and 10 LRA 2002, with consequences noted in ss 11 and 12. The most significant of these classes is:

- *absolute title* This is the strongest title a person can be registered with. It indicates that that person has a better right than anyone else to the land and is usually only registered by the registrar in circumstances where he is happy that the title is secure and cannot be challenged.
- A person registered with absolute title takes the land subject only to those interests entered on the register and those interests that override the register (defined under Sch 1: see 'Interests which override upon first registration'). Where registration of title is for the first time ie where unregistered land is being brought into the registered land system, those interests entered on the register will comprise those interests protected

by registration of land charges under the Land Charges Act 1972 (see chapter 4). (Where the registered proprietor is a trustee, he will also take the land subject to the provisions of the trust; where he is a lessee, he will also take the land subject to the provisions in the lease.) Where the title registered is of a leasehold estate, registration with absolute title guarantees that the lease has been validly granted.

A person may also be registered with:

- *possessory title*, where registration is based upon possession of the land, typically as an adverse possessor, rather than the provision of any title deeds, which the adverse possessor is unlikely to have. The registrar merely guarantees title as far as dealings post first registration are concerned; or

- *qualified title*, registered where there is a defect with the title, for example a lost deed, or where the registrar has a reservation about the title that cannot be ignored; or

- *good leasehold title*, in respect of leasehold estates, where the registrar is happy with the title granted to the tenant under the lease but not as to the title of the lessor.

Upgrading title

By virtue of s 62 LRA 2002, there is the possibility of upgrading a less than absolute title to absolute status, either by the registrar upon his own initiative, or upon an application typically made by the registered proprietor.

Third party proprietary interests affecting the land

When a person is registered as proprietor of a piece of land, in the circumstances outlined in 'Registration of title', you have already seen that they take the land subject to:

- any interests entered on the register relating to the estate they have just acquired. (Where registration is for the first time, and therefore at the time of acquisition the estate was unregistered, these will be those interests registered as land charges under the LCA 1972—see chapter 4); and

- any interests which override the register (outlined in Sch 1 where registration is for the first time, and Sch 3 where registration is to complete a subsequent transaction of an already registered estate).

Revision tip

Remember that exam questions often require you to compare rules of enforcing third party proprietary interests in registered land with those of unregistered land. Make sure you understand how the rules differ for different types of interests (link to chapter 4).

Interests entered on the register

These consist of those proprietary interests which, in principle at least, should have been entered on the register concerning the land to which they relate, in order to bind a purchaser of that land. The idea then is that a purchaser can inspect the register and discover any proprietary interests that both burden and benefit the land he intends to purchase. At the same time, holders of such proprietary interests have the certainty that by entering their interest on the register, they have protected that interest and made it enforceable against anyone who may come to the land.

The entry made to protect such interests can be either:

- a notice; or
- a restriction,

depending upon the type of interest.

Interests entered as a notice: by the registrar

It is important for you to remember that in certain cases, when creating an interest that has legal capacity (s 1(2) **Law of Property Act 1925** and discussed in chapter 2) over registered land, the creation of the interest must be completed by a process of registration (not to be confused with the process of registering title—see 'Registration of title'). The most significant of these are:

- expressly created easements equivalent in duration to one of the legal estates; and
- the grant of a legal charge.

Until registration takes place, the interest will not take effect at law, but merely in equity provided the formalities required in equity are present. (This process is discussed more fully in the relevant chapters which discuss the above interests.)

For now, what you must realize is that when the registrar receives an application to register one of these interests, and the registration process is carried out, the registrar must enter a notice on the charges section of the register relating to the land burdened by the interest so as to protect that interest and make it enforceable against anyone else who may come to the land (s 38 LRA 2002) (see 'What are the consequences of entering, or failing to enter, a notice?').

(A registrar will make a similar entry upon receipt of an application to register the grant of a lease of more than seven years to run created out of an already registered estate.)

Also remember that interests which override the register (see 'Interests which override the register') may be entered on the register by the registrar: s 37 LRA 2002. Where he makes such an entry, the interest concerned can no longer have overriding status.

Third party proprietary interests affecting the land

✳✳✳✳✳✳✳✳✳✳

Interests entered as a notice: by the holder of the interest (the person benefiting from the interest)

Rather than list those interests that can be entered on the register by the holder, s 33 LRA 2002 lists those interests that cannot be protected in this way, which include:

- interests under a trust (protected by entry of a restriction: see 'Interests entered as a restriction');
- leases of three years or less taking effect in possession (see chapter 6); and
- restrictive covenants between a landlord and tenant (discussed in chapter 7).

What types of interests are, therefore, protected in this way?

Table 3.1 shows examples of these types of interests.

Table 3.1 Interests entered as a notice

Interest	Description
Estate contracts	Includes contracts to buy freehold estates (see chapter 5), contracts to buy leasehold estates ie equitable leases (see chapter 6), options to purchase, and rights of pre-emption.
Restrictive covenants between freehold estate owners	Defined and discussed in chapter 13.
Equitable easements	Defined and discussed in chapter 12.
Rights to occupy the family home under the **Family Law Act 1996**	A spouse (and also now civil partners under the **Civil Partnership Act 2004**) has a right to occupy the family home which, if entered on the register, is enforceable against anyone coming to the land.
Estoppel rights	Examples identified in chapter 11.

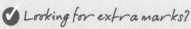 Looking for extra marks?

A right of pre-emption is an interest in land as soon as it is created: s 115 LRA 2002. This differs from rights of pre-emption created over unregistered land, whose status is governed by the decision in *Pritchard v Briggs* [1980] discussed in chapter 4.

Where will the notice appear on the register?

Notices are entered on the charges section of the register relating to the land affected by the interest: s 32 LRA 2002.

What are the consequences of entering, or failing to enter, a notice?

Remember, that entering a notice on the register in respect of an interest does not by itself mean that the interest is valid. Rather that, if it is, entry will have made it enforceable against a purchaser: see Figure 3.1.

Figure 3.1 Consequences of entering/not entering a notice

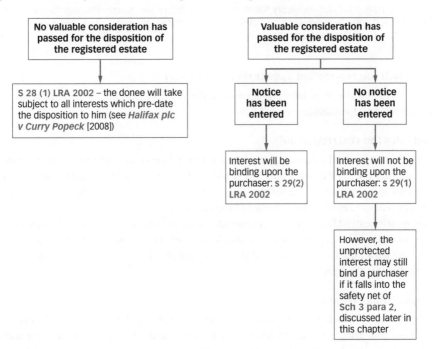

 Looking for extra marks?

Whilst mere notice of an interest, not protected by entry on the register, should not prevent a purchaser taking free from it, (subject only to it being overriding), equity has shown itself willing to intervene in cases of fraud. For example, see *Lyus v Prowsa Developments Ltd* [1982]: the unprotected right had been mentioned in the contract of sale, and a constructive trust was triggered preventing the purchaser from taking free from that right. (Contrast with the more recent decision of *Chaudhary v Yavuz* [2011] where the court declined to use equity as a means of enforcing an unprotected interest against a purchaser.) The difficulty lies in the fact that the term 'fraud' has been left to be defined on an ad hoc basis, with disagreements arising (see, for example, the contrasting views of the Court of Appeal and House of Lords in *Midland Bank Trust Co Ltd v Green* [1981], discussed in chapter 4).

Third party proprietary interests affecting the land

✳✳✳✳✳✳✳✳✳✳✳

Interests entered as a restriction

What type of interest is dealt with by entry of a restriction?

The most important type of interest dealt with in this way is the beneficial interest under a trust.

Revision tip

An exam question may not expressly tell you property is held under a trust. You may have to work this out based upon facts provided. A knowledge of circumstances as to when a trust may be implied is required (link to chapter 9).

Where will the restriction appear on the register?

It will appear on the proprietorship section of the register relating to the land affected by the interest: s 40 LRA 2002.

What does the restriction do?

Rather than identify the nature of the interest to which it relates, the restriction limits the way in which the registered proprietor can deal with the property. It lays down a specific procedure to follow when disposing of the property. Unless this procedure is followed, the registrar will not register the disponee of the property.

Where the restriction relates to a beneficial interest under a trust, it indicates that the property can only be disposed of where purchase monies are paid to at least two trustees (or a trust corporation). In other words, it stipulates that the disposal of the land complies with the mechanics of overreaching.

Overreaching: What is it?

A mechanism by which a purchaser of trust land can take the land free from the beneficial interests under that trust. It can only apply to those interests capable of existing without being attached to the land; predominantly (although not exclusively) beneficial interests under a trust, such interests being capable of existing in money as well as over land.

Overreaching: How does it work?

By paying purchase monies to at least two trustees or a trust corporation, in accordance with ss 2 and 27 LPA 1925, the interest is effectively detached from the land, so that the purchaser may take free from it. The interest now rests in the purchase monies paid, rather than existing over the land. Depending upon the terms of the trust, the trustees will then either distribute the money amongst the beneficiaries or will reinvest. For an example of successful overreaching, see *City of London Building Society v Flegg* [1988]. In contrast, look at *Williams & Glyn's Bank Ltd v Boland* [1981] for an example of a case where overreaching was unsuccessful.

What are the consequences of entering, or failing to enter, a restriction which relates to a beneficial interest under a trust?

Figure 3.2 illustrates the consequences of entering or not entering a restriction.

Figure 3.2 Consequences of entering or not entering a restriction

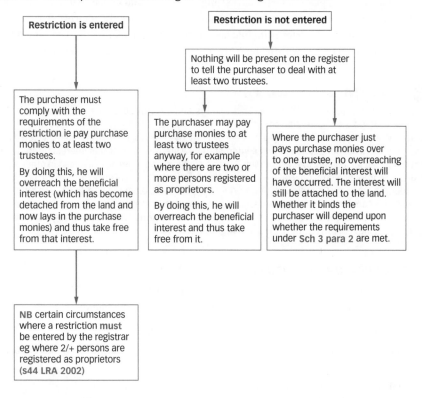

Why bother to enter a restriction if it means that your beneficial interest is going to be detached from the land and thus you may lose having somewhere to live?

The whole point of entering a restriction is to protect your interest. Where a restriction is entered and followed, although the process of overreaching that occurs means that your interest is detached from the land, and thus you may lose having somewhere to live, it is not destroyed. You still have a beneficial interest under a trust; it just now happens to exist over money. Such money may be reinvested in property so that you obtain somewhere to live once more, though this will depend upon the terms of the trust.

If no restriction is entered, and therefore no overreaching takes place to detach your interest from the land, your interest will only bind that purchaser where you can establish the requirements under **Sch 3 para 2 LRA 2002**, discussed below. Where you cannot meet these requirements, your interest will not bind that purchaser. Effectively, it has been destroyed by the purchase. You no longer have any interest at all.

Interests which override the register

These consist of third party interests affecting a piece of land which will bind a purchaser despite not appearing anywhere on the register. This category of interest therefore goes against the fundamental *mirror principle* (see 'Introduction'), that the register should accurately reflect not only who owns the land but any third party interests affecting it.

✅ *Looking for extra marks?*

Despite this imperfection with the registered land system, the **LRA 2002** did not take the opportunity to rid the registered land system of such interests, although it has reduced their number. Why allow for their continued existence? Perhaps because, for many of them, it would be unreasonable to expect the holder of the interest to take steps to protect that interest by entering it on the register. In addition, interests falling into this category can often be evidenced in other ways, for example through common usage ascertainable by making a physical inspection of the land itself.

A report by the Law Commission, made prior to the introduction of the **LRA 2002**, also noted that the wholesale abolition of such interests, without compensation payments to those affected, might contravene **Art 1 of the First Protocol of the European Convention on Human Rights 1950**, incorporated into English law by **s 1 Human Rights Act 1998**.

Interests which override upon first registration

When title to land is being registered for the first time, bringing the land into the registered system, interests listed under **Sch 1** will override registration, including:

- legal leases of seven years or less in duration (**para 1**);
- interests of persons in actual occupation (**para 2**) (see 'What is meant by "actual occupation"?'); and
- legal easements or profits (**para 3**).

Interests which override subsequent transactions of already registered land

Since the majority of dispositions concern land that is already registered, interests that override under **Sch 3 LRA 2002** are by far the most significant. Such interests are divided into three categories:

Sch 3 para 1

This incorporates legal leases of seven years or less. These will automatically bind a purchaser of the land, without the need for any further conditions to be met.

Third party proprietary interests affecting the land

(Remember:

- legal leases over seven years must have been substantively registered to make them legal. Consequently, they will automatically be entered on the register of the freehold land to which they relate (s 38 LRA 2002), so a purchaser of that land will be bound by them.

- Equitable leases must have been entered on the register as a notice by the holder of the interest in order to be binding upon a purchaser (s 32 LRA 2002 and see 'Interests entered as a notice by the holder of the interest (the person benefitting from the interest)'), although where the holder has failed to do so, he may be able to enforce the interest against the purchaser where he can establish the requirements under Sch 3 para 2.)

Sch 3 para 2

An interest will be binding upon a purchaser under this provision where the holder of the interest can establish:

- the interest he holds is a proprietary one, be it legal or equitable (and not excluded from this provision by the LRA 2002); and

- the interest existed at the time of the **disposition**; and

- they were in actual occupation of the land to which the interest relates and either:

  - the occupation would be obvious upon a reasonably careful inspection of the land; or

  - even if not obvious, the purchaser had actual knowledge of the interest.

This is provided they did not fail to disclose the interest if enquiry had been made of them.

On this last point, a purchaser should make enquiry of the actual holder of the interest; it is not enough to make enquiries of the registered owner: *Hodgson v Marks* [1971].

Where the holder can establish the above requirements, the interest he holds will only be binding to the extent of the land he actually occupies and no more (reversing the decision of *Ferrishurst Ltd v Wallcite Ltd* [1999]).

> ✅ *Looking for extra marks?*
>
> Where enquiries are made of the holder of the interest and he fails to disclose his interest, this will only prevent him from enforcing his interest under Sch 3 para 2, where it would have been reasonable for him to disclose. So, for example, a person who contributes to a purchase price of a property may not realize that this gives him a beneficial interest under a trust. In such circumstances, it may not be reasonable to expect the holder of the beneficial interest to disclose it when asked. How can you disclose something you yourself do not know about? If this was the case, the holder of such an interest would not be prevented from relying upon Sch 3 para 2.

What is meant by 'actual occupation'?

- Some physical presence on the land which itself has a degree of permanence and continuity.

- Temporary absences, even at the exact time of the disposition, may not prevent a finding of actual occupation, so long as the reason for such absence can be justified and is not too long, for example absence due to giving birth in hospital (*Chhokar v Chhokar* [1984]). Contrast *Stockholm Finance Ltd v Garden Holdings Inc* [1995] where absence from the property for over a year (combined with never having resided in the property for any lengthy period, using it just when visiting London from abroad) led the court to find no actual occupation.

- A persistent intention to return to the property may prove significant in a finding of actual occupation, such as in *Linklending v Bustard* [2010], where absence was due to being in a mental institution.

- The nature and condition of the land which is being claimed as occupied may be significant in determining the meaning of actual occupation—see *Lloyds Bank v Rosset* [1991].

- Actual occupation may be established through an agent (for example, a caretaker occupying on behalf of his employer). This will depend upon the facts of individual cases: see *Strand Securities v Caswell* [1965] and *Lloyds Bank plc v Rosset* [1991]. A minor cannot be in actual occupation on behalf of their parents: *Hypo-Mortgage Services Ltd v Robinson* (1997).

When must actual occupation be established?

It must exist at the time of the transfer of the land ie when the transfer deed is executed.

. . . .

Abbey National BS v Cann [1991] 1 AC 56, HL

A property was purchased with the aid of a mortgage by Cann, who was going to occupy it along with his mother. On the day of purchase, and thus when the charge in favour of the building society was being created, the mother was out of the country, although 35 minutes before completion, removal men started moving her belongings into the property. The charge was not completed by registration until a month later, by which time the mother was in physical occupation of the property. When her son defaulted on the mortgage payments, and the building society sought possession, it was held that the mother was unable to enforce her interest in the property as an overriding interest under the **Sch 3 para 2** equivalent that existed under the **LRA 1925**, which was in force at the time. Despite her being in actual occupation at the time of registration, the relevant time was held to be the date of transfer. To allow otherwise would be unfair to a purchaser who, having inspected the land and finding no-one present, would then be held bound by an interest held by someone who took occupation of the land between transfer and registration. Her acts of moving in at the date of transfer were deemed merely preparatory steps towards actual occupation; not actual occupation itself.

. . . .

(Remember, that when electronic conveyancing is established, transfer and registration will occur simultaneously; thus the problem envisaged above will be eradicated.)

✅ **Looking for extra marks?**

Thompson v Foy [2010] has questioned whether actual occupation must also exist at the date of registration.

Revision tip

A proliferation of case law exists on the issue of actual occupation. This is therefore often a good issue for discussion in an exam question, so be prepared to compare, contrast, and apply case law decisions.

Sch 3 para 3

Impliedly created legal easements (discussed in more detail in chapter 12) will bind a purchaser under this provision provided either:

- the person to whom the disposition is made actually knows about their existence; or
- the interest would be obvious upon reasonably careful inspection of the land; or
- the interest has been exercised in the year immediately preceding the disposition.

(Remember, expressly created legal easements and profits require registration to complete their creation. Consequently, they will automatically be entered on the register of the land which they burden, so will bind purchasers: **s 38 LRA 2002**. Equitable easements and profits must be entered on the register by the holder of the interest in order to be enforceable against purchasers: **s 32 LRA 2002**.)

Revision tip

Be sure you understand how to identify different types of interests and the formalities for their creation. An examiner may not always tell you the nature of the interest or whether it is legal or equitable (in cases where it could be either).

Transitional provisions

These provisions relate to interests created before the **LRA 2002** came into force and which had overriding status under the old **LRA 1925** rules. According to **Sch 12 LRA 2002**, some of these maintain their overriding status, in particular:

- legal leases of 21 years or less;
- legal easements and profits;
- rights of persons in actual occupation *or* in receipt of rent and profits from the land.

Altering the register

Section 65 and Sch 4 LRA 2002 lay down the provisions for making alterations to the register.

Indemnities

Provisions for compensating persons who suffer a loss as a result of mistakes in the register are governed by s 103 and Sch 8 LRA 2002.

 Key cases

Case	Facts	Principle
Abbey National BS v Cann [1991] 1 AC 56, HL	A mother was found not to be in actual occupation of a property, and thus have an overriding interest binding upon the building society, despite having moved some of her furniture into the property before completion took place and despite physically occupying the property at the time of registration.	The relevant time to establish actual occupation for the purpose of Sch 3 para 2 is the time of completion. Actual occupation will not be established upon mere preparatory acts to occupy.
Chhokar v Chhokar [1984] FLR 313, CA	A wife's beneficial interest under a trust was found to be binding on a purchaser of the property. Having paid purchase monies to just one trustee (the husband) no overreaching had taken place. The unoverreached interest, coupled with the fact that the wife was found to be in actual occupation at the time of purchase, despite being in hospital having a baby, gave her a binding overriding interest.	Temporary absence from the property will not prevent a finding of actual occupation for the purpose of Sch 3 para 2 provided there is some physical evidence of occupation present (here furniture and belongings remained in the property) coupled with an intention from the temporarily absent occupier to return.
City of London Building Society v Flegg [1988] AC 54	A property was purchased by a married couple with contributions provided by the wife's parents. The parents thus acquired a beneficial interest in the property. The property was mortgaged to the building society which later sought repossession. The building society was not bound by the parents' beneficial interests, having successfully overreached those interests when advancing mortgage monies to the married couple ie two trustees.	Successful overreaching requires payment of monies to at least two trustees. Once overreached, beneficial interests will not bind a purchaser, regardless of any actual occupation of the beneficiaries and any notice the purchaser may have of those interests.

Case	Facts	Principle
Linklending v Bustard [2010] EWCA Civ 424	A woman was found to be in actual occupation for the purpose of **Sch 3 para 2**, despite being absent from the property by reason of being in a mental institution.	In establishing actual occupation for the purpose of **Sch 3 para 2**, relevant factors may include an intention to return to the property, keeping furniture and personal effects at the property, regular visits to the property and continued payment of property outgoings.
Lloyds Bank plc v Rosset [1991] 1 AC 107	House of Lords held that a wife could not claim any binding interest against a bank to whom her husband had mortgaged a semi derelict property. Although approving Court of Appeal statements that she was in actual occupation, she was found to have no interest in the property.	In establishing actual occupation, look at the nature of the property. A semi derelict property may be occupied by virtue of the presence of builders and their supervision on site.
Strand Securities v Caswell [1965] Ch 958, CA	A father failed to establish that he was in actual occupation of a property by showing that his stepdaughter lived at the property. Although he used the property as a base when in London, such use was infrequent and he in no way treated the property as his home. His stepdaughter lived there for her own purposes and was in no way his agent.	Actual occupation for the purpose of Sch 3 para 2 cannot be established through occupation of another unless it can be shown that that other is your agent.
Williams & Glyn's Bank Ltd v Boland [1981] AC 487, HL	A bank was found to be bound by a wife's beneficial interest under a trust. Having advanced the mortgage monies to just one legal owner (the husband) it had not successfully overreached the beneficial interest and this, coupled with the fact that the wife was in actual occupation of the property, gave her an overriding interest binding upon the bank.	Successful overreaching requires payment of monies to at least two trustees. Where a beneficial interest has not been overreached, and the interest holder is in actual occupation of the land, it will bind a purchaser as an overriding interest.

 Exam questions

Problem question

Rory has just inherited a large piece of registered farmland from his uncle Stan. He has been approached by Natural Farming Ltd who wish to purchase the land for £300,000 so that they may use the land to expand their farming business. Rory is happy to sell but has been approached by several people who oppose the sale, namely:

1. his Auntie Vera, who claims to have an interest in the property by virtue of providing over half of the purchase monies when she and Uncle Stan purchased the land in 2011.

2. Malcolm, who leases part of the land for his own farming business. When asked by Rory whether he had any documentation to confirm this, he produced a document headed a deed and signed by both parties, witnessed and dated October 2012, which purported to grant him a 25 years' lease and which detailed the terms of that lease.

3. Peter, a neighbour, who has been using a short cut across the land to the main road. When asked by Rory whether he had any documentation to confirm this, he produced a valid deed that granted him a right of way across the land for the duration of his lifetime.

4. Larry, a homeless person, who Uncle Stan allowed to sleep in one of the disused barns on the land, for free when he needed to.

Are any of these rights binding upon Rory now that he has inherited the land from Uncle Stan and would any of these rights be binding upon Natural Farming Ltd if it went ahead with a purchase of the land?

See the Outline Answers section in the end matter for help with this question.

Essay question

The continued existence of overriding interests means that the objectives behind establishing a registered land system can never be met and the system itself can never be as efficient, certain, and just as was intended.

Discuss.

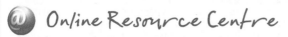

Online Resource Centre

To see an outline answer to this question log onto www.oxfordtextbooks.co.uk/orc/concentrate/

#4
Unregistered land

This is a topic area that may be examined in a self-contained question or as part of a question concerning another topic area. Frequently, it is combined with registered land. It can also appear in questions concerning a particular interest in land, for example an easements question or a restrictive covenants question, where the interest exists over unregistered land and issues arise regarding the ability to enforce that interest against a purchaser of that land.

Problem questions typically focus upon rules of enforcement of interests over unregistered land. For example, you may be told about various types of interests that exist over a piece of unregistered land. (Sometimes those interests will be clearly identified; other times you may have to work out what they are for yourself.) That land will then pass to a purchaser and you will be required to work out whether those interests will be binding upon that purchaser. Often, you will be asked to consider how your answer would differ had the land been registered land at the time of purchase. Sometimes, issues concerning incorrect searches against the Land Charges Register may also appear.

Essay questions may require you to analyse how, if at all, the mode of enforcement of third party interests in unregistered land improved upon the system that existed before the Land Charges Act was passed. Alternatively, you may be asked to compare and contrast the rules and principles of unregistered land with those of the registered land system.

Key facts

- Unregistered land is land where title has not been registered at the Land Registry. Proof of ownership therefore comes from an examination of title deeds relating to that land.

- Identification of any third party proprietary interests burdening a piece of unregistered land cannot be discovered by a search of the land register. Rather, an examination of the title documents and various registers, the most important of which is the Land Charges Register, is required to discover their existence.

- A search of the Land Charges Register is made against the names of previous owners of the land, not the property address. A purchaser is bound by all land charges he did not discover, either by failing to search against all relevant names, or searching against incorrect names.

- Legal interests over unregistered land bind the world, with the exception of the *puisne* mortgage, which requires registration as a land charge to be binding.

- Interests covered by the Land Charges Act 1972 must be registered as the appropriate land charge to bind a purchaser.

- Failure to register such an interest appropriately means that the interest will not bind certain types of purchasers of the land.

- A purchaser can take free of a beneficial interest under a trust in unregistered land where he successfully overreaches that interest.

- Where a purchaser has failed to overreach a beneficial interest under a trust, enforcement of that interest against him depends upon the doctrine of notice.

- Enforcement of pre-1926 restrictive covenants and equitable easements, and interests arising by estoppel, is also governed by the doctrine of notice.

Chapter overview

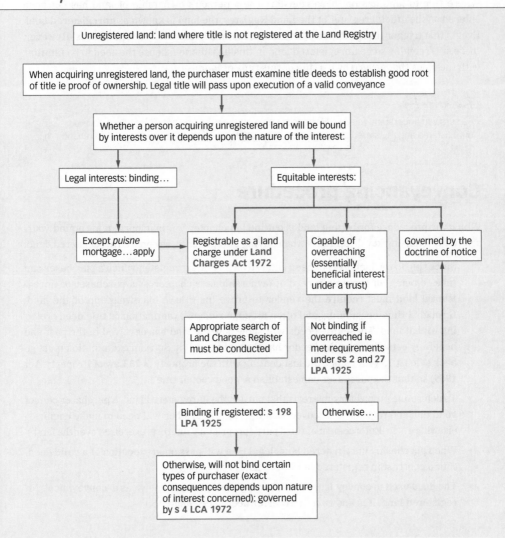

Introduction

Where title to land has not been registered ie a person's ownership of land has not been entered on the official register at the Land Registry, the land is known as **unregistered land**. Events that trigger the need to register title, discussed in chapter 3, are numerous. However, there still remains some unregistered land in this jurisdiction, hence the need to be familiar with the rules that govern ownership of this type of land.

Revision tip

Be sure you understand the key differences between the rules and principles which govern unregistered and registered land as this can be a key focus of an exam question (link to chapter 3).

Conveyancing procedure

Whilst the procedure for buying land is outlined in chapter 5, it is important to remind yourself of the following key differences when buying unregistered, as opposed to registered, land:

- Since title to the land has not been entered on an official register, which a purchaser can take as being an accurate record of ownership (see chapter 3), a purchaser of unregistered land must require the vendor to prove his title ie his ownership of the land, through a time-consuming, and often mistake ridden, examination of title deeds relating to that land. These title deeds will show how the land has devolved in the past and hopefully establish that the vendor has the right to sell it. Such an examination must go back at least 15 years since the last dealing with the property (s 23 Law of Property Act 1969) so that the purchaser can establish a 'good root of title'.
- To determine proprietary interests that burden the unregistered land, a purchaser cannot go to the land register to discover such interests, but rather will need to make enquiries elsewhere (see 'Enforcement of third party proprietary interests exercised over the land').
- When purchasing unregistered land, legal title will pass upon execution of a valid deed. (For a contrast in registered land, see chapter 5.)
- The deed used to convey legal title of unregistered land is known as a 'conveyance'. (In registered land, it is known as a 'transfer deed': see chapter 5.)

Enforcement of third party proprietary interests exercised over the land

In registered land, enforceability of such interests largely depends upon entry on the land register, with overriding interests being a notable exception: see chapter 3. With unregistered land, enforcement of these interests is governed by different rules, dependent largely upon whether the interest is legal or equitable in nature: see Figure 4.1.

Figure 4.1 Rules of enforcement in unregistered land

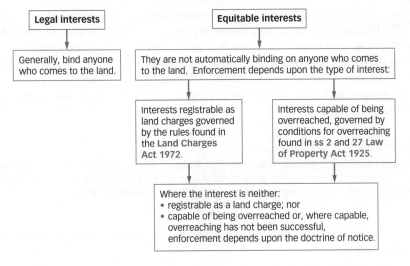

An exam question may not specifically identify whether an interest is legal or equitable. You must therefore know the rules regarding the formalities for creating interests (link to chapter 2).

Legal interests

A purchaser is bound by legal interests over unregistered land, subject to obtaining a waiver or release from the holder of the interest.

This may not be as harsh as it sounds. Generally, legal interests are created by deed and such documents should be kept with the title deeds so that a purchaser may discover their existence prior to making the decision to buy the land. Of course, there are exceptions; for example legal easements created impliedly by necessity (discussed in chapter 12). However, such rights may be (although not always) discoverable by the purchaser making a physical inspection of the land itself.

There is one exception of a legal interest that is not automatically binding upon a purchaser and that is the *puisne* **mortgage** (for a definition, see Table 4.1). Enforcement of this type of interest in fact depends upon registration as a land charge (see 'Interests registrable as land charges under the Land Charges Act 1972').

Equitable interests

Interests registrable as land charges under the Land Charges Act 1972

The basic principles

Interests that fall into this category must be registered as the appropriate land charge under the LCA 1972. Registration of the interest constitutes actual notice of that interest (s 198 LPA 1925 and explained in chapter 2). Consequently, that interest will bind anyone who comes to the land.

Where the interest has not been registered appropriately, it will be void against certain types of purchasers, whether the purchaser has knowledge of the existence of the interest or not. Notice is not relevant in the land charges system: s 199(1) LPA 1925; *Hollington Brothers Ltd v Rhodes* [1951].

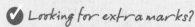

✔️ Looking for extra marks?

There may be a strong argument today to claim that where a purchaser takes title to land expressly subject to the rights of another, this will give rise to a constructive trust or that maybe such rights should be enforceable under the **Contracts (Rights of Third Parties) Act 1999**.

Which interests fall into this category and what type of land charge must they be registered as?

Governed by **s 2 LCA 1972**, the interests in Table 4.1 are the ones you should know.

✔️ Looking for extra marks?

According to the decision in *Pritchard v Briggs* [1980] a right of pre-emption is not an interest in unregistered land upon creation. It only becomes an equitable proprietary interest upon the vendor making the decision to sell. A decision to sell will activate any registration of a right of pre-emption as a Class C(iv) land charge, which, up until that time, remains dormant.

How does the holder of the interest register it as a land charge?

Application to register the interest as a land charge will be made to the Land Charges Department of the Land Registry at Plymouth. The interest should be registered as a land charge against the name of the estate owner at the time the interest is created and over whose estate the interest is to be exercised: s 3(1) LCA 1972. This is the name of the owner as it appears in the title deeds. The entry on the Land Charges Register will record the nature of the interest to be protected and the name of the person who claims to hold that interest.

How does the purchaser acquire knowledge of those interests registered as land charges?

The purchaser should conduct a search of the Land Charges Register to discover any land charges that have been registered and thus uncover any interests exercised over

Enforcement of third party proprietary interests exercised over the land

the land about to be purchased which will be binding upon him: see Table 4.1. This is typically conducted between exchange of contracts and completion (discussed in chapter 5). Where binding land charges are discovered after the purchaser has entered into a valid contract to purchase, **s 24 LPA 1969** entitles the purchaser to withdraw from the contract, provided he did not know about the existence of the land charge at the time of entering into it.

Table 4.1 Interests registrable as land charges under LCA 1972

Type of interest	Description	Land Charge
Puisne mortgages	A legal mortgage where the mortgagee does not take possession of the title deeds. This is because the mortgage is a second or subsequent mortgage over the property and the title deeds are with the first mortgagee.	Class C(i)
Estate contract	Includes contracts to buy freehold estates (see chapter 5), contracts to buy leasehold estates ie equitable leases (see chapter 6), options to purchase and rights of preemption (see chapter 5).	Class C(iv)
Restrictive covenants between freeholders created on/after 1 January 1926	Defined and discussed in chapter 13.	Class D(ii)
Equitable easements created on/after 1 January 1926	Defined and discussed in chapter 12.	Class D(iii)
Rights to occupy the family home under the **Family Law Act 1996**	A spouse (and also now civil partners under the **Civil Partnership Act 2004**) has a right to occupy the family home which, if registered as a land charge, is enforceable against anyone coming to the land. Although a statutory right, rather than a proprietary interest, enforcement is governed by the **LCA 1972**.	Class F

The search should be made against the names of the previous owners of the land, against whom land charges may have been registered. This has proven to be a major problem with the land charges system as purchasers may not always know the names against which they should be making their searches, especially the names of owners who owned the land many years ago and who therefore may not be uncovered when looking at the title deeds to acquire a good root of title, which requires just a minimum of 15 years investigation of title. Regardless of this fact, a purchaser would still be bound by land charges he had not been able to discover. To partly address this problem, **s 25 LPA 1969** provides a scheme whereby the purchaser can claim compensation for the existence of undiscoverable yet binding land charges, on condition that:

- he investigated good root of title and searched against the names of the estate owners revealed in this investigation; and
- he had no actual knowledge of the existence of the land charge(s) in question.

In addition, errors may be made where searches are made against incorrect names. Where this is the case, the land charge registered against the correct name is binding. Alternatively, where the search has been made against the correct name, but the land charge has been registered against an incorrect version of that name, the land charge will not bind: *Diligent Finance Co Ltd v Alleyne* [1972].

Where searches are made against the correct names, the purchaser acquires 15 working days' immunity so that any interests registered within this time will not bind him.

What are the consequences of failing to register an interest as a land charge?

These differ depending upon the type of interest and thus category of land charge that should have been registered: see Figure 4.2.

Figure 4.2 Consequences of failing to register an interest as a land charge

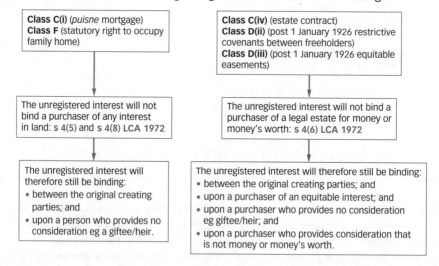

Class C(i) (*puisne* mortgage)
Class F (statutory right to occupy family home)

The unregistered interest will not bind a purchaser of any interest in land: s 4(5) and s 4(8) LCA 1972

The unregistered interest will therefore still be binding:
- between the original creating parties; and
- upon a person who provides no consideration eg a giftee/heir.

Class C(iv) (estate contract)
Class D(ii) (post 1 January 1926 restrictive covenants between freeholders)
Class D(iii) (post 1 January 1926 equitable easements)

The unregistered interest will not bind a purchaser of a legal estate for money or money's worth: s 4(6) LCA 1972

The unregistered interest will therefore still be binding:
- between the original creating parties; and
- upon a purchaser of an equitable interest; and
- upon a purchaser who provides no consideration eg giftee/heir; and
- upon a purchaser who provides consideration that is not money or money's worth.

Revision tip

Be sure you understand the precise effect an unregistered interest will have upon different types of purchasers. Look out, in exam questions, for people who inherit or who are gifted the property.

Enforcement of third party proprietary interests exercised over the land

When thinking about these consequences remember the following:

- Once an interest is void for non-registration, it cannot be revived upon a subsequent purchase of the land, even if the later purchaser is not one for value.

- A 'purchaser' for the purposes of s 4 LCA 1972, is any person who, for valuable consideration, takes any interest in land or a charge on the land: s 17(1) LCA 1972.

- A purchaser 'for money or money's worth' under s 4(6) LCA 1972 is one who provides valuable consideration either in the form of actual money or, alternatively, something that can be computed in financial terms, for example shares. It does not include someone who provided marriage as consideration, although marriage is itself recognized as valuable consideration elsewhere in land law (s 205(xxxi) LPA 1925) and indeed would be considered appropriate value for the purpose of s 4(5) and (8) in Figure 4.2.

- As long as the consideration provided by the purchaser is valuable (and in addition, where the land charge is one governed by s 4(6) LCA 1972, provided in the form of money or money's worth), the court will not enquire into the adequacy of the consideration provided.

- The fact that the purchaser has knowledge of the existence of the unregistered interest prior to the purchase will not mean that he will be bound by that interest. Notice has no role to play under the LCA 1972 and there is no requirement that the purchaser must be acting in good faith.

These last two points were confirmed in the key case of *Midland Bank Trust Co Ltd v Green* [1981]:

Midland Bank Trust Co Ltd v Green [1981] AC 513

A father gave his son an option to purchase the family farm. This estate contract was not registered by the son as a Class C(iv) land charge. The father later sold the farm to his wife for £500. Despite this being considerably less than the value of the land, and the wife having knowledge of the unregistered estate contract when she made the purchase, she was held to take free from that unregistered interest. Since the interest had not been appropriately registered, it would not bind her. The fact that she knew that the interest existed was deemed irrelevant. The court also felt it inappropriate to consider the adequacy of the consideration provided.

✅ Looking for extra marks?

When the case was heard by the Court of Appeal, Lord Denning felt that the £500 provided by the wife for the purchase was a 'gross undervalue'. Lord Everleigh said that the transaction was more akin to a gift of land coupled with a token £500 to meet the requirements under s 4 LCA 1972. The dealing between the father and his wife was deemed fraudulent and dishonest. However, Lord Wilberforce in the House of Lords disagreed, stating that it would be difficult to hold £500 as a nominal sum of money. In any case, provided the consideration was real, there would be no enquiry into whether the consideration was adequate; an expression he termed as one of transparent difficulty. On the issue of the wife not acting in good faith because she knew about the son's unregistered estate contract, Lord Wilberforce noted that the LCA 1972 did not include the words 'good faith' when describing a purchaser. He considered this omission a deliberate one and indeed thought that if acting in good faith had been a requirement of the purchaser, it would effectively be reintroducing an element of notice, which the LCA 1972 was aiming to avoid.

Interests capable of being overreached

Essentially, this relates to the beneficial interest under a trust (discussed in chapters 9 and 10). Not being capable of registration as a land charge, their enforcement against a purchaser of unregistered land primarily depends upon application of the conditions for overreaching laid down in **ss 2 and 27 LPA 1925**, discussed in chapter 3. These conditions operate exactly the same in unregistered land: see Figure 4.3.

Figure 4.3 Consequences of overreaching/not overreaching

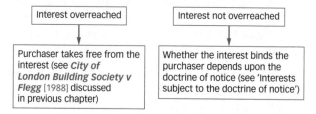

Interests subject to the doctrine of notice

The main interests that are still governed by this doctrine (and thus their enforcement is not dependent upon registration as a land charge) are:

- overreachable interests that have not been successfully overreached;
- restrictive covenants entered into between freeholders of land and created before 1 January 1926;
- equitable easements created before 1 January 1926; and
- interests arising by estoppel.

How does the doctrine of notice work?

An interest will only bind a person if he is not a *bona fide purchaser of a legal estate for value without notice*. To remind yourself as to how this operates, refer to the appropriate discussion in chapter 2.

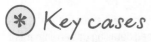

An exam question may require you to show how the doctrine of notice operates (link to chapter 2). It may also require you to assess its role in unregistered land today, so link with discussions in *Midland Bank Trust Co Ltd v Green* [1981].

✳ Key cases

Case	Facts	Principle
Diligent Finance Co Ltd v Alleyne [1972] 23 P&CR 346	A wife failed to register her Class F land charge against her husband's full name. The right was subsequently not binding upon a finance company who had correctly searched the register against the full name.	A land charge registered against the incorrect name, will not bind a purchaser who searches the register against the correct name.
Hollington Brothers Ltd v Rhodes [1951] 2 All ER 487	An equitable lease which had not been registered as an appropriate land charge, did not bind a purchaser of the reversion, despite the sale being expressly subject to the lease with a purchase price that reflected this fact.	An interest must be registered as a land charge, where appropriate, to bind a purchaser. Notice is irrelevant under the LCA 1972.
Midland Bank Trust Co Ltd v Green [1981] AC 513	An estate contract which had not been registered as a Class C(iv) land charge was not binding upon a purchaser who knew about it and who provided consideration that appeared to be undervalued.	A court is not to enquire about the adequacy of consideration provided by a purchaser in respect of application of the LCA 1972 rules. The knowledge of the purchaser is irrelevant.

Problem question

Josh has just purchased Willow House, a detached property with a garage and large garden. Title to the property is unregistered.

When the vendor, Guy, originally purchased the house, his wife, Marian, contributed a quarter of the purchase price, although the legal title was conveyed to Guy alone. Marian works in Italy and has to spend most of the week there, returning to stay in Willow House just at weekends. She does, however, leave many of her personal belongings in Willow House to make travelling between the countries easier. When a survey of the property was conducted prior to the purchase, it was on a weekday so Marian was out of the country. The surveyor noticed female belongings in the house and photos of Guy with a lady but made no enquiries as to who the lady was or who the female possessions belonged to. The surveyor did not mention anything about this to Josh.

Whilst Guy owned Willow House, he allowed Susie, the neighbour, to use a short cut across the garden of Willow House to get to the main road. Susie has a valid deed detailing this arrangement. Guy also allowed the garage to be leased to his friend Pete. This arrangement was drawn up in a document signed by both Guy and Pete, and gave Pete exclusive use of the garage for ten years.

Advise Josh as to whether Marian, Susie, and Pete have any rights that are enforceable against him.

How, if at all, would your answer differ, if Josh had been gifted Willow House rather than purchased it?

See the Outline Answers section in the end matter for help with this question.

Essay question

What were the perceived problems with the doctrine of notice? How did the land charges system seek to address these problems and was it successful in doing so?

@ Online Resource Centre

To see an outline answer to this question log onto www.oxfordtextbooks.co.uk/orc/concentrate/

#5
The freehold estate

The examination

How the material covered in this chapter appears in an exam paper will, to a large extent, be dependent upon individual approaches taken by different teaching institutions (and it is for this reason that no specimen exam questions have been provided at the end of this chapter). You must be guided by the tutorials and lectures that you have attended to ascertain where such material may appear within the exam and to what degree. For example, some institutions may not cover material concerning the characteristics of a freehold estate in any depth; others may, perhaps linking it to the concept of settled land and the creation of trusts (discussed in chapter 9). The material covered in relation to the creation of a freehold estate, the formalities and principles as to when equitable and legal ownership is established, applies elsewhere and you must be able to identify scenarios where such material is relevant for discussion.

Key facts

- The freehold estate is the largest of the two estates in land that has legal capacity and a person who holds a freehold estate over land is tantamount to being the owner of that land (although technically ownership rests with the Crown).

- The legal freehold estate is technically known as the fee simple absolute in possession and the characteristics of a legal freehold estate can be found from interpreting this technical definition.

- A contract for the transfer of a freehold estate must meet the requirements under **s 2 Law of Property (Miscellaneous Provisions) Act 1989.**

- Where the contract is to be varied, **s 2 LP(MP)A 1989** must be complied with when the variation is of a material term.

- A valid and specifically enforceable contract for the transfer of a freehold estate will give the purchaser an equitable interest in the land to be purchased, known as an estate contract.

- Legal title to the land will not pass to the purchaser until completion, which involves execution of a valid deed (**s 52 Law of Property Act 1925, s 1 LP(MP)A 1989**) and registration of title.

- The exact moment when legal title passes differs depending upon whether the land being purchased is registered (where title passes upon registration of title) or unregistered land (where title passes upon execution of a valid deed).

Chapter overview

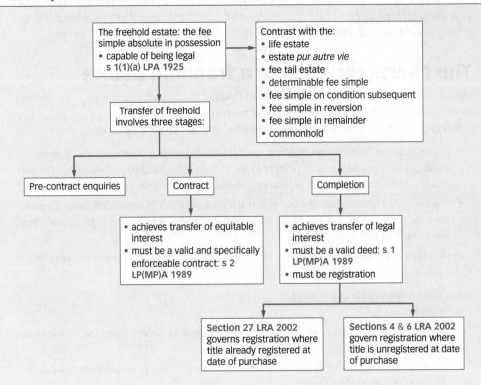

The freehold estate: the fee simple absolute in possession
- capable of being legal
s 1(1)(a) LPA 1925

Contrast with the:
- life estate
- estate *pur autre vie*
- fee tail estate
- determinable fee simple
- fee simple on condition subsequent
- fee simple in reversion
- fee simple in remainder
- commonhold

Transfer of freehold involves three stages:

Pre-contract enquiries

Contract

Completion

- achieves transfer of equitable interest
- must be a valid and specifically enforceable contract: s 2 LP(MP)A 1989

- achieves transfer of legal interest
- must be a valid deed: s 1 LP(MP)A 1989
- must be registration

Section 27 LRA 2002 governs registration where title already registered at date of purchase

Sections 4 & 6 LRA 2002 govern registration where title is unregistered at date of purchase

Introduction

The **freehold estate** is one of the recognized estates in land capable of being legal: s 1(1)(a) LPA 1925. It is the largest of the two estates that have legal capability, the other being the leasehold estate (see chapter 6).

The characteristics of a freehold estate

Whilst there is more than one type of freehold estate, the largest, and the only one that has legal capability, is the **fee simple absolute in possession**.

Holding this estate is as near to 'absolute ownership' as is possible to achieve since:

- its duration is without end, (unless the holder dies without heirs, at which point the estate dissolves and the land reverts to the Crown *bona vacantia*, illustrating the continuing technical ownership of land by the Crown: see chapter 1); and

- the holder's rights to use and possess the land are virtually unlimited, save for statutory limitations and subject to lesser estate holders' rights, whose estates have been carved out of that freehold estate.

The characteristics of this freehold estate can be identified by looking at the meaning of fee simple absolute in possession:

1. **It is an inheritable estate (*fee*)**
   This differs from:

   – a *life estate* which is not inheritable as it comes to an end upon the death of the grantee; and

   – an *estate pur autre vie*; again not inheritable as it comes to an end upon the death of someone other than the grantee.

   Both the *life estate* and the *estate pur autre vie* are types of freehold estates but neither have legal capability under s 1(1) LPA 1925 and can only exist in equity behind a trust.

2. **The estate is inheritable by anyone (*simple*)**
   Contrast with the *fee tail* estate where inheritability is curtailed to direct lineal descendants and sometimes only to those of a certain gender, for example *fee tail male*. Since 1 January 1997, when the Trusts of Land and Appointment of Trustees Act 1996 came into force, it is no longer possible to create this freehold estate of limited inheritance.

3. **The estate is perpetual and not liable to end prematurely upon the occurrence of a specified event (*absolute*)**

   This differs from:

   – A *determinable fee simple*: a fee simple estate that will be held until it is terminated automatically upon the occurrence of a specified event. For example, if Blackacre is granted to X until he qualifies as a solicitor, the fee simple he holds is not *absolute* and will terminate upon his qualification, if and when it occurs. Such fee simple estates can be ascertained by looking for words which limit the grant, for example 'whilst', 'until', 'during'.

- A *fee simple on condition subsequent*: where the fee simple is granted but is subject to a clause that if a particular condition is met in the future, the estate may be forfeited from the grantee. For example, Blackacre is granted to X on condition that he does not qualify as a solicitor. Such fee simple estates can be ascertained from wording in the grant that indicates the estate will last forever unless a condition limiting its duration is met, for example 'unless', 'provided that', 'on condition that'. It is normal when granting this type of fee simple that a right of entry is reserved for the grantor, entitling him to forfeit the estate in the event that the condition is fulfilled.

- A *fee simple on condition precedent*: this is where a fee simple is granted but which will only commence when a certain event has occurred; for example, granting Blackacre to X and his heirs when he reaches 21 years of age.

✅ Looking for extra marks?

What are the differences between a *determinable fee simple* and a *fee simple on condition subsequent*?

- A *determinable fee simple* terminates automatically when the determining event occurs, with the fee simple reverting back to the grantor. When the condition which allows for the estate to be forfeited is met in a *fee simple on condition precedent*, the fee simple remains vested in the grantee until such time as the grantor chooses to exercise his right to forfeit.

- A *determinable fee simple* can only ever exist in equity behind a trust. A *fee simple on condition subsequent* ranks as a legal estate. A fee simple subject to a right of entry is absolute according to the **Law of Property (Miscellaneous Provisions) Act 1989**, thus falling within **s 1(1)(a) LPA 1925**.

The courts have a greater tendency to strike out undesirable *conditions subsequent* than equivalent clauses in *determinable fee simples*. Whilst striking out the latter destroys the grant of the fee simple in its entirety, striking out the former, whilst it gets rid of the offending condition, will not destroy the grant of the fee simple which takes effect as a *fee simple absolute*.

4. The estate is one that gives the estate holder the present right to enjoy and possess (*in possession*).

    Possession need not be physical: **s 205(1)(xix) LPA 1925**. It can include being in receipt of rent or profits or having a right to receive the same. This is how a person can still hold the freehold estate even when a leasehold estate has been carved out of it and physical possession is with the tenant.

Are all freehold estates in possession?

No, the freehold estate may be:

- *in reversion*: a freehold owner may carve out a lesser estate, for example a life estate, from the fee simple estate. During the life interest, the freehold owner has parted with his present right to possess. When the life estate ends, the right to use and possess *reverts* to the freehold owner. So, during the existence of the lesser estate, the fee simple is not held in possession, but is being held *in reversion*.

- *in remainder*: a freehold owner may grant a lesser estate from the fee simple for use in the future. This lesser estate is then known as one that is *in remainder* ie it gives the grantee a present right but to future use and enjoyment of the land. For example, X holds the fee simple and leaves it in his will to his wife for life and thereafter to his son. The son's interest is held *in remainder*. He has to wait for the expiry of his mother's life interest before he has the right to use and enjoy the land.

Estates held *in reversion* or *in remainder* can only exist in equity behind a trust. Only fee simple estates held *in possession* have legal capability: **s 1 LPA 1925**.

The commonhold

This is a form of freehold estate that was introduced by the **Commonhold and Leasehold Reform Act 2002**. Key points to note are:

- The **commonhold** is intended to benefit blocks of flats and apartments where rights to possess and enjoy are usually based upon leasehold estates.

- It allows occupants, known as 'unit holders', to own the freehold of their flat/apartment.

- The freehold of the shared common parts within the building is held by a 'commonhold association', a private limited company that assumes responsibility for the management and upkeep of these shared common parts.

- Each unit holder becomes a member of the commonhold association. Collectively, they have the ability to control and manage the building in accordance with the 'commonhold community statement', which specifies the rights and duties of the commonhold association and unit holders.

Currently, few commonhold estates have been established, since the requirements to do so are difficult to meet and they have not proved popular with developers of blocks of flats who appear to still favour the creation of leasehold estates.

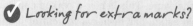

✅ Looking for extra marks?

Why create a commonhold rather than a long leasehold estate?

- Whilst the owner of a lease, even where the term of that lease is very long, essentially owns a wasting asset, the owner of a commonhold, a type of freehold estate, does not.
- Duties imposed upon unit holders by the commonhold community statement will equally apply to incoming unit holders as to outgoing ones, thus erasing problems of enforcing freehold covenants on the transfer of land (see chapter 13).

Formalities for transfer of a freehold estate

Pre contract stage

Involves numerous enquiries being made by the purchaser about the freehold title he wishes to purchase, and negotiations between the vendor and the purchaser, regarding such things as price, inclusion of chattels in the sale, time frame for the completion of the sale etc.

Contract stage

What does this achieve?

See Figure 5.1 for an explanation of what contract stage achieves at both common law and in equity.

Figure 5.1 Effect of a contract to purchase

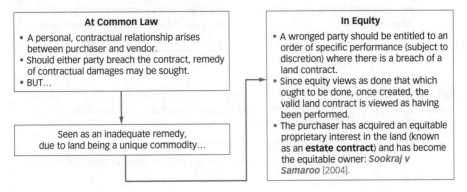

At Common Law	In Equity
• A personal, contractual relationship arises between purchaser and vendor. • Should either party breach the contract, remedy of contractual damages may be sought. • BUT...	• A wronged party should be entitled to an order of specific performance (subject to discretion) where there is a breach of a land contract. • Since equity views as done that which ought to be done, once created, the valid land contract is viewed as having been performed. • The purchaser has acquired an equitable proprietary interest in the land (known as an **estate contract**) and has become the equitable owner: *Sookraj v Samaroo* [2004].

Seen as an inadequate remedy, due to land being a unique commodity...

What about legal title?

This remains with the vendor, who effectively holds it on trust for the purchaser until such time as the sale is completed (see 'Completion stage'). Remember, this trust relationship does not reflect a usual trust: the vendor remains in possession of the property and can exclude the purchaser, although he must keep the land in the same condition as it was when the valid contract was made.

Revision tip

Remember that a person may acquire an equitable proprietary interest upon the completion of any valid contract relating to the creation/transfer of other estates or interests in land which is capable of specific performance. See chapter 6 and the discussion of the case of *Walsh v Lonsdale* (1882).

Formalities for transfer of a freehold estate

****

Formalities

All contracts must meet basic contractual formalities ie offer and acceptance, consideration, intention etc. However, where the contract has land as its subject matter, such as one for the transfer of a freehold estate, additional requirements must be met. These differ depending upon the date of creation of the contract.

Created pre 27/09/89	Created on/after 27/09/89
Contracts must comply with **s 40 LPA 1925** ie <ul><li>in writing (containing the essential terms and signed by the party against whom it is sought to be enforced); or</li><li>oral with either<ul><li>– written evidence signed by the party against whom it is sought to be enforced; or</li><li>– part performance.</li></ul></li></ul>	Contracts must comply with **s 2 LP(MP)A 1989** ie <ul><li>in writing;</li><li>containing all the terms; and</li><li>signed by both parties</li></ul>unless they fall into the exceptions in **s 2(5) LP(MP)A 1989**, in which case compliance with these three requirements is not necessary eg contracts to create leases of three years or less in duration.

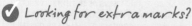 **Looking for extra marks?**

In addition to the statutory exceptions, remember various non-statutory exceptions have arisen as to when a contract need not be **s 2 LP(MP)A 1989** compliant, for example:

- lock-out agreements: *Pitt v PHH Asset Management Ltd* [1994];
- executed contracts ie those already performed: *Keay v Morris Homes (West Midlands) Ltd* [2012].

Section 2 LP(MP)A 1989 analysed

A contract which fails to satisfy all three requirements under **s 2** will be deemed void.

In writing

This can include typing, printing, and emailing (*J Pereira Fernades SA v Mehta* [2006]).

Containing all the terms

What terms?

The four 'P's:

- Parties, for example vendor and purchaser;
- Price, whether specifically or the mechanism by which it is to be calculated;
- Property ie land and estate, for example freehold;

- other Provisions. These include those terms that have been expressly agreed upon between the parties. Otherwise, standard terms and conditions will be implied, without the need for their express insertion.

Where?

The terms should be found either:

- in one document; or
- two identical documents where they are to be exchanged; or
- by reference to another document (s 2(2)).

Omissions

Where an essential term of the contract has been omitted, this would make the contract void. However:

- if you can establish that the omission is a mistake and that both parties had orally agreed to the omitted term but that the written document failed to reflect this, the court may allow rectification to correct the inaccurate written record: s 2(4) LP(MP)A 1989 and *Wright v Robert Leonard Developments Ltd* [1994]. Note *Oun v Ahmad* [2008], where an order for rectification was declined since the expressly agreed term had been deliberately omitted from the contract;
- where the term can be seen as part of a separate agreement not concerning the land, even if negotiated at the same time as the land contract, its omission from that land contract will not invalidate the latter. The ability to hive off parts of the arrangement into separate agreements is accepted: see, for example, *Tootal Clothing Ltd v Guinea Properties Management Ltd* (1992). Whether it can be seen as truly separate is ultimately a question of fact although the omitted term should not be a condition of the land contract. See, for example *North Eastern Properties Ltd v Coleman & Quinn Conveyancing* [2010]. Certainly, it is clear that the courts are keen to avoid parties using the strict formalities under s 2 LP(MP)A 1989 as a way of escaping their obligations.

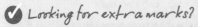

✅ Looking for extra marks?

For further case law examples of separate arrangements see *Record v Bell* [1991], where the courts were willing to find a 'collateral' contract regarding proof of title sitting alongside the land contract for sale, and *Grossman v Hooper* [2001].

Signed by both parties

Where the terms are incorporated by reference to another document, it is the incorporating document that must be signed by both parties (see *Firstpost Homes Ltd v Johnson* [1995].)

This requirement of a signature must be interpreted in accordance with its ordinary meaning. Printing a name on the document was rejected as a signature in *Firstpost*. The court identified the ordinary meaning as writing one's own name with one's own hand. Remember, however, that with technical advances, the ordinary meaning of a signature is likely to change.

Varying the contract terms

To do so may require you to comply with certain formalities but whether this will be the case depends upon the nature of the term that you are seeking to vary: *McClausland v Duncan Lawrie Ltd* [1997].

Varying a material term The variation must comply with s 2 LP(MP) A 1989. If it does not comply then: • the variation will be invalid; • the original terms of the contract will stand unless the oral variation is so fundamental that it amounts to a wholly new agreement, with the original agreement considered rescinded (*British & Benningtons Ltd v NW Cachar Tea Co* (1923)).	**Varying an immaterial term** No need to comply with s 2 LP(MP)A 1989.

Can contracts arise through correspondence?

The decision in *Hooper v Sherman* [1994], which allowed for a contract to arise from two letters, was not followed in the case of *Commission for the New Towns v Cooper (GB) Ltd* [1995]. Since no one letter contained all the terms and was signed by both parties, there was no document compliant with s 2 and thus no contract had arisen. This decision would seem to be the current position on this issue.

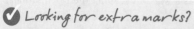

✅ Looking for extra marks?

Options to purchase are a specific type of land contract involving two key stages:

• the vendor grants the option to the purchaser, whereby the former agrees to keep open a specified offer to sell the freehold estate to the purchaser for a specified period;

• the purchaser may accept that offer at any time during the specified period on the terms as outlined in the option.

According to *Spiro v Glencrown Properties Ltd* [1991], it is the initial grant of the option that must comply with s 2, whilst the exercise of it need not. Since the exercise of the option is a unilateral act by the purchaser, to enforce s 2 compliance at this stage would be nonsensical. To require both parties to sign the exercise of the option, as s 2 requires, would destroy the whole purpose of an option. The purpose of s 2 is to record the mutual consent of the parties. Only the grant of the option depends upon this mutual consent.

Estoppel intervention

In some circumstances, equity may intervene to give a purchaser equitable rights even where no document compliant with s 2 LP(MP)A 1989 exists. This was the case in *Yaxley v Gotts* [2000] where the claimant had acted upon an oral agreement, to his detriment. The courts were willing to recognize that in equity he had an interest in the land. The defendant was thus estopped from asserting the true legal position that no valid contract existed.

In the recent House of Lords decision of *Cobbe v Yeoman's Row Management Ltd* [2008], it was emphasized that a proprietary estoppel would only exist where it was clear that the claimant believed he either had a certain interest in another's property or an expectation that he would acquire one. (Here, the claimant only had expectations of further negotiations to enter into a certain contract as regards a joint development project of land, rather than a certain interest in the land itself.) Further, Lord Scott noted *obiter* that proprietary estoppel could not be used as a way of enforcing an agreement that would otherwise be declared void for lack of meeting statutory requirements.

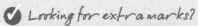 **✔ Looking for extra marks?**

Initially, some commentators saw the decision in *Cobbe v Yeoman's Row Management Ltd* [2008] as an attempt to severely curtail the use of estoppel. However, the later decision of *Thorner v Major & Others* [2009] (an inheritance expectation case) has suggested this is not the case. Perhaps the strictness applied in *Cobbe* can be partly explained because of the commercial, rather than familial, relationship between the parties. (If you think that estoppel will be examined in great detail, take a look at the opinions of the House of Lords in both cases. Estoppel is also considered in a little more detail in Chapter 11.)

Completion stage

Transfer of the legal interest

The exact time that this occurs will differ depending upon whether the title being purchased is registered or unregistered at the date of purchase.

Formalities

Deed

To pass legal freehold title, there must be a valid deed: s 52 LPA 1925. The current requirements for a valid deed are laid down in s 1(2) LP(MP)A 1989, as discussed in chapter 2.

Revision tip

Remember not to confuse the formalities for a valid deed with those for a valid contract. For example, whilst a contract must be signed by both parties, a deed need only be signed by the person granting the interest.

Formalities for transfer of a freehold estate

✳✳✳✳✳✳✳✳✳

Registration

Title will then have to be registered. This may be for the first time. Whether it is or not will determine when legal title actually passes to the purchaser.

Revision tip

Link to chapter 3 where the requirement to register a transfer of a freehold estate is considered in more detail.

The flowchart in Figure 5.2 illustrates the completion stage of a purchase.

Figure 5.2 Completion stage

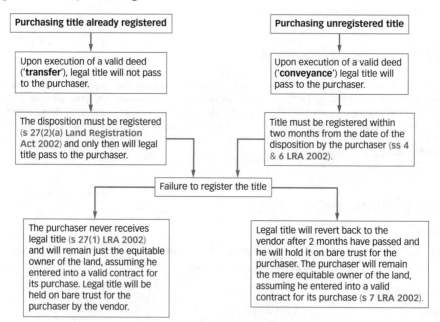

 Key cases

Case	Facts	Principle
Cobbe v Yeoman's Row Management Ltd [2008] 1 WLR 1752	Negotiations occurred between Cobbe and Yeoman's Row regarding development of a piece of land owned by the latter. Cobbe incurred expenses in undertaking works and obtaining planning under the impression that the land would be transferred to him for a joint development project. No written agreement was reached and Yeoman's Row pulled out of the deal once planning had been granted. A claim to proprietary estoppel by Cobbe was rejected.	For a successful estoppel claim there must be more than a general sense of unconscionability. The claimant must show a belief he has a certain property right in the land or an expectation that he will acquire one.
Commission for the New Towns v Cooper (GB) Ltd [1995] Ch 259	Faxes were exchanged amounting to an offer and acceptance regarding the sale of land. The exchange did not create a valid land contract.	For a valid contract in land to exist, there must be one document containing all the terms and signed by both parties.
Firstpost Homes Ltd v Johnson [1995] 1 WLR 1567	A letter regarding the sale of land, and which enclosed a plan identifying the land, was held not to constitute a valid contract under **s 2 LP(MP)A 1989**, as it had not been signed by both parties. Although both the letter and the plan had been signed by the vendor, the purchaser had only signed the plan. The typing of his name on the letter was not enough to constitute his signature.	It is the 'incorporating document' which must be signed by both parties. A 'signature' should be given its ordinary meaning.
McClausland v Duncan Lawrie Ltd [1997] 1 WLR 38	A completion date set for a Sunday was changed in an exchange of letters that did not comply with **s 2 LP(MP)A 1989**. The variation of the completion date was thus ineffective and the original agreement stood.	When seeking to vary a material term of the contract, the variation itself must comply with **s 2 LP(MP)A 1989**.

Key cases

✱✱✱✱✱✱✱✱✱✱✱✱

Case	Facts	Principle
Tootal Clothing Ltd v Guinea Properties Management Ltd (1992) 64 P&CR	An agreement for the grant of a lease coupled with an agreement that the tenant would carry out shop fitting works in a specified time in return for payment by the landlord. The lease was granted, the tenant carried out the works but the landlord refused to pay. An attempt by the landlord to argue there was just one contract which failed to incorporate all the terms in accordance with **s 2 LP(MP) A 1989**, and thus was invalid, was rejected.	The court found the existence of two agreements: one for the grant of the lease and one for the works. Thus the issue of the works need not have been incorporated in the same document as the lease for it to be enforceable.
Wright v Robert Leonard Developments Ltd [1994] NPC 49	An agreement related to the sale of a flat and furnishings, although the latter were not contained in the contract but in a separate schedule to which the contract made no reference. Upon removing the furnishings, the vendor's defence was that there existed no valid contract containing all the terms expressly agreed between the parties, since the written agreement failed to incorporate the furnishings. This was rejected. Convincing evidence existed to establish that the parties had agreed upon the inclusion of the furnishings in the sale and thus the contract, once rectified, was enforced.	If a contract appears invalid for not containing all the terms expressly agreed between the parties, where there is convincing evidence that the parties had agreed upon the omitted term, the court may order rectification of the contract, thus making it valid.
Yaxley v Gotts [2000] Ch 162	The claimant had reached an oral agreement with the father of the defendant that, if the latter bought a house and the claimant conducted substantial building works to convert the house into flats, he would be given the ground floor flats. In fact, the defendant bought the house. Unaware of this fact, the claimant carried out the works to the value of £9,000 and when the defendant sought to evict the claimant, the latter claimed an interest in the property. The court recognized the claimant had an interest in the property.	A person may be estopped from asserting the true legal position where it would be unconscionable to do so: where another has relied and acted upon a promise to their detriment.

#6
The leasehold estate

The topic of leases is a vast one and material on this topic has been divided into two separate chapters in this book. How much of this material is relevant to you will depend upon the course that you have studied. You must also be guided by your tutorials and lectures as to how the material, contained in both these chapters, may be combined in an exam question.

On the material covered within this chapter, typical problem questions require you to assess the status of occupants in a property: whether they occupy on the basis of a lease or licence. Sound knowledge of the principles used to distinguish the two is vital and good use of case law is key to doing well. As a general guide:

- Explain the key differences between a lease and a licence and the significance of these differences in terms of the issue you are being asked to consider.
- Assess whether the occupants enjoy exclusive possession. If no, occupancy can only be based upon a licence. If yes, remember to check that the occupants don't fall into the exceptions where a finding of exclusive occupation may not give rise to a lease.
- Where multiple occupiers, check for the four unities where seeking to establish a joint tenancy, rather than occupants holding individual leases.
- Assess whether there is certainty of term.
- Where a lease, assess the status of that lease by looking at compliance with formalities.

You may also have to assess whether any lease you find will bind a purchaser of the freehold.

As for essay questions, these too could focus on the distinction between a lease and a licence. Sometimes examiners require you to consider the differences between equitable and legal leases, both in terms of their creation and operation.

Key facts

- A lease is one of the estates in land capable of being legal: **s 1(1)(b) LPA 1925**.

- Without both certainty of term and exclusive possession there can be no lease (*Street v Mountford* [1985]), although the presence of both does not necessarily mean that a lease exists. Exclusive occupation could be based upon a licence (*Facchini v Bryson* [1952]).

- In addition to certainty of term and exclusive possession, a joint tenancy requires the four unities (*AG Securities Ltd v Vaughan* [1990]).

- Formalities for the creation of a legal lease differ depending upon the duration of the lease.

- Where these formalities have not been met, an equitable lease may exist provided there is a valid contract capable of specific performance (*Walsh v Lonsdale* (1882)).

- An equitable lease is not as good as the legal equivalent.

- The most common types of leases are fixed term and periodic.

- The process of terminating a lease by forfeiture differs depending upon the type of covenant breached. In each case, whether the property is residential or commercial will dictate the actual procedure to follow and may influence the tenant (and any sub-tenant's) ability to seek relief.

Chapter overview

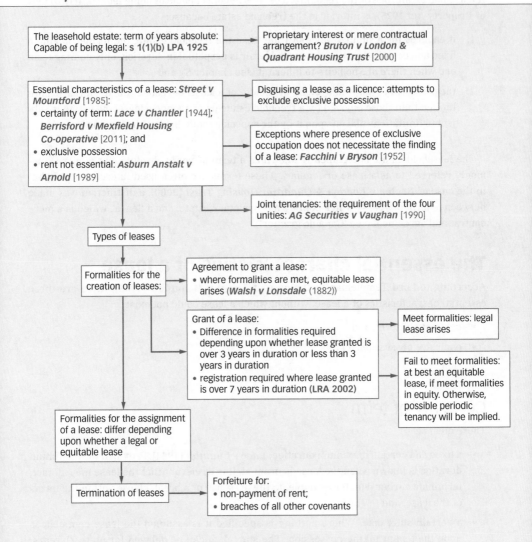

The leasehold estate: term of years absolute: Capable of being legal: **s 1(1)(b) LPA 1925**

→ Proprietary interest or mere contractual arrangement? ***Bruton v London & Quadrant Housing Trust*** [2000]

Essential characteristics of a lease: ***Street v Mountford*** [1985]:
- certainty of term: ***Lace v Chantler*** [1944]; ***Berrisford v Mexfield Housing Co-operative*** [2011]; and
- exclusive possession
- rent not essential: ***Asburn Anstalt v Arnold*** [1989]

→ Disguising a lease as a licence: attempts to exclude exclusive possession

→ Exceptions where presence of exclusive occupation does not necessitate the finding of a lease: ***Facchini v Bryson*** [1952]

→ Joint tenancies: the requirement of the four unities: ***AG Securities v Vaughan*** [1990]

Types of leases

Formalities for the creation of leases:

→ Agreement to grant a lease:
- where formalities are met, equitable lease arises (***Walsh v Lonsdale*** (1882))

Grant of a lease:
- Difference in formalities required depending upon whether lease granted is over 3 years in duration or less than 3 years in duration
- registration required where lease granted is over 7 years in duration (**LRA 2002**)

→ Meet formalities: legal lease arises

→ Fail to meet formalities: at best an equitable lease, if meet formalities in equity. Otherwise, possible periodic tenancy will be implied.

Formalities for the assignment of a lease: differ depending upon whether a legal or equitable lease

Termination of leases →

Forfeiture for:
- non-payment of rent;
- breaches of all other covenants

Introduction

A **leasehold estate**, one of the recognized estates in land capable of being legal (s 1(1)(b) Law of Property Act 1925), is inferior to the freehold estate because:

1. it endures for a smaller 'slice of time' than the freehold estate; the former having a fixed and certain duration, where the latter is perpetual in duration, only coming to an end when there are no heirs to inherit it (see chapter 5); and

2. the possessory rights enjoyed by the holder of a leasehold estate (the tenant) are more limited than those enjoyed by a freehold estate owner, since a leasehold estate is subject to limitations placed upon it by the superior estate holder (the landlord).

The leasehold estate is technically known as a **term of years absolute**, but is more commonly referred to as a **lease** or tenancy. These terms are often used interchangeably but in the case of *Bruton v London & Quadrant Housing Trust* [2000], a distinction was made between a 'term of years', which confers a proprietary estate, and a 'lease', which is a mere contractual agreement (see 'Capable grantor').

The essential characteristics of a lease

According to Lord Templeman in the case of *Street v Mountford* [1985], there are three essential characteristics of a lease, without which a lease could not exist:

- certainty of term; and
- exclusive possession; and
- rent.

Certainty of term

There must be:

- a fixed and certain maximum duration: *Lace v Chantler* [1944]. Provided the maximum duration is known when the lease is granted, it is irrelevant that the lease may, in fact, terminate earlier due, for example, to the presence of a break clause within the terms of the lease; and

- a certain start date. Where nothing is specified it is assumed the lease commences upon the tenant taking possession. The start date can be delayed for up to 21 years: s 149 LPA 1925.

The term itself can '*include a term of less than a year or for a year or years and a fraction of a year or from year to year*': s 205(1)(xxvii) LPA 1925.

What if the term appears uncertain?

The courts have shown willing to resolve the uncertainty by implying a periodic tenancy (see 'Periodic tenancy' for further discussion as to what this is), where:

- the tenant has taken possession; and
- has started paying rent by reference to a period.

(*Prudential Assurance v London Residuary Body* [1992])

The period implied would be calculated on the basis upon which the rent itself had been calculated, irrespective of how it was being paid: *Martin v Smith* (1874). The issue of uncertainty would thus be resolved since the law regards a periodic tenancy as a lease for a period (the fixed and certain term), followed by another lease for that period and so on until the lease is terminated in the appropriate way. Although, remember this approach was by no means automatic and the parties' intentions would be taken into account: *Javad v Aqil* [1991].

A recent development in resolving uncertainty

In *Mexfield Housing Co-operative Ltd v Berrisford* [2011], the Supreme Court found that an uncertain term should be treated as a lease for life and thus converted into a term for 90 years under s 149(6) LPA 1925. The reasoning was based upon the approach taken pre 1926 to such uncertain terms. The approach adopted in *Prudential* (see 'What if the term appears uncertain') was explained by the fact that the tenancy for life argument had neither been raised nor considered in that case.

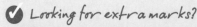 ✅ Looking for extra marks?

The Supreme Court went further and expressed clear disapproval for the requirement of certainty of term, suggesting that it should be abandoned altogether. The purpose of this requirement was also questioned in *Prudential*. Read the cases and consider the arguments for abolition. This could be a focus of an essay question on reform.

Exclusive possession

This is the ability to exclude all others from the property, including the landlord. Without exclusive possession a lease cannot exist. Possession of the land would instead be based upon a **licence** ie personal permission that creates no proprietary interest over that land. Exclusive possession is thus a key factor when distinguishing between a lease and a licence.

Attempts to disguise the creation of a lease as a licence

Landlords have often tried to disguise the creation of leases in order to avoid the numerous statutory benefits that a tenant enjoys. This they have done by attempting to create

The essential characteristics of a lease

✱✱✱✱✱✱✱✱✱✱✱

agreements between themselves and the occupiers of their land which appear to prevent exclusive possession from arising. At face value, this would suggest that such occupiers were licensees rather than tenants. The courts have been eager to detect such sham or pretence agreements which disguise as a licence something that in reality should be a lease, and thus ensure the occupiers receive the benefits to which they are entitled.

In deciding this issue, the courts must go beyond the form of the agreement, and rather look to the substance of the transaction: *Street v Mountford* [1985]. By looking at the reality of the arrangement, a court will then be better placed to assess whether the wording of the agreement, and the clauses that have been inserted, accurately reflect the nature of the arrangement or whether they have been inserted merely to act as a smoke screen to disguise as a licence what is, in reality, a lease.

✅ Looking for extra marks?

The courts' willingness to strike down pretence clauses has been criticized by some as ignoring the subjective intentions of the parties involved and the idea that parties are free to contract upon whatever terms they wish. Certainly, in the case of residential property there is a tendency to give less weight to freedom of contract in situations where people are desperate to find accommodation and thus might sign up to an agreement couched in any language and with any terms, in order to obtain shelter: *AG Securities Ltd v Vaughan* [1990]. However, in cases involving commercial parties, where equality of bargaining power exists, indications are that the courts may be more prepared to accept the parties' subjective intentions and give weight to the fact that the agreement has been labelled a 'licence': *National Car Parks Ltd v Trinity Development Co (Banbury) Ltd* [2002].

Attempts to exclude exclusive possession

Revision tip

Problem questions on the distinction between a lease and a licence often require you to compare and contrast case law to the facts in your exam question. Be sure to know both the key facts of each case *and* the legal reasoning behind each decision.

What factors will a court take into account when deciding whether clauses attempting to exclude exclusive possession are real or pretence?

- The relationship between prospective occupiers (where more than one).
- The course of negotiations.
- The nature and extent of the accommodation provided.
- The intended/actual mode of occupation.
  (*Stribling v Wickham* (1989))

Remember, this list is not exhaustive and other factors may be relevant depending upon the circumstances of each case.

Case law examples which demonstrate this:

Antoniades v Villiers [1990] 1 AC 417

A clause which stated the licensor was unwilling to grant exclusive possession and able to share, or invite others to share, the property with the licensees, was held a sham. The following were some of the key factors to influence the court:

- The occupiers were a quasi matrimonial couple, who had specifically asked for a double bed and clearly intended to occupy the property as a family home, thus making it unrealistic to introduce strangers to share with them.
- The accommodation was a small one-bedroomed flat; too small for others to share with the couple. This was evidenced by the fact that when they had a friend to stay, the conditions were very cramped.
- The clause to introduce others specified no maximum number. If real, any number of persons could be introduced to share with the couple. This was clearly unrealistic.
- The clause to introduce others had never been exercised.

Aslan v Murphy [1990] 1 WLR 766

A 'licence agreement' was held to be a lease. A key influence behind the decision was the nature of the accommodation. As a basement room 4ft3" by 12ft6", the ability of the licensor to introduce others to share with the occupant was clearly not operational.

Contrast the above with the following case:

AG Securities Ltd v Vaughan [1990] 1 AC 417

A clause stating that a maximum of three other persons could be introduced to share the property with the licensee, was held to be real and reflect the reality of the arrangement. The court was influenced by the fact that:

- Each occupant signed an agreement, which incorporated a clause that a maximum of three other people could be introduced to share the house with them. This was a realistic clause in relation to the shared occupation of a four-bedroomed house.
- This clause was actually exercised, indicating that it was not a mere pretence.
- The occupants were strangers who arrived at the property willing, presumably, to share with other persons they did not know, unlike the couple in *Antoniades v Villiers* [1990].

The essential characteristics of a lease

✱✱✱✱✱✱✱✱✱✱✱

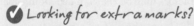 **Looking for extra marks?**

In the context of commercial premises, the extent of control the owner of the land retains over the premises and the business the occupier conducts there may be a key factor for the courts in deciding whether a lease or a licence exists. High degrees of control may be inconsistent with the occupier having exclusive possession and thus give rise to a licence. See, for example, *Esso Petroleum v Fumegrange* [1994].

Exceptions

Does the presence of exclusive possession necessitate the finding of a lease?

No. In *Facchini v Bryson* [1952], confirmed in *Street v Mountford* [1985], circumstances were highlighted whereby the factual enjoyment of exclusive occupation falls short of any conferment of a right to exclusive possession since overall control remains with the owner of the property. These exceptions include:

- occupancy based upon acts of friendship or generosity where there is no intention to create legal relations: *Marcroft Wagons Ltd v Smith* [1951];

- occupancy based upon family relationships: *David v LB Lewisham* (1977), although a family relationship between the occupant and the grantor will not automatically preclude the creation of a lease; it will depend upon the circumstances: *Nunn v Dalrymple* (1990);

- occupancy based upon service as an employee, where the provision of accommodation is for the better performance of the employee's duties: *Norris v Checksfield* [1991];

- occupancy as a lodger, where the provision of regular services, such as changing bed linen and cleaning the accommodation, prevents exclusive possession from arising: *Marchant v Charters* [1977]. This is provided that such clauses have not been inserted into the agreement to act as a smokescreen disguising the creation of a lease. In *Aslan v Murphy* [1990], the agreement stipulated that services would be provided, suggesting no exclusive possession for the occupant. The reality, however, was that in fact no services were ever provided and the clause had been inserted merely to camouflage as a licence what, in reality, was a lease.

Rent

In *Ashburn Anstalt v Arnold* [1989], it was established that rent is not essential to the finding of a lease. Indeed, the definition of a term of years absolute in s 205(1)(xxvii) LPA 1925 makes it clear that a lease can exist '*whether or not at a rent*'.

Revision tip

Where a lease is found to exist, you may be required to consider whether it is legal or equitable, which requires knowledge of formalities (see 'Formalities for creation').

Multiple occupation

Where more than one person is occupying the property on the basis of a lease, their occupation must either be on the basis of:

- each having separate leases; or
- having a joint tenancy between themselves.

Individual leases

Each occupant must have exclusive possession of a defined area, over which he has the ability to exclude all others, including the other occupants of the property. This may be possible, for example, in a situation where each occupant can claim a lease over his own bedroom in the property, with a licence to share the common parts. This possibility was recognized in an *obiter* statement in *AG Securities Ltd v Vaughan* [1990].

Joint tenancy

However, in situations where the property is such that individual leases are not possible, occupants will have to claim they have a joint tenancy; that together they are seen as a single entity entitled to exclusive possession of the whole. For this to exist, certainty of term and exclusive possession is not enough. The occupants must also share the four unities as stated in *AG Securities Ltd v Vaughan* [1990].

These are:

- *possession*: all occupiers are entitled to possess the whole of the property;
- *title*: all occupiers obtain their interest in the property by virtue of the same document. Technically, this requires all occupants to sign one single agreement. However, the courts are aware that landlords sometimes ask occupants to sign separate agreements purely to try and defeat unity of title and thus prevent a joint tenancy from arising:

. . . .

Antoniades v Villiers [1990] 1 AC 417

Despite the couple signing separate agreements, the court found unity of title. The reality was that one occupant would not have signed his agreement without the other also signing hers. The agreements were thus interdependent and could therefore be seen as a single transaction.

. . . .

- *time*: occupants must obtain their interest in the property at the same time; and
- *interest*: occupants must occupy the property with the same rights and obligations, for which they are jointly liable.

. . . .

Mikeover Ltd v Brady [1989] 3 All ER 618

Each occupant was found to be liable for just his own monthly payment. Therefore, no unity of interest was found to exist and occupancy of the accommodation was based upon a licence.

. . . .

Types of leases

Fixed term tenancy

A lease granted for a fixed term at the outset, for example a ten-year lease. The lease will not terminate until the end of the fixed term, subject to the presence of break clauses allowing for early termination, or a breach of covenant, which could lead to termination of the lease by forfeiture (see 'Forfeiture').

Periodic tenancy

A lease that is granted initially for a certain period (for example weekly, monthly, yearly) with the period automatically recurring until the lease is brought to an end, either by serving the appropriate notice period or through procedures following a breach of covenant. Typically the notice period has to equate to the period of the lease, for example a monthly periodic tenancy requires one month's notice. However, a yearly periodic tenancy requires six months' notice and a periodic tenancy over a dwelling house requires a minimum of four weeks' notice (**Protection From Eviction Act 1977**). Notice periods can also be specified by the parties themselves.

Remember, a periodic tenancy may be implied when a person takes possession and pays rent by reference to a period (See 'Certainty of term').

Tenancy at will

A personal relationship between the parties whereby a person is allowed to take possession of a property as a tenant but the agreement is such that either party can terminate the tenancy at will. Should the tenant start paying rent whilst in possession, a periodic tenancy may be implied, but only where there is sufficient intention between the parties.

Tenancy at sufferance

Where a tenant remains in possession once his lease has expired with neither the consent nor dissent of the landlord. If, and when, the landlord consents, a new tenancy will be created. However, in the meantime the possession of the property will not amount to a trespass as the initial possession was lawful.

Tenancy by estoppel

Arises in situations where the landlord has represented that he will grant a lease and the tenant has, quite reasonably, relied upon this representation to his detriment.

Formalities for creation

Capable grantor

As a general rule, a person purporting to grant a lease must be capable of doing so. However, this principle has been undermined by the decision in *Bruton v London & Quadrant Housing Trust* [2000] where a lease was recognized as having been created even though the grantor had no proprietary estate out of which to grant the lease.

> ✅ *Looking for extra marks?*
>
> In ***Bruton v London & Quadrant Housing Trust*** [2000], a charitable trust held a licence from Lambeth Council to use a block of flats for the purpose of providing short term accommodation for the homeless. The trust then gave a licence to Mr Bruton, a homeless person, to occupy a flat in return for a weekly 'licence' fee. The House of Lords felt that as Mr Bruton enjoyed exclusive possession for a term at a rent, in the absence of any exceptional circumstances, a lease had been created in his favour.
>
> According to Lord Hoffmann in this case, 'lease' or 'tenancy' are terms used to describe a contractual relationship between parties who are landlord and tenant. Whilst a lease will also often create a proprietary interest that is binding upon third parties, known as a 'term of years absolute', it was not an essential element of a contractual (or non-proprietary) tenancy. To make it binding upon a third party, the original grantor would need to have had an estate out of which to grant it. See the outcome in the case of ***London Borough Council of Islington v Green*** [2005]. On similar facts, a 'tenancy' was found not to be binding upon a third party.

Formalities for an agreement to grant a lease

In some cases, and especially for long leases, the parties may first enter into an agreement to create the lease. The formalities required differ depending upon the duration of the lease intended: see Figure 6.1.

Figure 6.1 Formalities for an agreement to grant a lease

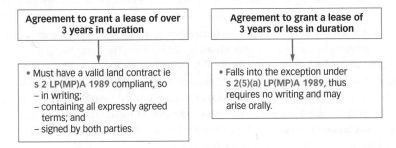

Agreement to grant a lease of over 3 years in duration	Agreement to grant a lease of 3 years or less in duration
• Must have a valid land contract ie s 2 LP(MP)A 1989 compliant, so – in writing; – containing all expressly agreed terms; and – signed by both parties.	• Falls into the exception under s 2(5)(a) LP(MP)A 1989, thus requires no writing and may arise orally.

Proprietary status of an agreement to grant a lease

The valid contract, provided that it is one capable of specific performance, transfers an equitable interest in the land to the transferee (the prospective tenant). Since equity views as done that which ought to be done, equity views the contract as having already been performed. As such, in the eyes of equity, the transferee at this stage already has an equitable lease: *Walsh v Lonsdale* (1882).

> *Revision tip*
>
> An equitable lease is a type of estate contract. The significance of the transferee having an equitable interest at this stage becomes apparent in circumstances where the freehold estate is transferred to a third party. Link to enforcement of third party interests against purchasers: chapters 3 and 4.

Formalities for the grant of a lease

Whether there has been a prior agreement to grant a lease or not, only once a lease has actually been granted, upon satisfaction of certain formalities outlined in Figure 6.2, will a legal leasehold estate be created in favour of the grantee.

> *Revision tip*
>
> Be alert, when reading an exam question, as to whether there has been merely an agreement to grant a lease, in which case at best only an equitable lease can exist (subject to satisfying formalities required by equity), or an actual grant of a lease, in which case a legal lease may exist (subject to satisfying formalities required at law).

Is an equitable lease as good as a legal lease?

An equitable lease can, of course, be converted into a legal lease by an order of specific performance. In the meantime, equity will uphold the rights of the parties as though the legal lease had already been granted. However, this does not make an equitable lease as good as having the legal equivalent, for the following reasons:

- The existence of an equitable lease is dependent upon the contract being capable of specific performance. This will not always be the case, as shown in *Coatsworth v Johnson* (1885). (This case has already been discussed in chapter 2.)
- Before the system of registration was introduced, it was easier to enforce legal proprietary interests against third parties than equitable ones; the latter being defeated when the land over which they were exercised fell into the hands of a *bona fide* purchaser for value of a legal estate without notice (see chapter 2). Whilst this distinction between legal and equitable proprietary interests has been eroded to some extent by the system of registration, there are still some clear examples of when legal proprietary interests are easier to enforce against third parties than equitable equivalents (see chapters 3 and 4 on enforcement of proprietary interests).
- An equitable lease is based upon the existence of a contract, which is not a conveyance. Thus on the creation of an equitable lease, the leaseholder will not receive certain benefits that he would have received had there been a conveyance. This is clearly visible when looking at the law of easements (see chapter 12).

- In leases created before 1996, the burden and benefit of tenant covenants will only pass to a successor in title where there has been a legal assignment of a legal lease. This clearly will not occur if the lease is merely equitable in nature (see chapter 7).
- A person who acquires merely an equitable lease, may be bound by other equitable interests created earlier over the property, since generally where the equities are equal, the first in time prevails: *Barclays Bank v Taylor* [1974].

Figure 6.2 Formalities for the grant of a lease

Leases of over 3 years in duration
- Must be granted by deed to create a legal lease: s 52 LPA 1925.
- A valid deed must comply with s 1(2) LP(MP)A 1989. It must be:
  - clear on its face;
  - signed by the grantor;
  - witnessed (attested); and
  - delivered (see chapter 2).
- Where the lease granted is over 7 years in duration, it must also be registered.
  - Where the lease is granted over unregistered land, registration is governed by s 4(1)(c) Land Registration Act 2002. Failure to register the lease within two months will mean that legal title, which passed upon execution of the valid deed, will revert back to the grantor, leaving the grantee with just an equitable lease at best.
  - Where the lease is granted over registered land, registration is governed by s 27(2)(b)(i). Failure to register will mean grantee never receives legal title.

Leases of 3 years or less in duration
- No deed is required to make such leases legal: s 52(2)(d) and s 54(2) LPA 1925 provided:
  - *it takes effect in possession*: possession includes receipt of rent or profits under s 205(1)(xix) LPA 1925. Section 54(2) LPA 1925 will not apply to future leases ie those leases that are to commence some time after they have been granted. Such future leases need to be granted by deed to be legal: *Long v Tower Hamlets LBC* [1998]; and
  - *at a best rent (ie market rent: Fitzkriston LLP v Panayi* [2008]*) that can reasonably be obtained without taking a fine.*

Position when fail to meet appropriate formalities:

Position at Law
- The failed attempt to create the legal lease means that the intended legal lease is void.
- However, if the tenant takes possession and starts paying rent by reference to a period, a periodic tenancy may be implied: *Prudential Assurance v LRB* [1992] (see earlier discussion).
- This will be a legal lease as it falls into the s 54(2) LPA 1925 exception. It will be less than three years in duration and thus no deed is required to make it legal, provided:
  - it takes effect in possession; and
  - at a best rent without taking a fine.

Position in Equity
- The failed attempt to create a legal lease may be viewed by equity as an agreement to create a lease.
- To be viewed as such there must be a valid contract ie s 2 LP(MP)A 1989 compliance as discussed above. Non-compliance with s 2 precludes an equitable lease analysis: *United Bank of Kuwait plc v Sahib* [1997].
- The contract must be capable of specific performance: *Coatsworth v Johnson* (1885).
- As equity views as done that which ought to be done, equity views the specifically enforceable contract as creating an equitable lease: *Walsh v Lonsdale* (1882).

Where a conflict exists between law and equity, the position in equity will prevail: *Walsh v Lonsdale* (1882).

Enforcement of leases against third parties

✶✶✶✶✶✶✶✶✶✶

Revision tip

This is a common topic for an essay question so when revising, be sure to make the links with material covered in the other chapters including chapters 2, 3, 4, and 12. Also make sure you understand the circumstances and formalities in which either equitable or legal leases arise.

Formalities for the assignment of an existing lease

The formalities required for transferring an existing lease from one party to another differ depending upon whether the lease in question is legal or equitable in nature: see Figure 6.3.

Figure 6.3 Formalities for the assignment of a lease

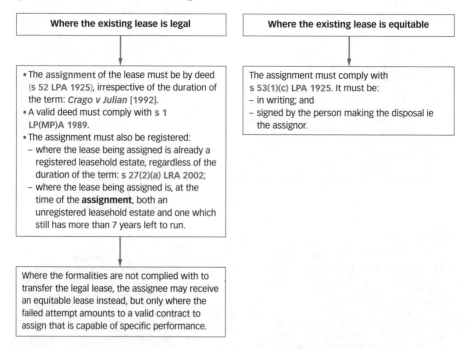

Where the existing lease is legal	Where the existing lease is equitable
• The assignment of the lease must be by deed (s 52 LPA 1925), irrespective of the duration of the term: *Crago v Julian* [1992]. • A valid deed must comply with s 1 LP(MP)A 1989. • The assignment must also be registered: – where the lease being assigned is already a registered leasehold estate, regardless of the duration of the term: s 27(2)(a) LRA 2002; – where the lease being assigned is, at the time of the **assignment**, both an unregistered leasehold estate and one which still has more than 7 years left to run.	The assignment must comply with s 53(1)(c) LPA 1925. It must be: – in writing; and – signed by the person making the disposal ie the assignor.

Where the formalities are not complied with to transfer the legal lease, the assignee may receive an equitable lease instead, but only where the failed attempt amounts to a valid contract to assign that is capable of specific performance.

Enforcement of leases against third parties

This is dealt with in detail in chapters 3 and 4. However, Figures 6.4 and 6.5 contain a brief overview as a reminder.

Registered land

Figure 6.4 Enforcement of leases: registered land

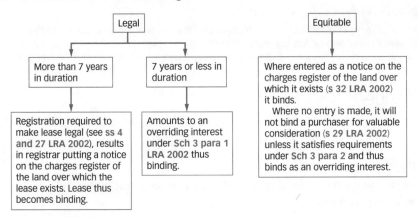

Unregistered land

Figure 6.5 Enforcement of leases: unregistered land

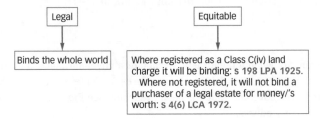

Termination of leases

Expiry

A fixed term lease will come to an end upon expiry of the term for which it was granted. (It cannot be brought to an end earlier than the term envisaged in the lease unless there exists some provision in the lease to do so, ie a break clause, or there has been some breach of a covenant in the lease allowing for forfeiture (see 'Forfeiture').)

Notice to quit

The parties to a periodic tenancy may give a notice to quit to bring the tenancy to an end. (See 'Periodic tenancy' for specific notice periods.) Where it is a joint periodic tenancy, notice to quit given by one of the joint tenants will be effective on all: *Hammersmith & Fulham LBC v Monk* [1992].

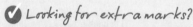

Consider the case of *Manchester CC v Pinnock* [2010] as regards the impact *Art 8 of the European Convention on Human Rights*, namely a right to respect a person's home, has on domestic law allowing one joint tenant to terminate the joint tenancy by serving notice to quit.

Surrender

This is where the landlord and tenant can agree that the tenant is going to give up the lease.

Merger

This occurs where the tenant obtains the freehold estate so that the freehold and leasehold estates become merged.

Repudiatory breach

In rare cases where a landlord may be in breach of his obligations, the tenant can accept the breach and walk away from the lease: *Hussein v Mehlman* [1992].

Forfeiture

Available as a remedy when a tenant is in breach of a covenant under a lease. It results in the lease being terminated. Two different procedures for forfeiting a lease exist depending upon the nature of the covenant that has been breached (see Figures 6.6 and 6.7). However, in common to both procedures:

- forfeiture is (generally) only an available remedy where there exists an express forfeiture clause (although note equitable leases where one is implied);
- the landlord loses his right to forfeit where he has waived his right ie
  - he is aware of the existence of the breach, either himself or through an agent; and
  - he does some unequivocal act which recognizes the continuation of the lease, for example accepting rent: *Central Estates (Belgravia) Ltd v Woolgar (No2)* [1972].

  Remember, where the breach is of a continuing nature, a waiver on one occasion will not preclude forfeiture for that breach where it continues in the future;

- a court order must be obtained where seeking forfeiture of a residential property (or one of mixed use: see *Patel v Pirabakaran* [2006]): s 2 Protection From Eviction Act 1977. Where there is no-one lawfully residing at the property, the landlord may peaceably re-enter without first obtaining a court order.

Figure 6.6 Forfeiture for non-payment of rent

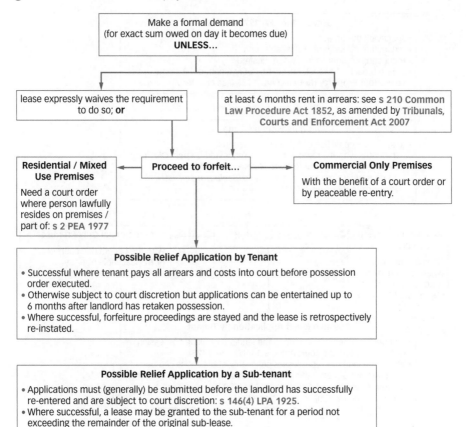

The requirement of a court order to re-enter residential leases recognizes a tenant's right to respect for his private life and home (**Art 8 ECHR**) and ensures his rights and obligations are determined only after a 'fair and public hearing' (**Art 6 ECHR**). Until recently, in the case of residential occupancy, the courts were not required to consider whether it was proportionate to evict the tenant, so long as relevant legislation had been satisfied. Following the case of *Manchester CC v Pinnock* [2010], the court has to consider whether it is proportionate to make a possession order, so as to be compatible with **Art 8 ECHR**. It remains to be seen what impact this will have on forfeiture proceedings.

✓ Looking for extra marks?

Termination of leases

✳✳✳✳✳✳✳✳✳✳✳✳

Figure 6.7 Forfeiture for all other breaches of covenants

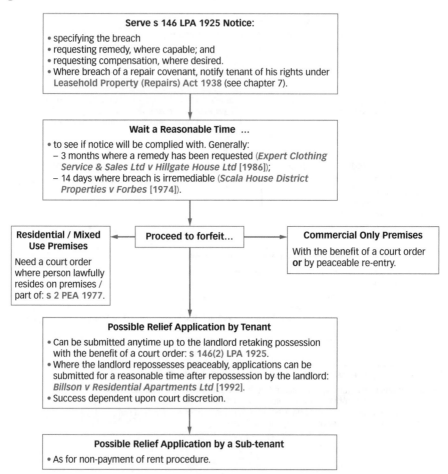

Serve s 146 LPA 1925 Notice:

- specifying the breach
- requesting remedy, where capable; and
- requesting compensation, where desired.
- Where breach of a repair covenant, notify tenant of his rights under Leasehold Property (Repairs) Act 1938 (see chapter 7).

Wait a Reasonable Time ...

- to see if notice will be complied with. Generally:
  - 3 months where a remedy has been requested (*Expert Clothing Service & Sales Ltd v Hillgate House Ltd* [1986]);
  - 14 days where breach is irremediable (*Scala House District Properties v Forbes* [1974]).

Residential / Mixed Use Premises

Need a court order where person lawfully resides on premises / part of: s 2 PEA 1977.

Proceed to forfeit...

Commercial Only Premises

With the benefit of a court order **or** by peaceable re-entry.

Possible Relief Application by Tenant

- Can be submitted anytime up to the landlord retaking possession with the benefit of a court order: s 146(2) LPA 1925.
- Where the landlord repossesses peaceably, applications can be submitted for a reasonable time after repossession by the landlord: *Billson v Residential Apartments Ltd* [1992].
- Success dependent upon court discretion.

Possible Relief Application by a Sub-tenant

- As for non-payment of rent procedure.

✅ *Looking for extra marks?*

When is a breach capable of remedy? In *Expert Clothing Service & Sales Ltd v Hillgate House* [1986], the court accepted that capability turned on whether the harm caused to the landlord by the breach is capable of remedy, rather than on whether the breach itself is capable of remedy. With this question in mind, most covenants are capable of remedy. This view has been endorsed recently in *Akici v LR Butlin* [2006].

There are exceptions however. A breach of an alienation covenant is still considered incapable of remedy: *Scala House and District Property v Forbes* [1974]. Some breaches of user covenants where the property is used for immoral purposes are also considered incapable of remedy where a stigma has attached to the property: *Rugby School (Governors) v Tannahill* [1935]. However, if the immoral user is stopped quickly enough, so that no stigma has been given the chance to attach to the property, the breach may be considered remediable: *Ropemaker Properties Ltd v Noonhaven Ltd* [1989].

✅ *Looking for extra marks?*

Where a landlord has a choice as to whether to obtain a court order to possess or not, he must weigh up the advantages and disadvantages. The advantages of proceeding without a court order are that it saves time and money. The disadvantage is the potential criminal liability which may result under **s 6 Criminal Law Act 1977**, should there be any use, or a threat to use, violence for the purpose of gaining entry against anyone on the premises opposed to that entry. Indeed, the courts appear to disapprove of peaceable re-entry. In *Billson v Residential Apartments Ltd* [1992] Nicholls LJ declared that it cannot be right 'to encourage law abiding citizens to embark on a course of conduct which is a sure recipe for violence'.

✅ *Looking for extra marks?*

When deciding whether to exercise discretion in favour of a tenant seeking relief, the general view taken by the court is that forfeiture is merely security for non-payment of rent (Lord Greene MR in *Chandless-Chandless v Nicholson* [1942]). As such, where the tenant pays all outstanding sums, or provides evidence that such sums will be paid in the immediately foreseeable future, relief is likely to be granted. There are, of course, exceptions. Where the landlord has already let the property out to a third party, relief may not be granted if this would unfairly affect the innocent third party: *Stanhope v Haworth* (1886). In respect of a sub-tenant, application relief may not be granted where the sub-tenant is present on the property unlawfully: *St Marylebone Property Co v Tesco Stores* (1988).

(✱) *Key cases*

Case	Facts	Principle
AG Securities v Vaughan [1990] 1 AC 417	Four separate licence agreements had been signed on different days relating to the occupancy of a four-bed flat. Each agreement stipulated for different payment amounts and each excluded exclusive possession and stipulated sharing with a maximum of three other people. Held to be licences.	Look to the nature of the accommodation and the relationship between the occupiers when considering whether a clause excluding exclusive possession is real or a sham. All four unities must exist for a joint tenancy to arise.

Key cases

✳✳✳✳✳✳✳✳✳✳✳

Case	Facts	Principle
Antoniades v Villiers [1990] 1 AC 417	A cohabiting couple signed separate but identical licence agreements contemporaneously giving them the right to occupy a small one-bed flat. The agreement stipulated exclusive possession had not been granted and the licensor had the ability to invite others to share the flat. Held to be a lease.	Look to the nature of the accommodation and the relationship between the occupiers when considering whether a clause excluding exclusive possession is real or a sham. Signing separate agreements will not defeat unity of title provided the agreements can be seen as interdependent.
Aslan v Murphy [1990] 1 WLR 766	Licence agreement in respect of a tiny basement room, to which the licensor retained keys. The agreement excluded exclusive possession and required the occupant to vacate the premises for 90 minutes each day. It was held to be a lease.	Look to the nature of the accommodation when considering whether a clause excluding exclusive possession is real or a sham. There is no magic in the retention of keys. Look at the purpose for which keys have been retained.
Bruton v London & Quadrant Housing Trust [2000] 1 AC 406	A licensee of a block of flats purported to give a homeless person a licence over one of the flats. The House of Lords found the homeless person to have a 'lease' since he enjoyed exclusive possession for a term at a rent.	An apparent distinction exists between a lease, which amounts to a mere contractual arrangement, and a term of years which is a proprietary interest.
Prudential Assurance Co Ltd v London Residuary Body [1992] 2 AC 386	A 'tenancy' had been granted over a strip of land until such time as it would be required back for the purpose of widening the road. Whilst it was held that this was an uncertain term, the House of Lords upheld the finding of a periodic tenancy.	There must be certainty of term for a lease to exist. Where the term appears uncertain, if the tenant has taken possession and started paying rent by reference to a period, a court may be willing to imply a periodic tenancy has been created
Street v Mountford [1985] AC 809	Occupancy was based upon a 'licence agreement' which gave M, in return for a weekly 'licence fee', exclusive occupancy of a self-contained flat. Despite the agreement containing a clause stating a tenancy was not intended to arise, M was found to have a tenancy.	Where an agreement satisfies the characteristics of a lease (exclusive possession, certainty of term, at a rent) a tenancy will be found (subject to exceptions). One must look to the substance of the transaction and not just its form.

Case	Facts	Principle
Walsh v Lonsdale (1882) 21 Ch D 9	A seven-year lease was granted to W in writing but not by deed. W went into possession and started paying rent and an issue arose which required determining whether his occupation was based upon a legal periodic tenancy or a seven-year equitable lease. He was held to occupy on the basis of the latter.	Where a valid contract to grant a lease exists that is capable of specific performance, as equity sees as done that which ought to be done, this arrangement creates an equitable lease. Where a conflict exists between law and equity, equity prevails.

 Exam questions

Problem question

Carrie is the freehold owner of a large house. She has converted the top floor into a self-contained flat, consisting of two bedrooms, a bathroom, kitchen, and large living room. In December last year, she placed an advertisement in a local university paper stating 'flat available for immediate occupation at £400 a month'.

Friends Raj and Sally applied. Each signed separate 'licence' agreements on the same day which contained a number of identical terms including:

1. the licensor reserves the right to increase the number of occupants of the flat by one;
2. the licensor will provide laundry services to the licensee on a weekly basis and retains a key for this purpose;
3. the licensee shall be responsible to pay a licence fee of £200 per month.

To date Carrie has provided no laundry services and has only used the keys to access the flat once in order to retrieve something from the loft, when she gave Raj and Sally 24 hours' notice.

Advise Raj and Sally as to their legal status.

What difference would it make to your answer if Raj and Sally were strangers and they had replied to the advertisement independently of one another, signing the agreements on different days?

See the Outline Answers section in the end matter for help with this question.

Essay question

The distinction between an equitable lease and a legal lease lies in its creation and no further. Discuss.

 Online Resource Centre

To see an outline answer to this question log onto www.oxfordtextbooks.co.uk/orc/concentrate/

#7
Covenants in leases

The examination

The extent to which the material covered in this chapter is relevant to you will depend upon the course that you have studied. You must be guided by your tutorials and lectures when working out how much is relevant to you and also the way in which different issues within the topic of leases will be combined in a question. Remember that material covered here may be combined with material covered in chapter 6 on leases. A problem question concerning breach of **covenants**, for example, may involve issues of forfeiture. You may be required to assess whether a lease exists in the first place (rather than a licence) before considering liability for apparent breach of covenants.

Essay questions on issues covered within this chapter often focus upon statutory changes that occurred in 1995 regarding enforcement of leasehold covenants. Some examiners focus upon the way in which the law balances the interests of landlords and tenants and whether the law tends to favour the rights of one above the other.

Key facts

- Leasehold covenants are promises made between a landlord and tenant. They can be express or implied; positive or negative in nature.

- An express covenant to repair should not include work that renews virtually the whole of the property in one go, brings completely new improvements to the property, or requires the correction of design faults with the property unless such faults are causing physical damage to the property which itself falls within a covenant to repair.

- Certain repair obligations are impliedly imposed upon a landlord by common law and statute, notably the **Landlord and Tenant Act 1985**.

- Remedies available for breach of a repair obligation include forfeiture, damages, and **specific performance**.

- Covenants not to assign or sub-let may be absolute or qualified. Where qualified, a landlord must not refuse consent unreasonably: **s 19(1)(a) Landlord and Tenant Act 1927**.

- Covenants are enforceable between the original covenanting parties based upon the contractual relationship they share.

- The enforcement of covenants between successors in title depends upon whether the burden and/or benefit of the covenants have passed. Rules governing this differ depending upon whether the lease was created before or after 1 January 1996 when the **Landlord and Tenant (Covenants) Act 1995** came into force.

Chapter overview

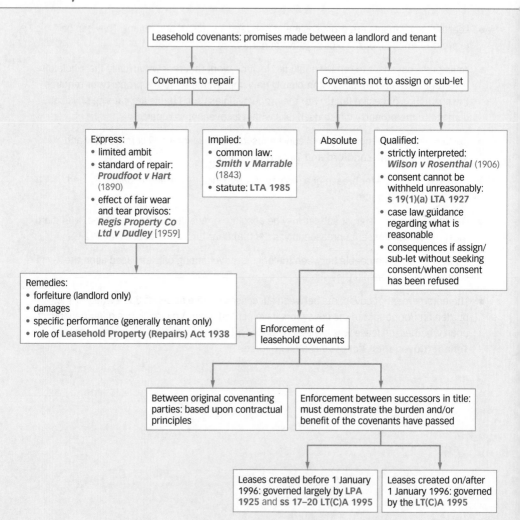

Introduction

Leasehold covenants are promises that are made between a landlord and his tenant, regulating the relationship between them and the way in which a leasehold estate is enjoyed. Both the landlord and the tenant will enter into a variety of covenants for the benefit of the other party.

The covenants may be either express or implied. The nature and extent of liability imposed by express covenants will be a matter of negotiation between the parties. Implied covenants, which can occasionally be expressly excluded from the lease (where it is allowed), may impose burdens on either the landlord or the tenant. An example of a landlord's implied obligation is a covenant to allow the tenant quiet enjoyment ie to allow the tenant to take exclusive possession of the property without any interference. An example of a tenant's implied obligation is a covenant not to commit waste.

Covenants, whether express or implied, may be either positive (for example, to repair) or negative (for example, prohibiting change of use to the property).

Covenants to repair

These may be express, burdening either the landlord or the tenant or, in some circumstances, both. For example, the landlord may promise to keep the exterior of the property in good repair whilst the tenant promises to do the same with the interior.

An implied obligation to repair can also be imposed upon a landlord (see 'Implied covenants to repair'), but not a tenant.

Express covenants to repair

The extent of liability imposed

The following should be borne in mind when considering the scope of an express covenant to repair:

- The exact wording of the covenant may give guidance. For example, a covenant that stipulates the covenantor must '*keep the property in good and substantial repair*' (rather than merely '*maintain the property ...*') requires him to put the property into a good state of repair at the start of the lease term and maintain such a state throughout the term (see *Credit Suisse v Beegas Nominees Ltd* [1994]).

- Whilst an express covenant to repair will inevitably require some element of renewal, to replace whatever is in a state of disrepair, liability should not extend to renewal of virtually the whole of the property in one go: *Lister v Lane* [1893]. Ultimately, it is a question of degree and looking at how much of the property is to be affected by the repair required: *Ravenseft Properties Ltd v Davstone (Holdings) Ltd* [1980]. There may also be a linked issue of costs. Where the costs of the repair work required are close to the overall value of the property as it existed before it fell into disrepair, the work required may fall outside the ambit of the covenant: *Brew Brothers v Snax (Ross) Ltd* [1970].

- Whilst an express covenant to repair should not impose an obligation to make new improvements to the property, for example putting in a damp proof course where none previously existed, an improvement may occur as a by product of the repair itself, for example replacing a broken boiler with a modern version: *Pembury v Lamdin* [1940].

- An express covenant to repair should not itself impose an obligation to correct design faults with the property, as originally constructed: *Post Office v Aquarius Property Ltd* [1987]. However, if that fault causes disrepair to the property which can only be fixed by correcting the design fault from which it flows, the correction of that design fault may fall within the ambit of the covenant to repair.

The standard of repair required

The standard is to be determined according to the age, character, and locality of the property *at the time that the lease was granted*: *Proudfoot v Hart* (1890). The repair works should be to a standard fit for a reasonably like-minded tenant of the type likely to take a lease of that property.

When does liability arise?

Under a tenant obligation, liability arises as soon as the property falls into a state of disrepair, even where the tenant is unaware of this. Whereas, under a landlord obligation, since a landlord generally has no access to the property, liability will arise only once he has been given notice of the disrepair.

The effect of a fair wear and tear proviso

An express covenant to repair may exempt a tenant from liability for fair wear and tear. However, if this fair wear and tear leads to other disrepair to the property, which itself falls into the ambit of the express covenant to repair, and the only way to correct this consequential disrepair is to correct the fair wear and tear from which it flows, a tenant may be required to do so, despite the existence of the fair wear and tear exemption: *Regis Property Co Ltd v Dudley* [1959].

Implied covenants to repair

These burden the landlord and override any express obligations to the contrary. They include:

- Where a house is let furnished, an obligation to ensure that the house is fit for human habitation at the start of the lease term: *Smith v Marrable* (1843).

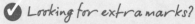

Looking for extra marks?

Whilst the implied obligation to ensure a house is fit for human habitation is a common law obligation imposed upon a landlord in respect of the condition of a dwelling, its impact is curtailed by application to furnished dwellings only. It is true to say that the courts have in the past tended to adopt a rather *laissez-faire* approach when it comes to regulating the condition of rented property, seeing it as a matter of negotiation between the parties (in the absence of any statutory control). This approach, however, assumes that equality of bargaining power will exist between the parties, which is not always the case. A change of direction from the courts can be seen in the case of *Lee v Leeds CC* [2002], where the Court of Appeal indicated that where property is let for social housing, a landlord should be obliged to take steps to ensure that it is not in such a condition that a tenant's right under **Art 8 of the European Convention on Human Rights 1950** is infringed, namely respect for private family life and the home.

- In respect of leases of houses at a (extremely) low rent, an obligation to keep the property in a fit state during the term of the lease: s 8 Landlord and Tenant Act 1985.

- Sections 11 to 14 Landlord and Tenant Act 1985:

  An obligation for the landlord to keep in repair the structure (something essential to a building's appearance, stability, or shape: *Re Irvine's Estate v Moran* (1992)), exterior (including drains, gutters, and external pipes) and installations of a house, for the supply of water, gas, electricity, and for sanitation and heating. It does not extend to the correction of design faults with the property (*Quick v Taff-Ely BC* [1986]) unless the design fault is itself causing disrepair to the structure, exterior, or installations of the house. If the only way to fix this disrepair is to correct the design fault from which it flows, a landlord will be obliged to do so under this Act: *Staves & Staves v Leeds CC* (1990).

  The obligation only applies to leases of dwelling houses granted on/after 24 October 1961 for a term of less than seven years. The landlord's liability will only arise once he has notice of such disrepair: *O'Brien v Robinson* [1973]. Upon notice, he will be liable not only for the disrepair to the structure, exterior, or installations as appropriate, but also for any disrepair that is consequential to this, provided he has notice of such consequential damage and provided the tenant has acted promptly in notifying the landlord so as to mitigate the loss.

  In determining the standard to which the landlord is required to repair, regard must be had to the age, character, and prospective life of the dwelling house and its locality.

Specific remedies for breach of repairing covenants

Forfeiture

Available to the landlord and has the effect of bringing the lease to an end.

Covenants not to assign or sub-let the property

✳✳✳✳✳✳✳✳✳✳

Revision tip

Link your revision here to material on forfeiture covered in chapter 6.

Damages

Under s 18 Landlord and Tenant Act 1927, damages must not exceed the amount by which the value of the reversion in the premises is diminished owing to the existence of the breach. Damages are not recoverable where the premises are to be demolished or intended structural alterations would render the repairs valueless.

✅ **Looking for extra marks?**

Where either forfeiture or damages is sought by a landlord for breach of a tenant's repairing obligation in respect of a lease granted for more than seven years and with at least three years remaining, the Leasehold Property (Repairs) Act 1938 will apply.

Upon commencing the action, the landlord must serve notice on the tenant of the tenant's right to serve a counter notice within 28 days claiming protection from the Act. Where the tenant correctly serves the counter notice, the landlord is precluded from taking any further action without first obtaining leave from the court. Such leave will typically be given where the court considers:

- the cost of doing the repairs now will be less than if the repairs were left and done in the future; or
- there is a risk of substantial damage to the property if the repairs are not carried out immediately; or
- immediate repair is necessary in order to prevent a substantial decrease in the value of the reversion.

Specific performance

This is available to a tenant: *Jeune v Queens Cross Properties* [1974]. Where the breach is of a landlord's implied covenant to repair under ss 11–14 and s 17 LTA 1985 provides for the availability of this remedy.

It is more rarely given in favour of the landlord; perhaps where the lease does not provide for the alternative remedy of forfeiture: *Rainbow Estates Ltd v Tokenhold Ltd* [1999].

Covenants not to assign or sub-let the property

Where a lease is silent as to whether a tenant can assign or **sub-let** the property, a tenant may do either freely. However, most leases contain either an absolute or qualified covenant not to assign or sub-let the property.

Absolute covenants

These prohibit any assignment or sub-letting of the property, subject only to the landlord changing his mind upon request.

Qualified covenants

These allow an assignment or sub-letting of the property but only with the landlord's consent. They are interpreted strictly by the court. A qualified covenant precluding sub-letting the whole of the property without the landlord's consent will not prohibit the sub-letting of part of that property: *Wilson v Rosenthal* (1906).

When considering the issue of consent, you must take into account the following points:

- A landlord must not unreasonably withhold consent: **s 19(1)(a) Landlord and Tenant Act 1927**, which overrides any express provision to the contrary.

- Apart from refusal on grounds of discrimination (for example, race or sex) guidance as to what will be unreasonable must be taken from case law.

- In *International Drilling Fluids Ltd v Louisville Investments (Uxbridge) Ltd* [1986], it was declared that the purpose of a qualified covenant is to protect the landlord from having his premises used/occupied by an undesirable tenant in an undesirable way. The grounds for refusal must have something to do with the relationship of landlord and tenant, for example refusing because the tenant is already in serious breach of another covenant in the lease.

> ✅ *Looking for extra marks?*
>
> Lord Bingham, in the case of **Ashworth Frazer Ltd v Gloucester CC** [2001], identified three principles by which a court should be guided in determining whether a landlord's refusal is unreasonable. If you think this may be an area that will be examined, it would be useful to read his judgment.

- In addition, you should consider:
    - the effect a refusal will have on the tenant. Where the detriment caused to the tenant far outweighs any benefit the landlord is gaining by refusing consent, such refusal may be considered unreasonable; and
    - in respect of commercial leases granted on/after 1 January 1996, whether the ground(s) given for refusal is one identified in the lease. If yes, refusal cannot be considered unreasonable: **s 22 Landlord and Tenant (Covenants) Act 1995** which adds **s 19(1A)** to the **LTA 1927**.

- Ultimately, the burden of proof rests with the landlord: **s 1(6) Landlord and Tenant Act 1988**.

The consequences

- Assigning or sub-letting the lease without first seeking consent, where such consent is required, will amount to a breach of the qualified covenant, even if the landlord could not have reasonably refused consent: *Eastern Telegraph Co Ltd v Dent* [1899].

- Where consent has been sought but refused, the tenant really has three options:

  - accept the landlord's refusal and abandon any attempt to assign or sub-let.

  - ignore the refusal and go ahead with the assignment or sub-letting anyway. Whilst the disposition itself would (usually) be effective (*Old Grovebury Manor Farm Ltd v W Seymour Plant Sales & Hire Ltd (No 2)* [1979]), it will be in breach of covenant and thus the tenant will risk proceedings for damages or, more seriously, forfeiture. Arguably, the proposed assignee or sub-tenant would not wish to go ahead with the disposition where they know it is in breach of covenant since, with such knowledge, they would be unlikely to succeed in getting relief in any subsequent forfeiture proceedings (see chapter 6).

  - Seek a court declaration that the consent is being unreasonably withheld, which will take time and money.

Enforcement of leasehold covenants

Enforcement between the original parties to the lease

Enforceability of covenants between the original parties to the lease (see Figure 7.1) is based upon their contractual relationship to one another; the parties have **privity of contract**.

Figure 7.1 Enforcement between original parties

L

↓

T

Liability extends to all the covenants in the lease, regardless of whether they touch and concern the land or not, and such liability continues, in principle, for the entire duration of the lease term.

Enforcement between successors in title to the original parties to the lease

When either the lease or the reversionary interest is passed on to a successor in title, will the benefit and burden of the covenants in the lease pass to that successor?

- Leases *originally* created on/after 1 January 1996 are governed by the **Landlord and Tenant (Covenants) Act 1995**.

- Leases *originally* created before this date are largely governed by the **Law of Property Act 1925**.

Remember that **ss 17–20** of the **LT(C)A 1995** apply equally to pre, as well as to post, 1996 leases.

✅ *Looking for extra marks?*

The **LT(C)A 1995** provisions are mandatory and cannot be excluded or modified in some way: **s 25**. Note, however, the decision of the House of Lords in *London Diocesan Fund v Phithwa* [2005], where a more controversial interpretation of s 25 was adopted.

Revision tip

The changes to the law brought about by the **Landlord and Tenant (Covenants) Act 1995** is a popular area for discussion in an essay question. You should know the key changes brought about by the Act (see 'Assignment of the lease', 'Assignment of the reversion', and 'sub-tenants') and be able to reflect upon the motivation and fairness of these changes.

Assignment of the lease

Figure 7.2 illustrates the assignment of the lease.

Figure 7.2 Assignment of the lease

When the original tenant (T) assigns his lease to his assignee (A), will the burden of covenants entered into by T pass to A?

Table 7.1 explains T's position post assignment.

Enforcement of leasehold covenants

✱✱✱✱✱✱✱✱✱✱

Table 7.1 Position of T—post assignment

Pre-1996 Lease	Post-1996 Lease
T remains liable throughout the entire duration of the lease term, as originally envisaged, on all the covenants of the lease due to privity of contract:	T will automatically be released from liability for all tenant covenants upon assignment (**s 5 LT(C) A 1995**), unless:
Thursby v Plant (1668). This continuing liability is reinforced by **s 79 LPA 1925**. T retains the right to pursue breaches committed by the landlord, before the assignment to A took place: City & Metropolitan Properties Ltd v Greycroft Ltd [1987].	1. the breach is of a purely personal covenant to him: **BHP Petroleum GB Ltd v Chesterfield Properties Ltd** [2000]; or 2. the breach was committed whilst T was the tenant: **s 24 LT(C)A 1995**; or 3. the assignment was an *excluded assignment* under **s 11 LT(C)A 1995**; typically one in breach of covenant. T's liability continues until a non-excluded assignment occurs, at which point T's liability will cease; or 4. T entered into an Authorized Guarantee Agreement under **s 16 LT(C)A 1995**, whereby he guarantees the performance of the covenants *by his immediate assignee* only.

In respect of either a pre or post-1996 lease, remember the following two points:

- Where T retains liability, either on the basis of privity of contract under a pre-1996 lease, or, for example, an AGA under a post-1996 lease, he cannot be held liable for a breach of covenant, where such covenant had been varied after the assignment took place and the variation was such that the landlord had an absolute right to refuse: **s 18 LT(C)A 1995**. Note however liability for increased rent following activation of a foreseen rent review clause: *Friends Provident Life Office v British Railways Board* [1996].

- To pursue T for rent or any other fixed charge owed by A, L will first have to serve upon T a default notice, governed by **s 17 LT(C)A 1995**. The notice must be served within six months of the monies becoming due, notifying T of the amount owing and the fact that T is to be pursued for this sum. This procedure prevents L from allowing a debt to increase whilst T has no knowledge of the breach or indeed the fact that he is to be held responsible for the sums owed.

> ✅ *Looking for extra marks?*
>
> Authorized Guarantee Agreements usually arise in circumstances where the tenant requires the landlord's consent to an assignment of the lease and the landlord makes his consent conditional upon the tenant entering into an AGA. Where the lease is silent, this condition must be reasonable. In commercial leases that expressly stipulate this as a condition to granting consent, there is no issue of reasonableness.

What could T do if held liable for a breach committed by A?

Whether a pre- or post-1996 lease, the following options are available to T:

- Employ the *Moule v Garret* (1872) principle: where you are compelled to pay damages for the legal default of another, you can go against that other to recover the sums you paid.

- Recoup sums paid via an indemnity covenant. These are only exercisable against your immediate assignee. Thus if A assigned the lease to A2, who commits a breach for which T is held liable, T would utilize his indemnity covenant to recoup the money from A, who would do the same to recoup the money from A2. Where there is a complete chain of indemnity, ultimately the person left out of pocket should be the person who has committed the breach (here A2). However, if there is a break in the chain, for example A is insolvent or has disappeared, T would not be able to skip over A and try and claim monies back from A2: *Re Mirror Group (Holdings) Ltd* (1993). Indemnity covenants may be express or, in the case of pre-1996 leases only, implied:

  - into assignments of leases over unregistered land for valuable consideration: s 77 LPA 1925; and

  - into assignments of leases over registered land, regardless of value: Sch 12 para 20 LRA 2002.

- Where there has been full payment of monies requested in a s 17 LT(C)A 1995 default notice, request an overriding lease under s 19 LT(C)A 1995. The request must be made in writing and within 12 months of the payment being made. L would then have to grant an overriding lease, within a reasonable time. The term of the overriding lease would be equal to that of the remaining term of the lease plus three days and on essentially the same terms. The effect of the overriding lease would be to put T in the position of A's immediate landlord and thus give T landlord powers over A, including the right to forfeit the lease. T's overriding lease would then become a lease in possession which T could then assign (or sub-let) to a more attractive tenant, less likely to breach the covenants in the future. In doing so, not only does T get rid of the defaulting tenant but it also enables him to recoup some of the money he may have paid out for a breach he did not commit.

Table 7.2 explains A's position post assignment.

Table 7.2 Position of A—Post assignment

Pre-1996 lease	Post-1996 lease
As A (generally) does not enjoy a privity of contract relationship with L, he will only be liable if the burden of the covenants passed to him under *Spencer's Case* (1583). To do so:	As A (generally) does not enjoy a privity of contract relationship with L he will only be liable if the burden of the covenants passed to him under s 3 LT(C)A 1995. This will pass the burden

Enforcement of leasehold covenants

✱✱✱✱✱✱✱✱✱✱

Table 7.2 (continued)

Pre-1996 lease	Post-1996 lease
1. the covenant must 'touch and concern' the land ie affect the landlord and tenant in their capacity as such: **Breams Property Investment Co Ltd v Stroulger** [1948]; and	of all tenant covenants except those expressed to be personal to the original party (**s 3(6) LT(C) A 1995**).
2. there must be **privity of estate** ie a direct relationship of landlord and tenant must exist between the parties L and A: **Purchase v Lichfield Brewery Co** [1915]; and	
3. there must have been a legal assignment of a legal lease.	

Revision tip

Link point (2) in Table 7.2 to chapter 6 and the discussion whether an equitable lease is as good as a legal one. (Since an equitable lease does not give an estate in land, rather an equitable right to specific performance of a contract to grant a lease, the equitable tenant has no estate with which to create a privity of estate relationship.)

In respect of either a pre- or post-1996 lease, remember the following:

- Although A will generally not enjoy a privity of contract relationship with L, such a relationship will arise if A enters into the covenants directly with L after the assignment takes place thus creating a contractual relationship between them (as illustrated under a pre-1996 lease in the case of *Estates Gazette Ltd v Benjamin Restaurants Ltd* [1994]).

- Where the burden of the covenants has passed to A, he cannot be made liable for breaches that occurred before the assignment to him, unless such breaches are of a continuing nature (for example a breach of a covenant to repair), in which case A's liability for that breach will commence from the date of the assignment: *Grescot v Green* (1700) (pre-1996 lease); s 23 LT(C)A 1995 (post-1996 lease).

- Where a landlord has the choice as to whether to pursue T or A for the breach, he is free to choose either party, or both simultaneously, provided that he does not obtain double recovery.

When the original tenant (T) assigns his lease to his assignee (A), will the benefit of covenants T enjoyed pass to A?

Table 7.3 explains T's and A's positions regarding the benefit of covenants post assignment.

Table 7.3 Position of T and A regarding the benefit

POSITION OF T	
Pre-1996 lease	**Post-1996 lease**
T retains the right to pursue breaches committed by the landlord, before the assignment took place: *City & Metropolitan Properties Ltd v Greycroft Ltd* [1987].	When the benefit of covenants passes from T to A under **s 3 LT(C)A 1995**, T retains the right to pursue breaches committed by the landlord whilst he was tenant: **s 24 LT(C)A 1995** (unless the right to do so has been expressly assigned to his successor, A)
POSITION OF A	
A will only be able to pursue those breaches committed by the landlord after the assignment has occurred, provided he can establish the benefit of the covenants passed to him by meeting the *Spencer's Case* (1583) requirements.	A only acquires the right to pursue breaches that occur after the assignment to him has taken place, unless the right to pursue pre-assignment breaches has been expressly assigned to him: **s 23 LT(C)A 1995**.

Assignment of the reversion

Figure 7.3 illustrates the assignment of the reversion.

Figure 7.3 Assignment of the reversion

When the original landlord (L) assigns his reversionary interest to his assignee (L2), will the burden of covenants L entered into pass to L2?

Table 7.4 explains L's position post assignment.

Table 7.4 Position of L—post assignment

Pre-1996 lease	Post-1996 lease
L remains liable throughout the entire duration of the lease term, as originally envisaged, on all the covenants of the lease due to privity of contract: *Stuart v Joy* [1904]. This continuing liability is reinforced by **s 79 LPA 1925**.	L remains liable until such time as he is released from liability under **s 6 LT(C)A 1995**. The procedure for seeking release is governed by **s 8 LT(C)A 1995**, although release is not possible where the assignment is an excluded one under **s 11 LT(C)A 1995**. Even where a release has been successfully obtained, it will not be effective in respect of:

Enforcement of leasehold covenants

✳✳✳✳✳✳✳✳✳✳✳✳

Table 7.4 (*continued*)

Pre-1996 lease	Post-1996 lease
	1. purely personal covenants: *BHP Petroleum GB Ltd v Chesterfield Properties Ltd* [2000]; or
	2. breaches that were committed by L whilst he was the landlord: **s 24 LT(C)A 1995**.

What could L do if held liable for a breach committed by L2?

Whether a pre- or post-1996 lease, the following options are available to L:

- use the *Moule v Garret* (1872) principle as discussed earlier; or
- recoup sums paid using indemnity covenants, as discussed earlier. This is only possible where they have been expressly provided for.

Table 7.5 explains L2's position post assignment.

Table 7.5 Position of L2—Post assignment

Pre-1996 lease	Post-1996 lease
As L2 does not enjoy a privity of contract relationship with T, he will only be liable if the burden of the covenants passed to him under **s 142 LPA 1925**, which passes the burden of covenants having reference to the subject matter of the lease. This means the same as 'touch and concern': *Hua Chiao Commercial Bank Ltd v Chiaphua Industries Ltd* [1987] (see *Spencer's Case* (1583)).	As L2 does not enjoy a privity of contract relationship with T, he will only be liable if the burden of the covenants passed to him under **s 3 LT(C)A 1995**. This will pass the burden of all tenant covenants except those expressed to be personal to the original party (**s 3(6) LT(C)A 1995**).

In respect of either a pre- or post-1996 lease, remember that where the burden of the covenants has passed to L2, he cannot be made liable for breaches that occurred before the assignment of the reversion to him, unless such breaches are of a continuing nature (for example a breach of a covenant to repair), in which case L2's liability for that breach will commence from the date of the assignment (*Duncliffe v Caerfelin Properties Ltd* [1989] (pre-1996 lease); s 23 LT(C)A 1995 (post-1996 lease)).

When the original landlord (L) assigns his reversionary interest to his assignee (L2), will the benefit of covenants L enjoyed pass to L2?

Table 7.6 explains L's and L2's positions regarding the benefit of covenants.

Table 7.6 Position of L and L2 regarding the benefit

POSITION OF L	
Pre-1996 lease	**Post-1996 lease**
L loses the right to pursue any breach of tenant covenants upon assignment; even in respect of those breaches committed whilst he was the landlord. The benefit to do so passes to his successor upon assignment under **s 141 LPA 1925**: *Re King* [1963].	Where released from the burden of landlord covenants under **s 6 LT(C)A 1995**, L would also cease to be entitled to the benefit of covenants under the lease, save the right to pursue those breaches that occurred before he ceased to be so entitled: **s 24(4) LT(C)A 1995**, (unless that right has been expressly assigned to his successor, L2).
POSITION OF L2	
L2 will acquire upon assignment the benefit of all covenants which have reference to the subject matter of the lease (**s 141 LPA 1925**) including the right to pursue breaches that occurred before the assignment took place: *Arlesford Trading Co Ltd v Servansingh* [1971].	L2 will not be able to pursue breaches of tenant covenants that occurred before the assignment unless either: 1. the right to do so had been expressly assigned to him upon the assignment of the reversion: **s 23 LT(C)A 1995**; or 2. the breach was of a continuing nature in which case he could pursue but only as from the date of assignment.

Sub-tenants

Figure 7.4 illustrates the position of sub-tenants.

Figure 7.4 Sub-tenants

What is the position of ST?

Table 7.7 explains the position of ST.

Table 7.7 Position of ST

Pre-1996 lease	Post-1996 lease
In principle, L cannot enforce covenants directly against ST as there is neither privity of contract nor privity of estate between them: *South of England Dairies Ltd v Baker* [1906]. Instead,	ST could be held directly liable to L for a breach of a *restrictive* covenant: **s 3(5) LT(C)A 1995**. (Satisfaction of the other requirements under *Tulk v Moxhay* (1848) is not required.)

Key cases

✱✱✱✱✱✱✱✱✱✱

Table 7.7 *(continued)*

Pre-1996 lease	Post-1996 lease
L would have to seek remedy against T, assuming ST's breach put T in breach of a covenant in his headlease. T might then be able to recoup his losses from ST, assuming an express indemnity covenant existed between them. However, direct enforcement between L and ST is possible where the requirements under *Tulk v Moxhay* **(1848)** are met. These requirements are discussed in chapter 13 and will only aid in the enforcement of restrictive covenants.	

Remember, notice will be satisfied under *Tulk v Moxhay* (1848), by virtue of **s29(2)(b) LRA 2002** where registered land, and by the subtenant being deemed to have either actual or constructive notice where unregistered land (*Hall v Ewin* (1887)).

Revision tip

The case law concerning enforcement of leasehold covenants highlighted earlier is used to provide authority for principles of law. It is unlikely, therefore, that you need to concern yourself with revising the facts of these cases.

 Key cases

Case	Facts	Principle
Brew Brothers Ltd v Snax (Ross) Ltd [1970] 1 QB 612	Seepage from drains damaged foundations of a property, causing a wall to tilt. Repairs held outside the scope of the tenant's express covenant to repair, since would have cost the same as the value of the premises if totally rebuilt.	Where the cost of repair works amounts to a significant proportion of the value of the property itself, the works may be deemed to fall outside the ambit of a repair covenant.
Lister v Lane [1893] 2 QB 212	A tenant was held not liable to rebuild a house which had to be demolished due to its wooden foundations having rotted.	Where works would affect the whole or substantially the whole of the building, making the building different from the one demised, such works are likely to fall outside the ambit of a repair covenant.

Case	Facts	Principle
Post Office v Aquarius Property Ltd [1987] 1 All ER 1055	Basement built with porous cement so basement flooded when water table rose, though this caused no physical damage to the building. Tenant not liable to correct the design fault.	Repair does not require the correction of design faults unless the design fault causes further physical damage to the property and the only way to correct this physical damage is to correct the design fault from which it flows.
Quick v Taff-Ely Borough Council [1986] QB 821	Lack of insulation around single glazed windows caused condensation resulting in damage to house contents and decoration. Landlord not liable to repair this design fault with the windows.	Repair does not require the correction of design faults unless the design fault causes further physical damage to the property and the only way to correct this physical damage is to correct the design fault from which it flows.
Ravenseft Properties Ltd v Davstone (Holdings) Ltd [1980] QB 12	Stone cladding on a block of flats cracked and was in danger of falling off the building, due to a failure to install expansion joints. Tenant was held liable under his covenant to repair. The work required repair to only a trivial part of the building in total and the improvement would not change the nature of the building.	Whether repair falls into the ambit of an express covenant to repair is a question of degree. Where it involves giving the landlord back something wholly different from that which he demised, it will fall outside the ambit.

 ② Exam questions

Problem question

In January 2013, Constance, the freehold owner of a flat, granted Miriam by deed a six-year lease over the flat at a rent of £7,000 per annum. The lease contained, *inter alia*, covenants:

1. to keep the premises in good and substantial repair;
2. not to assign or sub-let the whole or any part of the premises without the consent of the landlord.

Six months later, Miriam was offered a job in France and so, with the consent of Constance, she assigned her lease to Patrick.

On a recent visit to the premises, Patrick gave Constance a letter, requesting that she consent to a sub-let of the property to his friend, George, who had just returned from a gap year in South America. Constance told Patrick that George had approached her about renting a different flat

Exam questions

✱✱✱✱✱✱✱✱✱✱✱

she owned. Patrick informed Constance that he had changed his mind about renting this other flat when he found out that sub-letting from Patrick would be cheaper.

On the same visit, Constance noticed that a patch of damp had appeared near to the window frame in the kitchen. Upon a closer inspection she noticed that the window frame was actually cracked. It had been letting in the rain which, she concluded, must have been the cause of the damp. When she asked Patrick whether he knew about this problem he said that he did. He had been meaning to tell her about it but kept forgetting. When she told him that it was his responsibility to do the repairs, he said he had no money but that if she allowed him to sub-let to George he would use this income to do the repairs.

Advise Constance as to her rights and remedies, if any.

What difference, if any, would it make to your answer if the lease had initially been granted to Miriam in 1994 for a term of 30 years?

See the Outline Answers section in the end matter for help with this question.

Essay question

To what extent has the **Landlord and Tenant (Covenants) Act 1995** eradicated the perceived problems that existed in relation to the enforcement of leasehold covenants prior to the Act coming into force?

 Online Resource Centre

To see an outline answer to this question log onto www.oxfordtextbooks.co.uk/orc/concentrate/

#8

Adverse possession

Problem questions will require you to identify the requirements to prove **adverse possession**, namely factual possession and the intention to possess, with reference to case law. Following this, you will be required to explain the process which would end the paper owner's rights. An important point is to establish which rules apply; knowing the rules for registered and unregistered land both before and after the **Land Registration Act 2002**.

Essay questions commonly focus upon how easy/difficult it is to establish an adverse possession claim and you will frequently be required to make comparisons between the rules that operate in unregistered and registered land, often with analysis of the changes introduced by the **LRA 2002**. This may be linked to human rights issues and a consideration of the moral and social policies that underlie the law relating to adverse possession.

Key facts

- To establish adverse possession of any type of land there must be:
  - factual possession of the land by the adverse possessor; and
  - the adverse possessor must have the requisite intent to possess.
- In unregistered land, after 12 years' adverse possession the paper owner will be statute barred from seeking recovery of his land.
- In registered land:
  - where 12 years' adverse possession are completed prior to 13 October 2003, then the paper owner will hold the property on trust for the adverse possessor;
  - where 12 years' adverse possession are completed after 13 October 2003, then the paper owner will no longer be statute barred but must comply with the new rules under the **LRA 2002** (which radically altered the rules in relation to registered land).
- Leasehold land can be subject to adverse possession but this will not act against the freeholder unless there is a period of adverse possession against him after the lease expires.
- Whilst human rights issues have been raised about this area of law, recent European case law suggests that no human rights are violated by the existence of this law.

Chapter overview

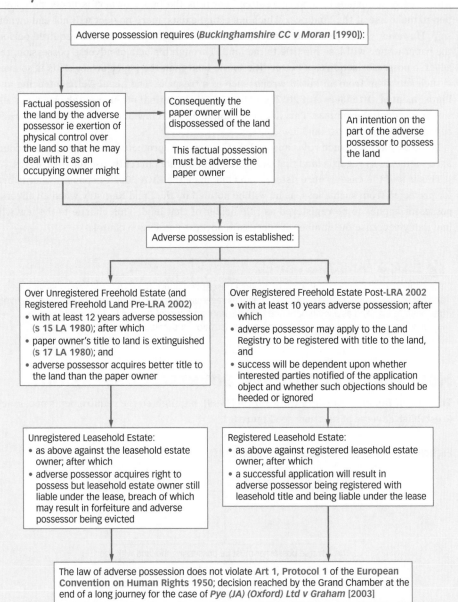

Adverse possession requires (*Buckinghamshire CC v Moran* [1990]):

Factual possession of the land by the adverse possessor ie exertion of physical control over the land so that he may deal with it as an occupying owner might

Consequently the paper owner will be dispossessed of the land

This factual possession must be adverse the paper owner

An intention on the part of the adverse possessor to possess the land

Adverse possession is established:

Over Unregistered Freehold Estate (and Registered Freehold Land Pre-LRA 2002)
- with at least 12 years adverse possession (**s 15 LA 1980**); after which
- paper owner's title to land is extinguished (**s 17 LA 1980**); and
- adverse possessor acquires better title to the land than the paper owner

Over Registered Freehold Estate Post-LRA 2002
- with at least 10 years adverse possession; after which
- adverse possessor may apply to the Land Registry to be registered with title to the land, and
- success will be dependent upon whether interested parties notified of the application object and whether such objections should be heeded or ignored

Unregistered Leasehold Estate:
- as above against the leasehold estate owner; after which
- adverse possessor acquires right to possess but leasehold estate owner still liable under the lease, breach of which may result in forfeiture and adverse possessor being evicted

Registered Leasehold Estate:
- as above against registered leasehold estate owner; after which
- a successful application will result in adverse possessor being registered with leasehold title and being liable under the lease

The law of adverse possession does not violate **Art 1, Protocol 1** of the **European Convention on Human Rights 1950**; decision reached by the Grand Chamber at the end of a long journey for the case of *Pye (JA) (Oxford) Ltd v Graham* [2003]

Introduction

An owner of an estate in land (hereafter known as the paper owner) is under no obliga-tion to make use of the land over which his estate exists; mere neglect will not end owner-ship. However, where that land is adversely possessed by another for the required period, the paper owner will lose his title to the land. Through his acts of adverse possession, the adverse possessor acquires a better title to the land than the paper owner. This is so even if such acts stem from an initial wrong, such as a trespass. The Legal Aid, Sentencing and Punishment of Offenders Act 2012, s 144 makes it a criminal offence to take such posses-sion in residential premises. This does not change the civil law in this area and is generally beyond the scope of most land law courses.

In the past at least, such rules ensured that landowners protected their rights and encour-aged vigilance as regards land that they owned but did not currently use for themselves.

This is still the case in unregistered land but since the LRA 2002 the paper owner is bet-ter protected from such a loss, as he will be notified by the Land Registry when an adverse possessor applies to be registered as title holder of that land. This change to the law will inevitably decrease the number of successful adverse possession claims.

> ☑ *Looking for extra marks?*
>
> The continued recognition of the law of adverse possession under the LRA 2002 seems inevitable and necessary to achieve certainty and finality as regards ownership claims over land. This objective has been recognized as a legitimate one by the European Court of Human Rights. In addition, by keeping the rules intact for unregistered land, registration of that land may be encouraged.

How do you establish adverse possession?

The case of *Buckinghamshire CC v Moran* [1990], highlighted the requirements necessary to establish adverse possession: see Figure 8.1.

Figure 8.1 Adverse possession requirements

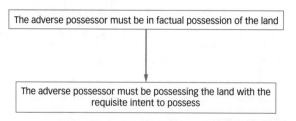

These requirements have been confirmed in *Pye (JA) (Oxford) Ltd v Graham* [2003], and apply equally whether the disputed land is registered or unregistered.

Revision tip

Many of the fundamental principles of adverse possession are discussed in *Pye (JA) (Oxford) Ltd v Graham* [2003] so a good understanding of this case is essential.

Factual possession by the adverse possessor

The adverse possessor must demonstrate a sufficient degree of physical control over the land in question. What is required is evidence that the adverse possessor has been able to deal with the land as an occupying owner might be expected to deal with it and that no-one else has done so (*Powell v McFarlane* (1977)).

Pye (JA) (Oxford) Ltd v Graham [2003] 1 AC 347

After the defendant's grazing licence expired, they continued to farm the land for over 12 years, during which time the land was accessed through a padlocked gate, for which the paper owner did not have a key. The defendants had shown factual possession of the land since they had used the land as their own, in a way which would be normal for an owner of that land to use it and contrary to the paper owner's wishes.

Dispossession of the paper owner will be a consequence of factual possession

Possession is exclusive so when the adverse possessor goes into factual possession he will necessarily dispossess the paper owner (per Lord Browne-Wilkinson in *Pye*). This does not require that the paper owner be driven out of his land, although this would obviously be clear dispossession. Nor will it be assumed merely by the fact that the land is not currently being used by the paper owner (*Tecbild Ltd v Chamberlain* (1969)). It may even occur in circumstances where the paper owner does not realize that he has been dispossessed, such as where a person remains on land belonging to the paper owner when a licence to do so has expired (*Pye*).

What degree of physical control is required to find factual possession?

This will obviously vary depending upon:

- whether possession takes place following the paper owner discontinuing his own possession or rather being dispossessed of his land (the former perhaps requiring a lesser degree of activity than the latter); and
- the type, state, and location of the land in question.

Examples have included:

- enclosing the land by the erection of fences: *George Wimpey & Co Ltd v Sohn* [1967];
- padlocking a gate which provides the only access to the land in dispute: *Buckinghamshire CC v Moran* [1990].

How do you establish adverse possession?

✳✳✳✳✳✳✳✳✳✳✳

What is important for you to remember when assessing whether there is a sufficient degree of physical control of the land by the adverse possessor, is the following:

- The possession cannot be presumed from mere temporary or trivial acts by the adverse possessor.

....

Tecbild Ltd v Chamberlain (1969) 20 P&CR 633, CA

The claimants sought to establish sufficient physical control of the land by establishing that their children played on the land whenever they wished and that their horses were tethered and exercised there. Such acts were deemed to be 'mere trivial acts of trespass' and thus insufficient to establish factual possession of the land.

....

The courts will assess from all the evidence if the adverse possessor has established exclusive possession. So an accumulation of trivial acts may amount to factual possession.

> ### Revision Tip
>
> An exam problem question may often have acts which begin as quite trivial, with later acts being more substantial. The examiner will require you to apply the facts to establish when possession has been enough.

- The possession must be open ie the sort of possession that the paper owner, with reasonable diligence could discover (**s 32(1) Limitation Act 1980**).
- It is the effect of the adverse possessor's actions over the land that is important when establishing whether they have exerted a sufficient degree of physical control and not their motivation for taking such actions.

....

Hounslow LBC v Minchinton (1997) 74 P&CR 221, CA

The adverse possessor had fenced part of the disputed land so as to prevent her dogs from escaping when she exercised them there. Although the motivation for her action had been to prevent her dogs from escaping, the effect of her action was to keep out the whole of the world from the land. It was the objective effect of her action, rather than her subjective motivation which, when taken into account with other things she had done on the land, deemed her to have assumed sufficient physical control of the land.

....

Factual possession must be adverse to the paper owner

Remember:

- possession with permission of the paper owner cannot be adverse (*Smith v Lawson* (1997));
- possession need not be inconsistent with the future intended use of the land by the paper owner to be adverse:

Buckinghamshire CC v Moran [1990] Ch 623, CA

The defendant adverse possessor possessed the claimant's land but only with an intention to do so until such time as the claimant went ahead with plans to build a bypass over it. Despite this limited intention, his desire to possess the land for himself as long as he could for his own benefit was enough to establish that the possession was adverse. The defendant's knowledge of the intended future use of the land would not, by itself, prevent the possession from being adverse.

✔ *Looking for extra marks?*

There was a move by Lord Denning in *Wallis's Cayton Bay v Shell-Mex and BP [1975]* to use the argument of implied licence identified in *Leigh v Jack* (1879). Essentially, where the use of the land was not inconsistent with the intended future use of the paper owner, then there was, by implication, permission from the paper owner to occupy the land until he wanted to use it for himself. Thus possession would not be adverse. Although this is rejected by the **Limitation Act 1980 Sch 1 para 8(4)**, it was revived, briefly, in *Beaulane Properties Ltd v Palmer* [2005]. This may form the basis of an essay question.

Intention to possess

Often such intention can be found when looking at the adverse possessor's actions on the disputed land. The acts required to establish a sufficient degree of physical control on the land (see 'What degree of physical control is required to find factual possession') may well indicate the existence of the requisite intent to use the land 'in the way in which a full owner would and in such a way that the owner is excluded' (Lord Hutton in *Pye (Oxford) Ltd v Graham* [2003]). In *Buckinghamshire CC v Moran* [1990], the court acknowledged that there could be a link between actions conducted on the land and finding the necessary intent.

However, where the actions of the adverse possessor could be open to more than one interpretation, and thus his intention ambiguous, he will not be deemed to have the requisite intent. His intention must be clear for all to see, and especially the paper owner.

Powell v McFarlane (1977) 38 P&CR 452

The adverse possessor was a 14-year-old boy who had been grazing his cow on the disputed land. The court declined to find an intention to possess from just these actions. When taking into account his age, it was not clear that his intention was to possess the land for his own benefit for as long as he could.

When trying to establish the requisite intention to possess, you must remember the following:

- The adverse possessor need not have an intention to dispossess; merely an intention to possess. So he could adversely possess the land without knowing it: *Hughes v Cork* [1994].

- The adverse possessor need not have an intention to own the disputed land; merely an intention to possess it for as long as he can for his own benefit. So, in the case of *Lambeth LBC v Blackburn* (2001), where the adverse possessor's intention was to stay in the council house until evicted, intention to possess was found. As Lord Hoffmann said in *Buckinghamshire CC v Moran* [1990] it is the intention to possess, not the intention to own, that is relevant.

- If the adverse possessor believes that he has the consent of the paper owner to be on the land, this will defeat any claim for adverse possession.

Establishing adverse possession of unregistered land

The principle

A claim of adverse possession of unregistered land is based upon limitation of actions. The paper owner has 12 years in which to remove the adverse possessor s 15(1) LA 1980. After that any action is barred and the title to the land extinguished (s 17 LA 1980).

Revision tip

Remember that the operation of s 15 LA 1980 not only applies to unregistered land, but also to registered land where the period of adverse possession expired before the LRA 2002 came into force.

Twelve years' adverse possession

The 12 years may be completed by more than one successive adverse possessor (*Williams v Usherwood* (1982)). However, there must not be a break in the adverse possession. A successful recovery of the land would stop the clock running and any later adverse possession would start the clock ticking again from the beginning.

Remember, that the title acquired by the adverse possessor will be subject to all proprietary rights that burden the land, whether legal or equitable, registered in accordance with the Land Charges Act 1972 or not, and irrespective of whether the successful adverse possessor had notice of those rights or not.

Subsequent dealings with the adversely possessed land

There is now every incentive to register the land, and if possession can be proved the land can be registered.

Establishing adverse possession of registered land

This is now governed by the provisions in the **LRA 2002** which has fundamentally changed the way in which a claim for adverse possession can be recognized as regards registered land. It will apply to all adverse possession claims of registered land that commenced after the Act came into force in October 2003.

Revision tip

Establish the date that adverse possession began. Add 12 years. If this brings you to before 13 October 2003 then the old registered land rules apply (so 1990 + 12 = 2002). That means that the registered owner would hold the land on trust for the adverse possessor (**s 75 LRA 25**). If it brings you after that date (1992 + 12 = 2004) then the new registered land rules apply.

✅ *Looking for extra marks?*

Particular focus of an essay question may require you to understand the motivation for changes. Lord Browne-Wilkinson expressed his unhappiness at the old rules in relation to registered land in his judgment in *Pye (Oxford) Ltd v Graham* [2003], whilst seeing their value in unregistered land. The changes under the **LRA 2002** protect ownership and the investment potential in land. Evidentially, a system based upon registration rather than possession should protect those who are registered as owners over possessors. Arguably, the new law also sits more comfortably with the **European Convention on Human Rights 1950**. In reality, the introduction of the new law may have been motivated largely by the need to facilitate e-conveyancing.

The principle

A claim of adverse possession of registered land post-2003 is not based upon limitation of actions (**s 96 LRA 2002**). Instead the adverse possessor must take positive steps to apply to the Land Registry to be registered with title to the land.

Ten years' adverse possession

After a minimum of ten years of adversely possessing a piece of land (see 'How do you establish adverse possession?'), as the same rules apply to this part of the process (**Sch 6 para 11 LRA 2002**), the adverse possessor can apply to the Land Registry to be registered with title to the land that he is adversely possessing.

Remember that:

- The possession must be for a period of ten years immediately preceding the adverse possessor's date of application: **Sch 6 para 1(1) LRA 2002**.

Establishing adverse possession of registered land

✳✳✳✳✳✳✳✳✳

- The estate adversely possessed need not have been registered at the Land Registry throughout the entirety of this period: **Sch 6 para 1(4) LRA 2002**.

- No application can be made when the current registered proprietor is unable, due to mental disability, to make decisions on the application or to communicate those decisions: **Sch 6 para 8 LRA 2002**.

On application the Land Registry will notify the registered title holder and other interested parties (ie a mortgagee) of the application (**Sch 6 para 2 LRA 2002**) who then have 65 working days to submit an objection.

If no objection is submitted then the adverse possessor will be duly registered as title holder.

If there is an objection then the paper owner has two years in which to remove, or give permission to, the adverse possessor. If they have not done this the adverse possessor can make a further application and they will be registered as title holder (**Sch 6 para 6 LRA 2002**). See Figure 8.2 for further explanation of such objections.

Figure 8.2 Ten years' adverse possession—objections

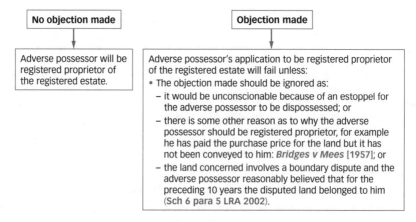

The effect of a successful claim

Where an application to be registered as title holder is successful, the applicant's name will be substituted for that of the former proprietor. The effect is to transfer the estate to the applicant.

The adverse possessor will be subject to virtually all proprietary rights that burden the land. As chargees are notified of an adverse possessor's application to be registered as title holder, they have the opportunity to raise objections to the application. Where they fail to do so, they cannot later claim to enforce their charge against the new registered owner (unless registration followed, ignoring any objections made, based upon one of the three grounds stated in Figure 8.2, in which case the registered charge can be enforced against the new registered title holder).

Subsequent dealings with the adversely possessed land

Where the adverse possessor has successfully been registered as the new owner, it will have no impact on any further dealings with that land, which will occur in much the same way as any registered estate.

Where the adverse possessor has not made an application to be registered as title holder, yet continues to adversely possess the land, his rights, such as they are, will bind any successor to the paper owner who provides no consideration for the transfer of the land. Where the successor provides consideration, the adverse possessor's rights may constitute an overriding interest under Sch 3 para 2 LRA 2002 provided certain conditions are met (discussed in full detail in chapter 3). Such rights could therefore be binding upon that successor. Should the adverse possessor stop possessing the land, even after he has successfully completed ten years' adverse possession, he will no longer be deemed in actual occupation of the land and thus have no rights enforceable under Sch 3 para 2 LRA 2002.

Revision tip

Link the previous discussion, concerning dealings with adversely possessed land, to material covered in chapter 3.

Adverse possession of a leasehold estate

By the tenant

Remember that in order to establish adverse possession, the possession must be without the permission of the paper owner. It is for this reason that a tenant cannot claim adverse possession against his landlord whilst his lease still exists. Even if, during the term of the lease, the tenant possesses more of the landlord's land than is actually demised, this will not amount to adversely possessing that land. Instead, the demised premises are seen as having been extended.

By someone other than the tenant

The possession is adverse to the leaseholder's estate not the freeholder (the landlord). Only when the lease expired would the possession be adverse to the freeholder. To achieve a better title than anyone to the land, the adverse possessor must adversely possess the land against both the leasehold and freehold estate owners. This can take some time, as seen in Figures 8.3 and 8.4.

Where possession is in relation to an unregistered leasehold estate

Remember that the clock does not begin to tick against the unregistered freehold owner until the lease has expired, regardless of the fact that the adverse possessor may have already completed 12 years' adverse possession against the leasehold estate owner.

Adverse possession of a leasehold estate

****

Figure 8.3 Adverse possession of an unregistered leasehold estate

> The adverse possessor completes 12 years' adverse possession against the leasehold estate owner, after which the leasehold estate owner's title is extinguished and he is statutorily barred from seeking recovery of the land: LA 1980.

> Having extinguished the leasehold estate owner's title, there is nothing to assign to the adverse possessor. He is thus not liable (generally) on the terms of the lease. Instead, until the original lease expires, the dispossessed leasehold estate owner remains liable. Where he breaches any of the lease terms, the landlord can bring forfeiture proceedings against him. If successful, the lease will be terminated; the landlord regains his right to possess the land and can thus take action to evict the adverse possessor.

> Provided there has been no such eviction of the adverse possessor, once the lease expires, a further 12 years of adverse possession against the unregistered freehold owner will extinguish the latter's title and he will be statute barred from seeking recovery of the land.

Where possession is in relation to a registered freehold estate subject to a registered lease

Figure 8.4 Adverse possession of a registered freehold estate subject to a registered lease

> The adverse possessor completes 10 years' adverse possession against the registered leasehold estate owner (ie tenant). He can now apply to the Land Registry to be registered as the title holder of the leasehold estate: Sch 6 para 1 LRA 2002.

> Upon receiving the application, the Land Registry notifies all interested parties who are given the opportunity to submit an objection to the application (as with adverse possession of a freehold estate, discussed above).

> Where the application is successful, the adverse possessor will be registered with title to the leasehold estate. In effect, there has been a statutory assignment of the lease to him thus he is liable on all the terms of the lease: Sch 6 para 9 LRA 2002 and *Central London Commercial Estates Ltd v Kato Kagaku Ltd* [1998].

> Where the adverse possessor completes a further 10 years of adverse possession against the registered freehold estate owner, he will be entitled to apply to the Land Registry to be registered with title to the freehold estate. (These applications have been discussed previously.)

Human rights

It was argued in *Pye v UK* (2007) that the law on adverse possession was incompatible with Art 1, Protocol 1 of the European Convention on Human Rights 1950, (enacted into English law by the Human Rights Act 1998), namely the peaceful enjoyment of his possessions save where it is in the public interest that he be deprived of them. However, after a long series of appeals, the Grand Chamber has held that principles of adverse possession are compatible with the Convention. The use of limitation periods, through which adverse possession operates in respect of pre-2003 actions, are a common feature of legal systems. The law of adverse possession operates to control land use rather than deprive people of their property. Such control is not contrary to Art 1 when it is a proportionate response to a legitimate public interest.

Revision tip

The question of whether adverse possession can be seen as 'land theft' and links to human rights arguments can form the basis of an essay. Be prepared to consider the justification for the law of adverse possession and, in particular, consider arguments and analysis stemming from the appeals journey of *Pye* (the decision itself and articles on the case which followed).

✅ Looking for extra marks?

In *Beaulane Properties Ltd v Palmer* [2005], on facts similar to *Pye* but the expiration of 12 years' adverse possession occurred after the Human Rights Act 1998 had come into force (rather than before as in *Pye*), the Deputy Judge of the High Court felt that the law was not compatible with the Convention. He achieved compatibility by reviving the principle from *Leigh v Jack* (1879) (see 'Factual possession must be adverse to the paper owner'). Read his judgment and consider if his reasoning was correct in the light of the reasoning of the Grand Chamber in *Pye*.

✳ Key cases

Case	Facts	Principle
Buckinghamshire CC v Moran [1990] Ch 623, CA	Possession of land over which the paper owner intended to build a bypass in the future. The adverse possessor knew this and intended to possess until such action was taken.	An adverse possessor's knowledge of the intended future use of the land will not prevent possession from being adverse. The adverse possessor must intend to possess the property for his own benefit for as long as he can.

Case	Facts	Principle
Hounslow LBC v Minchinton (1997) 74 P&CR 221, CA	Enclosure of land by adverse possessor to prevent her dogs escaping when exercised there.	It is the objective effect of an adverse possessor's actions, rather than his subjective motivations, which must be considered when establishing a sufficient degree of physical control to amount to factual possession of land.
Powell v McFarlane (1977) 38 P&CR 452	14-year-old boy grazed his cow on disputed land.	Where the actions of an adverse possessor could be open to more than one interpretation, thus his intention is ambiguous, the requisite intent cannot be found.
Pye (JA) (Oxford) Ltd v Graham [2003] 1 AC 347	Farming of grazing land by the defendants, initially on the basis of a grazing licence, but once expired and a request for renewal refused, without such a licence. Defendants' padlocked gate giving access to the land, with no key being given to paper owner. Defendants acquired title to the land by adverse possession.	An adverse possessor must be dealing with the land in a way an occupying owner would, to the exclusion of others and contrary to the paper owner's wishes. Willingness to possess land with permission will not prevent possession from being adverse until such permission is given.
Tecbild Ltd v Chamberlain (1969) 20 P&CR 633, CA	Acts relied upon by claimants to establish physical possession of land were tethering and exercising their horses on the land and allowing their children to play on the land.	Factual possession of the land will not be established by mere temporary and trivial acts of trespass.

(?) Exam questions

Problem question

Fred was the registered freehold proprietor of a large country estate (The Elms). The property consists of a large house, some fields, and a wooded area. The estate was unoccupied from 1998. At some point in the future Fred planned to turn the property into a country house hotel. In the summer of 1999 George and Hilly, who have nowhere to live, break off a padlock on the gate which provides access to the wooded area. They pitch a tent in the wood. In 2000 George and Hilly fit their own padlock to the existing gate and in 2001 they build a more permanent structure made out of corrugated iron and old packing cases. In May 2002 they are joined by their friends Ian and John. In 2007 George and Hilly are given a council flat. Ian and John remain in place. In late 2010, Fred decides not to go ahead with the development and the whole estate is sold to a chain of hotels—Town and Country Hotels Ltd. In early 2011 Ian and John are discovered by builders working on the redevelopment but they refuse to leave.

Advise Ian and John and Town and Country Hotels Ltd.

See the Outline Answers section in the end matter for help with this question.

Essay question

The scope of adverse possession, and the ability to acquire land by stealth, has been severely curtailed by the **Land Registration Act 2002**, resulting in a law that can be morally justified. Discuss.

 Online Resource Centre

To see an outline answer to this question log onto www.oxfordtextbooks.co.uk/orc/concentrate/

#9
Trusts of land

The examination

This is an area that is closely linked with co-ownership of land (discussed in chapter 10) and also with trusts of the family home, which is not discussed in any great detail in this book but is covered in the Equity and Trusts book that accompanies this series.

Since trusts of land are a relatively new concept to land law, introduced by the **Trusts of Land and Appointment of Trustees Act 1996 (TLATA)**, examiners often require an analysis of the legislative changes brought about by **TLATA 1996**; why they were necessary and how trusts of land differ from their predecessor, the trust for sale. Issues regarding the sale of trust property, the powers of trustees, and rights of beneficiaries may also be a focus of an exam question, with a need to contrast the position pre and post **TLATA 1996**.

Key facts

- Whilst strict settlements created before **TLATA 1996** and governed by the **Settled Land Act 1925** can continue to exist, the creation of new successive interests must be by way of a trust of land.

- The creation of concurrent interests in land generally now occurs by way of a trust of land, governed by **TLATA 1996** and replacing their forerunner, trusts for sale.

- Trusts of land may be expressly or impliedly created and where implied, may be resulting or constructive trusts.

- Whilst the key feature of the trust for sale was that trustees had a duty to sell the trust land, with a power to postpone, under a trust of land trustees have the power to sell, but need not do so.

- Key provisions of **TLATA 1996** include:
  - **ss 6–8**: governing the extent of trustees' powers over the trust property;
  - **s 11**: governing the circumstances in which trustees have a duty to consult beneficiaries when exercising their powers;
  - **ss 12–13**: governing the rights of beneficiaries to occupy the trust property; and
  - **ss 14–15**: governing the right of an interested party to make an application to the court for an order to resolve a dispute over trust land (see chapter 10).

Chapter overview

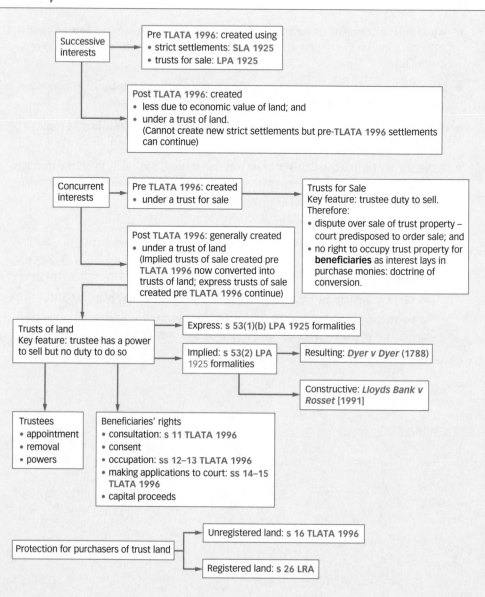

Successive and concurrent interests in land

Pre TLATA 1996

Successive interests in land were created when an estate owner disposed of his estate, either *inter vivos* or by will, to a number of people in succession; for example A leaves his freehold estate to B for life; remainder to C in fee simple. Both B and C acquired interests in the land: B acquired a life estate and C acquired a fee simple in remainder. Since 1925, neither of these interests could exist as legal estates in land (see s 1 Law of Property Act 1925 and chapter 5). Devices were therefore established to allow for the creation of such successive interests, namely:

- a strict **settlement**, governed by the Settled Land Act 1925; or
- a **trust for sale**, governed by the LPA 1925.

As well as the creation of successive interests, concurrent interests in land arose where more than one person was entitled to enjoy and possess the land at the same time. The creation of such concurrent interests resulted either from an express intention, where legal title to an estate was conveyed to two or more people, or it was implied from the circumstances (discussed later). Whatever the circumstances in which they arose, concurrent interests existed behind a trust for sale.

Post TLATA 1996

Concurrent interests and, to a much lesser extent, successive interests are still created today. However, devices established for their creation have been fundamentally overhauled by TLATA 1996. Key changes include:

- an inability to create new strict settlements: s 2 TLATA 1996, although strict settlements that already existed before TLATA 1996 can continue and remain governed by SLA 1925;
- the creation of any successive interests after 1 January 1997 must now take effect as a **trust of land**, governed by TLATA 1996 (s 1 TLATA 1996);
- the creation of concurrent interests now generally exist behind a trust of land, which, to a large extent, has replaced trusts for sale.

Successive interests

Successive interests are limited by statute to prevent land from being off the market for too long. However, they do still arise ie a lifetime interest for A to live in a property, with an interest in remainder to B when A dies. These successive interests take effect under a trust of land, governed by TLATA 1996 (see 'Trusts of land' for a more detailed discussion).

Successive interests created before TLATA 1996, which took effect under a strict settlement governed by the SLA 1925, can continue to exist but are becoming increasing rare and therefore less frequently a topic for examination.

Concurrent interests and the role of trusts

Where land is vested in one person, he becomes the sole owner of that land. No distinction is made between legal and equitable ownership.

Where land is conveyed so as to create concurrent interests, where more than one person is entitled to enjoy and possess the land at the same time, such land will be held by way of a trust. A distinction is therefore made between those who hold legal title as trustees on trust and those who hold the equitable title as beneficiaries. Whilst holding the legal title merely confers upon you fiduciary duties and administrative responsibilities in managing the trust property, it is the holding of the equitable title that confers true value and substance of owning a property since it determines beneficial enjoyment of the land.

Prior to TLATA 1996, the trust established in the creation of concurrent interests was a trust for sale.

Trusts for sale

Trusts for sale are defined in s 205(1)(xxix) LPA 1925. A key feature of a trust for sale is that the trustees had a duty to sell the trust property. This duty did not have to be acted upon immediately, since trustees also had a power to postpone sale. Nevertheless, the overriding duty to sell meant:

- Where a dispute arose between concurrent owners as to whether the land should be sold or not, and a subsequent application was made to the court under s 30 LPA 1925 to request a court order to settle the dispute, the court would be predisposed towards ordering a sale (see chapter 10).

- The beneficiaries under a trust for sale did not have a right to occupy the trust property since their interests were seen as resting in purchase monies rather than the land itself. This was known as the doctrine of conversion and has since been abolished under s 3 TLATA 1996.

- As social attitudes changed and land was beginning to be appreciated more for its use, as a place to live, rather than its economic value, postponement of the duty to sell became commonplace. The idea behind a trust for sale, that trustees had a duty to sell, was becoming inappropriate.

This last point was the principal motivation for wishing to replace trusts for sale with a new type of trust that was not focused upon an underlying duty to sell: the trust of land.

The effect of TLATA on trusts for sale

- All trusts for sale *impliedly created by statute* before TLATA 1996 came into force have been automatically converted into trusts of land on 1 January 1997: s 5 and Sch 2 TLATA 1996.

- Trusts for sale *expressly created* before TLATA 1996 came into force, can continue to exist as trusts for sale. Indeed, it remains possible even now to create new express trusts for sale. However, the trustees of these trusts for sale have an irreducible power to postpone sale indefinitely, despite any express contrary intention: s 4 TLATA 1996. To some extent, therefore, trusts for sale have lost their key feature and thus their continued creation may be somewhat pointless.

Trusts of land

Trusts of land are defined in s 1 TLATA 1996 as being any trust of property which consists of or includes land whether expressly or impliedly created; whether arising before or after 1 January 1997. Unlike a trust for sale, trustees under a trust of land have no duty to sell, but merely a power to do so.

Trusts of land may be:

- express; or
- implied, of which there are two types:
  - resulting; and
  - constructive.

Revision tip

The creation of trusts, and particularly the circumstances in which implied trusts will arise, is dealt with in more detail in the Equity and Trusts book accompanying this series. You must be guided by your individual course as to how much knowledge of this topic you require for your land law examination.

Express trusts of land

When do they arise?

An express trust of land may arise when there is a self declaration by the legal owner that it is being held on trust, or land is conveyed to another to be held on trust. All express trusts of land require compliance with the formalities in s 53(1)(b) LPA 1925. They must be evidenced in writing and signed by the person declaring the trust.

The effect of an express declaration of trust

Generally, and assuming the express declaration satisfies the formalities above, it will be conclusive as to the nature and extent of the beneficial rights held under the trust of land: *Pettitt v Pettitt* [1970]. The conclusive nature of the express declaration can only be rebutted with evidence of fraud or, in rare circumstances, where evidence is produced showing the express declaration does not accurately reflect the intention of the parties.

Implied trusts of land

These are discussed in greater detail in the Equity and Trusts book accompanying this series. The focus of this chapter is to look at actual trusts of land themselves, however they arise. Implied trusts do not need the formalities of an express trust in land (s 53(2) LPA 1925).

Resulting trusts

A legal owner may be required to hold the land on trust for those who have contributed to the purchase of the land, their share being in proportion to their contribution: *Dyer v Dyer* (1788).

Of course, it is possible to rebut the presumption of a resulting trust where it is clear that the contributor did not intend to acquire a beneficial interest in the property or where the contribution was intended to be a gift or a loan.

> #### Example
>
> Alex provides one third of the purchase monies for the purchase of a property by Bert. Whilst legal title is vested in Bert, a resulting trust will be imposed and he will hold the property on trust for himself as to two thirds and Alex as to one third, since beneficial interests under a resulting trust are proportionate to contributions made.

Constructive trusts

Constructive trusts in land arise in limited situations outlined by Lord Bridge in *Lloyds Bank plc v Rosset* [1991], based upon the intention of the parties:

- *express common intention*—Where there is evidence that the parties expressly reached an agreement, arrangement, or understanding that the beneficial ownership of the property was to be shared. Following such agreement there must be detrimental reliance. This can be a broad range of actions and is not limited to direct financial contributions to the home.

- *inferred common intention*—Where there is no express discussion, then such an intention can be inferred from conduct. The conduct which will infer this intention is direct contributions towards the purchase of the property, whether initially or ongoing, such as the payment of mortgage installments. Indirect financial contributions, such as decorating the house, will not suffice to establish the requisite common intention. The position is different for married couples or civil partnership where the division of property is regulated by the **Matrimonial Proceedings and Property Act 1970** and the **Family Law Act 1996**. There has been much debate on the basis of the inference being purely for direct financial contributions which are discussed further in the Equity and Trusts book accompanying this series.

The value of the interest under a constructive trust will depend upon all the conduct that has taken place between the parties: *Stack v Dowden* [2007].

Revision tip

If this is an area that you think will be examined, look at the relevant section in the Equity and Trusts book accompanying this series where there is greater analysis of recent decisions.

Trustees of land

Appointment

Who appoints?

Trustees can be appointed by other trustees under the provisions of **s 36 Trustee Act (TA) 1925**. The court has power to appoint trustees under **s 41 TA 1925**. Beneficiaries, who act unanimously and of capacity, can also appoint trustees under **s 19 TLATA 1996**. All of these provisions are subject to any express clause in the trust document.

Who can be appointed?

Anyone who is *sui juris* and willing to act. Trustees can also be beneficiaries under the trust. However, their role as trustees (the duties and responsibilities that it brings) remains quite distinct from beneficial enjoyment they derive from being equitable title holders.

Number of trustees?

A maximum of four trustees can hold legal title (see chapter 10). A trust of land can exist with just one trustee but remember (from chapters 3 and 4) that a minimum of two trustees is required to give valid receipt and allow for overreaching to occur under **ss 2 and 27 LPA 1925**.

Formalities for appointment

A trustee should be appointed by deed. Where this occurs, the trust property is automatically vested in the trustee, with the already existing trustees as joint tenants without the need for a separate transfer: **s 40 TA 1925**.

Removal

A trustee may retire from being a trustee: s 36 TA 1925. However,

- he may not do so, where there is not going to be a simultaneous appointment of a new trustee, without first seeking consent of his co-trustees; and

- he may not do so if, upon his retirement, just one trustee remains.

Beneficiaries can also remove trustees under s 19 TLATA 1996, meeting the same requirements as for appointment.

Formalities

Retirement should be by deed. The remaining trustees will automatically be vested with the legal estate to hold as joint tenants without the need for a separate transfer: s 40 TA 1925.

Where the trustee is also a beneficiary

If a trustee is also a beneficiary then retirement as a trustee will not stop that person from being a beneficiary under the trust. Likewise, where a trustee does dispose of his beneficial interest in the property (s 53(1)(c) LPA 1925), he will still remain a trustee of that property until such point as he retires, is removed, or dies.

Powers

As a starting point, trustees of land have 'all the powers of an absolute owner': s 6(1) TLATA 1996.

What do these powers entail?

They include:

- the power to sell, lease, mortgage, grant options, easements etc. (Remember that a purchaser will only take free from beneficial interests existing behind the trust where the mechanics of overreaching have been satisfied: discussed in chapters 3 and 4 regarding registered and unregistered land respectively.);

- the power to acquire freehold or leasehold estates, whether for investment or for occupation by a beneficiary under the trust: s 6(3) TLATA 1996;

- the power to exclude or restrict the rights of one or more of the beneficiaries to occupy the trust land: s 13(1) TLATA 1996 (see 'Occupation');

- the power to delegate their trustee functions to one or more of the beneficiaries of full age: s 9(1) TLATA 1996;

- the power to transfer trust land to the beneficiaries, where they are of full age and capacity, and absolutely entitled to the land, even where the beneficiaries do not require it.

What duties does a trustee owe when exercising these powers?

As the home is a trust asset then decisions to sell will be regulated by **s 1(1) Trustee Act 2000**, a trustee is under a duty to exercise 'such care and skill as is reasonable in the circumstances'. Regard shall be had to experience and any special knowledge the trustee may have when assessing whether an appropriate level of care and skill has been exercised.

How are these powers curtailed?

- The powers are only available to the trustees for the purpose of exercising their functions as trustees: **s 6(1) TLATA 1996**.

- The powers can be excluded or restricted by express provision in the disposition creating the trust of land: **s 8(1) TLATA 1996**.

- The powers must not be exercised in a way that contravenes any other enactment, rule of law, or equity: **s 6(6) TLATA 1996**.

- When exercising these powers, trustees must have regard to the rights of the beneficiaries: **s 6(5) TLATA 1996**. They must, for example, get the best possible return for the trust property.

- So far as practicable, and in the absence of express contrary intention, trustees must consult beneficiaries of full age and beneficially entitled to an interest in possession in the trust land when exercising their powers. Trustees should then give effect to the wishes of the beneficiaries and, where dispute between the beneficiaries exists, give effect to the wishes of the majority in value so far as is consistent with the general interests of the trust: **s 11(1) TLATA 1996**. It is for the trustees to decide what is in the general interest of the trust.

- The exercise of the powers may be made subject to the consent of the beneficiaries but only where this is expressly provided for in the trust instrument or by a court order.

Delegation of their powers

All trustees may jointly delegate their powers to beneficiaries entitled to an interest in possession in the trust land: **s 9 TLATA 1996**.

Rights of beneficiaries

These include:

Consultation

As discussed (see 'How are these powers curtailed?'), in most circumstances beneficiaries have a right to be consulted when trustees exercise their powers: **s 11 TLATA 1996**.

Rights of beneficiaries

✳✳✳✳✳✳✳✳✳✳✳

Consent

As discussed (see 'How are these powers curtailed?'), where required, trustees' exercise of power may be subject to obtaining the consent of beneficiaries.

Occupation

Revision Tip

Examiners often focus on how the law has changed since the introduction of **TLATA 1996**. The issue of occupation is one such area where comparisons between pre and post **TLATA 1996** can be made.

Pre TLATA—under trusts for sale

Whilst a beneficiary who was also a legal owner of the property, had a right to occupy the property, the position was less certain for beneficiaries who did not also hold legal title as trustees. Their right to occupy would depend upon:

- Whether they were already in actual occupation of the property. If they were, their right to occupy was safeguarded by virtue of **s 14 LPA 1925**. If they were not, it seemed they had no right to insist upon taking occupation of the property.

- In addition, where the purpose of the trust was not to provide a home for the beneficiaries, such beneficiaries would find it hard to insist upon a right to occupy the trust property: *Barclay v Barclay* [1970].

Remember, that under a trust for sale, where trustees had a duty to sell, beneficial interests were seen as resting in the sale proceeds, rather than the land itself (*the doctrine of conversion*), which seemed to tip the balance against them having rights of occupation (see 'Trusts for sale').

Post TLATA—under trusts of land

When does a beneficiary have a right to occupy trust property?

As before **TLATA 1996**, a beneficiary who is also a legal owner of the trust property has a right to occupy that property. **Sections 12** and **13 TLATA 1996** govern rights to occupy trust property by beneficiaries who are not also the legal title holders.

According to **s 12 TLATA 1996**, a beneficiary is entitled to occupy trust property at any time if at that time:

- the purpose of the trust includes providing land for beneficiaries to occupy; and

- such land is both available (so not, for example, already leased to a tenant) and suitable for occupation (so not, for example, an office block unsuitable for residential occupation or a situation where the beneficiary seeking occupation does not get along with the other occupiers).

How are disputes resolved?

Trustees can exercise their powers to restrict or exclude one or more, but not all, of the beneficiaries from occupying the land. In doing so, the trustees:

- must act unanimously; and
- must act reasonably.

In acting reasonably, trustees must have regard to factors specified under s 13(4) TLATA 1996 namely:

- the intentions of the person(s) who created the trust;
- the purpose for which the land is held; and
- the circumstances and wishes of all beneficiaries entitled to occupy under s 12.

When exercising their power to restrict or exclude occupation, trustees may impose financial or other conditions on the beneficiary/beneficiaries occupying, for example:

- to pay for any repairs to the property or other expenses the property incurs;
- to pay an occupation rent to those beneficiaries whose rights to occupy have been restricted or excluded, as a way of compensation: *Dennis v McDonald* [1982], where a male partner was allowed to continue to occupy the property but ordered to pay rent to the female partner who had left the property due to his violence. The obligation to compensate does not extend to beneficiaries who voluntarily vacate the property. In the case of *Murphy v Gooch* [2007] the moving out of a co-owner due to relationship breakdown, was deemed to be constructive exclusion and thus not voluntary, accordingly giving rise to the payment of occupation rent.

Trustees even have the power to physically partition the land, where appropriate, to allow different beneficiaries the ability to occupy exclusively different parts of the building: *Rodway v Landy* [2001].

What is clear is that in exercising this discretion, a beneficiary already in occupation should not be removed and prevented from occupying without either his consent or court approval (where the court would consider criteria under s 13(4) listed under s 13(7) TLATA 1996).

Making an application to court

Beneficiaries have a right to make an application to the court under s 14 TLATA 1996 to request a court order, for example to settle a dispute between beneficiaries as to whether the trust land should be sold or not (see chapter 10) or to resolve disputes over the trustees' allocation of rights to occupy.

Capital proceeds

Where trust land is sold, and beneficial interests are successfully overreached (see chapters 3 and 4) beneficiaries have a right to the capital proceeds where their interests now lie, proportionate to the interest they held in the land.

Protection for a purchaser of trust land

Unregistered land

Although trustees of land have a power to sell trust property subject to the limits discussed, by virtue of s 16 TLATA 1996 even if they exceed their powers a purchaser will take free from any beneficial interest if:

- he satisfied the requirements of overreaching; and
- had no actual notice that the disposition to him was in breach of trust.

Registered land

Section 16 TLATA 1996 does not apply to registered land. It is assumed that any restrictions on the rights of the trustees to deal with the land have been entered as a restriction on the register for the purchaser to see. A valid sale of the property will not occur unless such restrictions as have been entered are complied with. No further protection therefore need be afforded to the purchaser.

However, in the case where such restrictions are not present, s 26 LRA 2002 appears to provide purchasers of registered land with adequate protection. The effect of this provision seems to be that a purchaser takes an unimpeachable title to the registered land even in circumstances where the trustees have acted in breach of the trust.

 Key cases

Case	Facts	Principle
Lloyds Bank plc v Rosset [1991] 1 AC 107	A wife assisted substantially in the renovation of the family home, legal title to which was vested solely in her husband. The House of Lords declined to find that a constructive trust had arisen as a result of her work on the property.	In the absence of any express agreement, arrangement, or understanding between the parties that the property is to be shared beneficially, upon which a party relies to his detriment, a constructive trust may arise where such common intention can be found from the conduct or mutual dealings between the parties. However, such conduct must amount to a direct contribution to the purchase of the property.
Stack v Dowden [2007] 2 AC 432	An unmarried couple, having lived together for 18 years, bought a house to live in with their four children. The lady contributed more than 50% of the purchase monies, with legal title being registered in their joint names. No declaration of trust was made indicating how the beneficial interest should be held. Upon the relationship breaking down, the House of Lords affirmed that where there is a joint tenancy at law, the starting point is to assume a beneficial joint tenancy (ie equal shares). However, taking into account all dealings between the parties (especially the fact that they had always kept their financial affairs separate), the lady was deemed to be entitled to a higher than 50% share in the house.	The quantum of a beneficial interest under a constructive trust should be calculated with regard to the whole course of dealing between the parties and not merely by reference to the actual financial contributions.

 Exam questions

Problem question

Alan is the sole legal owner of 'Bleak House'. The property was largely purchased with his savings. A quarter of the price was paid by his son Bill and Bill's partner Claire. Bill and Claire live in the property.

Alan has fallen out with Bill and wishes to sell the property. He has found a buyer, David.

Exam questions

✱✱✱✱✱✱✱✱✱✱✱

Alan seeks your advice on the following questions:

1. whether he can sell the property without consulting Bill and Claire;

2. whether he can ask Bill and Claire to leave the house so that it has vacant possession and is therefore more saleable;

3. whether Alan can sell the house without the consent of Bill and Claire;

4. whether David will take free of any interests if he does complete the sale.

See the Outline Answers section in the end matter for help with this question.

Essay question

The provisions contained within the **Trusts of Land and Appointment of Trustees Act 1996** now make sure that a correct balance is achieved between the rights of trustees and those of beneficiaries under a trust.

Discuss.

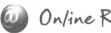 Online Resource Centre

To see an outline answer to this question log onto www.oxfordtextbooks.co.uk/orc/concentrate/

#10
Co-ownership

The examination

This topic area may be examined alone or combined with other aspects of law, notably trusts of land (discussed in chapter 9) and/or principles governing enforcement of beneficial interests behind a trust against purchasers of trust land (discussed in chapters 3 and 4).

Problem questions are common and may require you to:

- assess the fact that the property is co-owned and held on trust and consequently analyse how the property is held both at law and in equity;
- work through a series of events in chronological order assessing how, if at all, the event changes the way property is being held at law and in equity. Such events inevitably involve either a death of a co-owner or an event which could possibly amount to a severance;
- consider how a court would deal with applications to sell trust property either by one of the co-owners themselves or by a trustee in bankruptcy, where one of the co-owners has been declared bankrupt;
- consider the consequences should the co-owned property be sold, both in relation to the co-owners and the purchaser.

An essay question may focus on analysis of severance or require you to assess how the **Trusts of Land and Appointment of Trustees Act 1996 (TLATA)** has changed the law of co-ownership from that which existed before the Act was passed.

Key facts

- Co-owned property can be held by way of a joint tenancy or a tenancy in common.

- Co-owned property is held on trust and, since **TLATA 1996**, this is generally a trust of land.

- Legal title can only be held as a joint tenancy, by a maximum of four people. Equitable title can be held as a joint tenancy or a tenancy in common by an unlimited number of people.

- A joint tenancy in equity, but not at law, can be severed to create a tenancy in common.

- Methods of severance are outlined in **s 36 Law of Property Act 1925**, which itself confirms methods of severance recognized in *Williams v Hensman* (1861).

- Disputes between co-owners as to whether the co-owned property should be sold can be resolved by making an application to the court requesting a court order to settle the dispute under **s 14 TLATA 1996**. The court shall have regard to factors listed under **s 15 TLATA 1996** upon reaching a decision.

- Applications for sale by a trustee in bankruptcy upon a co-owner being declared bankrupt are also made under **s 14 TLATA 1996** but in reaching a decision the court shall have regard to factors listed under **s 335A Insolvency Act 1986**.

Chapter overview

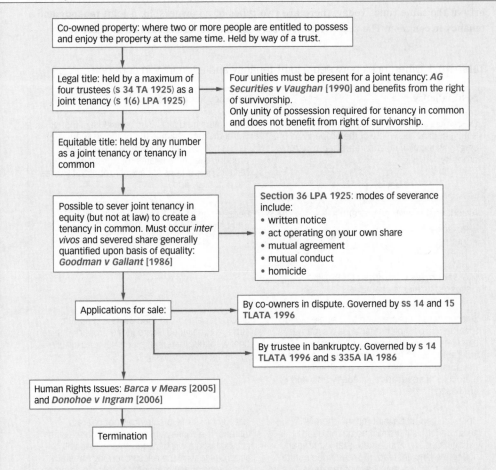

Co-owned property: where two or more people are entitled to possess and enjoy the property at the same time. Held by way of a trust.

Legal title: held by a maximum of four trustees (s 34 TA 1925) as a joint tenancy (s 1(6) LPA 1925)

Four unities must be present for a joint tenancy: *AG Securities v Vaughan* [1990] and benefits from the right of survivorship.
Only unity of possession required for tenancy in common and does not benefit from right of survivorship.

Equitable title: held by any number as a joint tenancy or tenancy in common

Possible to sever joint tenancy in equity (but not at law) to create a tenancy in common. Must occur *inter vivos* and severed share generally quantified upon basis of equality: *Goodman v Gallant* [1986]

Section 36 LPA 1925: modes of severance include:
• written notice
• act operating on your own share
• mutual agreement
• mutual conduct
• homicide

Applications for sale:

By co-owners in dispute. Governed by ss 14 and 15 TLATA 1996

By trustee in bankruptcy. Governed by s 14 TLATA 1996 and s 335A IA 1986

Human Rights Issues: *Barca v Mears* [2005] and *Donohoe v Ingram* [2006]

Termination

Types of co-ownership

Co-owned property is where two or more people are entitled to possess and enjoy the property at the same time. Today, there are two types of co-ownership: a **joint tenancy** and a **tenancy in common**. The key differences between the two are explained in Table 10.1:

Table 10.1 Differences between a joint tenancy and a tenancy in common

Joint tenancy	Tenancy in common
Co-owners are together seen as a single legal entity; holding the whole of the property as one single owner, with no separate shares in the property.	Co-owners hold a distinct, individual, although as yet undivided, share in the property ('undivided' as it is not possible to say which part of the property the share relates to). The share often reflects proportions initially contributed towards the purchase price.
All four unities must be present: • Possession • Interest • Title • Time (*AG Securities v Vaughan* [1990] and discussed further in chapter 6).	Requires only unity of possession, although others may be present.
Since joint tenants are seen as a single owner together, no one joint tenant has a separate share in the land that he may deal with independently of the others. Instead, each has the potential to claim a separate share through a process of **severance** (in equity only and discussed further below).	Since a tenant in common owns a separate, although undivided, share in the property, he can deal with this share in his lifetime, for example, by selling or mortgaging it.
Upon the death of a joint tenant, there is no share for his heirs to inherit. The death extinguishes any entitlement that joint tenant had to the land. Instead, the co-owned estate 'survives to' the remaining joint tenant(s). This is known as the **right of survivorship**. Through this process, the last remaining joint tenant, when all the others have died, will become the sole owner of the land, at which point co-ownership will cease.	The right of survivorship does not operate. Instead, the share will pass in accordance with provisions in a will or, where there is no will, in accordance with the rules governing intestacy. The shares of any remaining tenants in common will remain unaffected by the death, (unless they inherited the share of the dead tenant in common).

The imposition of a trust

Wherever there is co-owned property, it will be held by way of a trust. This trust may be expressly created or may arise in circumstances where, out of a desire to do justice, a trust is imposed to give recognition to a person's interest in the land where legal title has not been vested in them.

> ### Revision tip
>
> Whilst the creation of implied trusts is explained briefly in chapter 9, a more detailed discussion can be found in the Equity and Trusts book that accompanies this series.

Before 1997, the type of trust imposed upon co-owners was a *trust for sale*: ss **34** and **36 LPA 1925**. Today, following **TLATA 1996**, which came into force on 1 January 1997, such trusts are now generally *trusts of land*.

> ### Revision tip
>
> Some examiners may require you to analyse differences between the two types of trust. An understanding of material covered in chapter 9 will therefore be required.

As trust property, there are two levels of ownership: legal and equitable.

The legal title

Those on the legal title are the trustees of the property, responsible for the overall management and administration of the property, which must be carried out in accordance with their duties and responsibilities as trustees (discussed in chapter 9).

Who?

There can only be a maximum of four legal title holders. Where there are more than four, those who will be deemed to hold the legal title will be the first four who are named on the conveyance and who have capacity to be a trustee: s **34 Trustee Act 1925**.

Whilst no statute specifies a minimum number of people who should hold legal title, ideally there should be at least two as this will aid overreaching upon subsequent transactions of the property (see chapters 3 and 4).

How?

The only way in which legal title can be held is as a joint tenancy: ss **1(6)** and **34 LPA 1925**.

> ### Example
>
> Property is conveyed to Anna, Bert, Camilla, Duncan, Edward, and Freda. Bert is 14 years old. Legal title will be held by Anna, Camilla, Duncan, and Edward as joint tenants. Bert cannot hold legal title as, at 14 years old, he does not have the capacity to be a trustee. Freda cannot be on the legal title at this stage as there are already four people on the legal title (the first four named with capacity).

The imposition of a trust
✳✳✳✳✳✳✳✳✳✳

(Remember, that when a minor, such as Bert, reaches 18 years old he will not automatically become a trustee and hold legal title, even if events have occurred in the interim whereby there no longer exists the maximum four trustees (perhaps following the death/retirement of original trustees). Where a gap on the legal title exists making it possible for him to become a trustee having reached 18 years old, Bert may be appointed as one, following appropriate formalities, as discussed in chapter 9.)

The equitable title

Those on the equitable title hold a beneficial interest in the property. The value and substance of owning a co-owned property comes from holding the equitable title.

Who?

There is no maximum number of people who can be on the equitable title. Those on the equitable title may also differ from those on the legal title.

How?

The equitable title can be held as either a joint tenancy or a tenancy in common. The flow chart in Figure 10.1 provides a guide as to how to determine whether the equitable title is held as a joint tenancy or a tenancy in common.

Revision tip

When assessing the initial equitable position it is vital that you consider the points in the order outlined in Figure 10.1. For example, an express declaration of a joint tenancy could not prevail where the four unities are missing. This is why you must look for the unities first.

✅ Looking for extra marks?

Occasionally, express declarations may be contradictory, for example to hold as 'beneficial joint tenants in common in equal shares'. For case law analysis as to how the court deals with such contradictions compare *Martin v Martin* (1987) with *Joyce v Barker Bros* (1980). Ultimately how a court determines what a contradictory express declaration means rests upon the construction of the whole document in which those words are contained. Where contradictions appear throughout, the fairest result is to declare a tenancy in common.

Figure 10.1 How to determine the equitable ownership

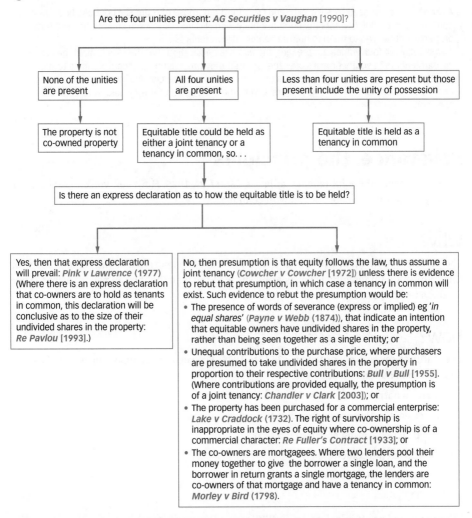

In *Stack v Dowden* [2007], the House of Lords inferred that in the context of family homes where there is a legal joint tenancy, the presumption of a tenancy in common arising through unequal contributions to the purchase price should not apply unless one of the parties could provide evidence to the contrary. This approach seems to have been confirmed in the recent case of *Jones v Kernott* [2011]: a joint tenancy should only be displaced if the parties' common intention could justify it in the light of their whole course of conduct. Both cases are discussed further in the Equity and Trusts book that accompanies this series.

Example

A property is purchased by Mike, Nils, and Olive for the purpose of running a boutique hotel. Mike contributes £100,000 towards the purchase price with Nils and Olive each contributing £50,000. The property is conveyed to them to hold as beneficial joint tenants.

Assuming all four unities are present, the express declaration that they are to hold the property as joint tenants in equity prevails over the fact that they provide unequal contributions to the purchase price, and that the property is to be used for a commercial activity. Only if no express declaration is present, would these facts lead to the conclusion that they hold as tenants in common.

Severance: the principles

You cannot sever the joint tenancy at law: **s 36(2) LPA 1925**. However, you can sever a joint tenancy in equity to create a tenancy in common.

Why?

The principal motivation would be a desire to escape the operation of the right of survivorship. Whilst a joint tenant has no separate share in the land that he can pass to a chosen successor, a tenant in common does.

How?

The ability to sever is governed by **s 36 LPA 1925**. The recognized modes of severance under this provision include:

- written notice; or
- other acts or things which include:
    - an act operating on your own share;
    - mutual agreement;
    - mutual conduct; and
    - homicide.

(All recognized as effective modes in *Williams v Hensman* (1861).)

When?

Whatever the method of severance, it must take place during the lifetime of the severing tenant. This is why it is not possible to sever by will as a will does not take effect until the death of the person to whom it relates: *Re Caines* [1978]. (Severance may be possible by execution of mutual wills showing a common intention to sever: see 'Mutual conduct'.)

Result?

A successful severance will have no effect on how the legal title is held.

> ✅ *Looking for extra marks?*
>
> Where a severing tenant is also a joint tenant at law, he will remain so even after successful severance in equity. If he wished to remove himself from legal title, he would need to:
>
> - release his legal estate to other joint tenant(s): **s 36(2) LPA 1925**; or
> - retire as a trustee: **ss 39 and 40 TA 1925**; or
> - be removed from the trust: **s 19 TLATA 1996**.

Severance only affects the equitable title. By severing, the co-owner will acquire a separate and distinct, if yet undivided, beneficial share in the land and become a tenant in common in equity.

Generally, severance has a unilateral effect ie only the co-owner who is severing will be affected and become a tenant in common. The other joint tenants will remain as joint tenants between themselves.

Example 1

Claus, Gill, and Victor hold property on trust for themselves as beneficial joint tenants:

| **LAW** | Claus, Gill, Victor | *Joint tenants* |
| **EQUITY** | Claus, Gill, Victor | *Joint tenants* |

Gill successfully severs. The position would then be:

LAW	Claus, Gill, Victor	*Joint tenants* (no change to legal title)
EQUITY	Claus, Victor	+ Gill
	Joint tenants	*Tenant in common*

Where there are only two joint tenants in equity and one decides to sever, this action will have a bilateral effect, with both becoming tenants in common in equity. You cannot be a joint tenant by yourself.

Example 2

Claudine and Gemima hold property on trust for themselves as beneficial joint tenants:

| **LAW** | Claudine, Gemima | *Joint tenants* |
| **EQUITY** | Claudine, Gemima | *Joint tenants* |

Claudine successfully severs. The position would then be:

LAW	Claudine, Gemima		*Joint tenants* (no change to legal title)
EQUITY	Claudine	+	Gemima
	Tenant in common		*Tenant in common*

Generally, the severed share is quantified on the basis of equality, irrespective of the initial contributions made to the purchase price of the property: *Goodman v Gallant* [1986]. In other words, where there are *x* number of joint tenants at the time of severance, the severing tenant's severed share will equate to 1/*x*th.

So, in example 1 earlier, Gill's severed share would be one third; in example 2, Claudine and Gemima would each have a half.

This principle of equality is subject to express contrary intention.

Modes of severance

Written notice: s 36(2) LPA 1925

- This can be a unilateral action by the severing joint tenant with no requirement to get the consent of the other joint tenants.

- The written notice need not comply with any particular form. Whilst it must be in writing, it need not state that it is a s 36 notice; nor must it be signed by the severing joint tenant: *Re Draper's Conveyance* [1969].

- The notice must convey an unequivocal and irrevocable intention to sever immediately: *Harris v Goddard* [1983]. This requires the severing joint tenant to communicate a clear desire to regard himself from this point on as having a distinct and realizable share in the property and therefore no longer wishing to benefit from the right of survivorship. This may be achieved expressly, for example 'I wish to sever the joint tenancy now', or may have to be implied. Compare and contrast *Re Draper's Conveyance* [1969] with *Harris v Goddard* [1983] both of which concerned divorce documentation (see Key cases).

✅ *Looking for extra marks?*

In the case of *Nielson-Jones v Fedden* [1975], it was suggested that divorce documentation should never amount to effective written notice as it is not sufficiently irrevocable. However, this criticism has not held much weight. It is difficult to see what type of document would not be considered revocable.

- The notice must be served on all the other joint tenants in equity. This can be achieved by:

  - handing the notice over to them personally; or

  - leaving it at their last known place of abode or business in person or posting it to that address: s 196(3) LPA 1925. The severing joint tenant must be able to establish that the notice arrived at that address. If he uses registered post, he can take advantage of s 196(4) LPA 1925, which declares notice to have been sufficiently served where it is addressed to the person(s) on whom it should be served, sent to the appropriate address, and not returned undelivered. Where he uses normal post, he would have to prove that the notice actually arrived: *Kinch v Bullard* [1999].

However, remember that the notice does not need to have been read by the intended recipients for it to be effective. Look at the facts in *Re 88 Berkley Road* **[1971]** (see Key cases) which establishes this.

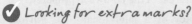

Looking for extra marks?

There has been some suggestion that written notice is not available as a means of severance where the names on the legal title do not mirror those who hold beneficially in equity; for example, where A and B hold on trust for X, Y, and Z. This has come from a technical interpretation of **s 36(2) LPA 1925** and specifically the words 'where a legal estate … is vested in joint tenants beneficially'. Arguably, a more liberal interpretation of the section should be taken allowing all equitable joint tenants the opportunity to sever by this method.

An act operating on your own share

This is where the joint tenant acts unilaterally to sever his beneficial interest in the co-owned property, and sometimes his acts may even be concealed from the other joint tenants. The act must have a final and irrevocable character that precludes the severing joint tenant from claiming, by the right of survivorship, any interest in the joint tenancy.

There are numerous acts that fall into this mode of severance:

- *total alienation* ie where the severing tenant sells or disposes of his beneficial interest in the co-owned property. This includes entering into a specifically enforceable contract to sell: *Brown v Raindle* **(1796)**. To be an effective disposal, and thus an effective severance, there must be compliance with **s 53(1)(c) LPA 1925**.

Example

Vlad, Anish, and Pete are legal joint tenants holding property on trust for themselves as beneficial joint tenants.

LAW	Vlad, Anish, Pete	*Joint tenants*
EQUITY	Vlad, Anish, Pete	*Joint tenants*

Anish sells his share to Gabriel. The position would now be:

LAW	Vlad, Anish, Pete		*Joint tenants*
EQUITY	Vlad, Pete	+	Gabriel
	Joint tenants		*Tenant in common*

Remember, severance does not affect the legal title. Should Anish no longer wish to be a trustee of the property he no longer holds a beneficial interest in, he should take action to remove himself from the legal title, for example by retiring as trustee.

Anish could have sold his share to one of the other joint tenants, for example Vlad. The position would then be:

LAW	Vlad, Anish, Pete		*Joint tenants*
EQUITY	Vlad, Pete	+	Vlad
	Joint tenants		*Tenant in common*

Modes of severance

✳✳✳✳✳✳✳✳✳✳

It is quite possible for one co-owner to be both a joint tenant and a tenant in common in equity of the same property: *Wright v Gibbons* (1949).

* *Partial alienation* ie where the severing tenant mortgages (*First National Securities Ltd v Hegarty* [1985]) or leases his beneficial interest in the co-owned property.

* *Involuntary alienation* for example bankruptcy of a joint tenant: *Re Pavlou (A Bankrupt)* [1993]. Upon bankruptcy, the severed share will vest in the bankrupt's trustee in bankruptcy (see 'Applications for sale by a trustee in bankruptcy').

* *Commencement of litigation* where it concerns the court taking direct action on the joint tenancy itself. This is despite the fact that court proceedings could be discontinued and therefore arguably are neither final nor irrevocable. Provided the intention to sever can be seen as final at the time of commencing proceedings, this will be sufficient: *Re Draper's Conveyance* [1969].

A mere unilateral oral declaration of an intention to sever is insufficient to amount to severance. To be effective, it would have to be incorporated into a written document. This is to avoid any issues that might arise from uncertainty.

Mutual agreement

Form

The agreement:

* must be between *all* beneficial joint tenants: *Wright v Gibbons* (1949);
* can be oral or in writing;
* need not be contained within a specifically enforceable contract (*Burgess v Rawnsley* [1975]). The fact that the agreement may be legally unenforceable was further illustrated in *Hunter v Babbage* [1994]. A divorcing couple's agreement to sell the matrimonial home and split the proceeds was held effective severance, despite being contained in a *draft* consent order which had yet to receive court approval;
* must be fixed and unchanging so it probably needs to go beyond an 'agreement in principle', which suggests that the parties have reserved the right to change their positions: *Gore and Snell v Carpenter* (1990).

Content

The agreement must convey an unequivocal common intention to sever, whether express or implied. (An example of implied common intention could be where joint tenants agree that upon death their interests should pass to their child: *McDonald v Morley* (1940).)

A mere agreement just to sell the co-owned property is not sufficient, as it does not eliminate the possibility of holding the sale proceeds as a joint tenancy to which the right of survivorship applies: *Nielson-Jones v Fedden* [1975]. If the agreement was to sell the co-owned property *and* split the sale proceeds, this would be sufficient as it shows a clear intention on the part of the joint tenants to see themselves as having distinct shares in the co-owned property.

Burgess v Rawnsley [1975] Ch 429

A couple (H and R) purchased a property, each contributing half towards the purchase price, which they held as legal and equitable joint tenants. Upon their relationship breaking down, negotiations began for H to buy R out. Initially, R orally agreed to sell her interest in the property to H for £750. She then revoked that agreement and demanded a higher price. H then died before negotiations were concluded. The Court of Appeal held that there had been effective severance prior to H's death. By both parties reaching the initial agreement, although later revoked, it indicated a common intention that they have separate shares in the property and that the right of survivorship should no longer operate between them.

✔ Looking for extra marks?

In the case of *Davis v Smith* [2011] it was accepted that a mere agreement to sell a jointly owned property, or indeed accept a subject to contract offer on that property, would not itself sever the joint tenancy. Such action would not be inconsistent with a joint tenancy continuing and applying to the sale proceeds. However, by indicating that sale proceeds from the property (and other jointly owned assets) would be divided in a balanced way, and by seeking legal advice, the parties had done enough to demonstrate a common intention to sever. In finding severance, the courts should concentrate on what actually passes between the parties, both words and conduct, and pay little attention as to what was in the mind of one of the parties which may have been communicated to a third person.

Mutual conduct

* Where there is no express or implied agreement to sever, it may be possible to infer from the conduct of the joint tenants that the interests of them all are to be treated as tenancies in common.

* There must be a clear intention from the joint tenants' course of dealings with the property that the right of survivorship should no longer operate between them. In *Greenfield v Greenfield* (1970), the co-owned property was physically divided. Severance had not resulted from this conduct as it seemed apparent that the co-owners were still happy for the right of survivorship to operate.

* The execution of mutual wills, directing where each joint tenant's 'share' should go upon death, indicates a common intention that their interests in the co-owned property be severed and that the right of survivorship should no longer operate: *Re Wilford's Estate* (1879).

- In the case of *Burgess v Rawnsley* [1975], Sir John Pennycuick noted that negotiations between joint tenants in relation to each other's share in the property, could serve to indicate a common intention to sever, even where such negotiations fail to result in a final agreement. However, it was his opinion that a mere offer from one joint tenant to buy the other out for £X, and that other makes a counter offer of £Y, would be insufficient to indicate a common intention to sever.

Homicide

A person cannot benefit from the right of survivorship where he unlawfully kills another joint tenant: *Cleaver v Mutual Reserve Fund* [1892]. His action of unlawful killing, therefore, generally severs his interest.

Applications for sale by co-owners in dispute

Where a dispute arises between co-owners as to whether a co-owned property should be sold, it is possible for an application to be made to the court requesting a court order to resolve that dispute.

Pre TLATA—under trusts for sale

Under a trust for sale, trustees had a *duty* to sell, with a statutory power to postpone. When a court received an application requesting a court order to settle a dispute between co-owners as to whether to sell the trust property or not under s 30 LPA 1925, it was predisposed towards ordering a sale. This assumption to sell would be lost in cases where the co-owners had agreed, prior to the acquisition of the trust property, only to sell if all co-owners agreed. In such cases, a court would only order a sale where such agreement was forthcoming.

A further consideration that might persuade a court to postpone an order to sell would be if the purpose for which the trust property had been purchased, for example to provide a home, was continuing and thus could still be fulfilled.

Post TLATA—under trusts of land

When an interested party, which includes a beneficiary, makes an application to the court by virtue of s 14 TLATA 1996, requesting an order to settle a dispute regarding whether to sell a co-owned property, the court should have regard to factors listed in s 15 TLATA 1996, namely:

- the intention of the person(s) who created the trust;
- the purpose for which the property subject to the trust is held;

- the welfare of any minor who occupies or might reasonably be expected to occupy any land subject to the trust as his home;
- the interest of any secured creditor of any beneficiary;
- the circumstances and wishes of the beneficiaries or the majority of them, having regard to the size of their interests.

The s 15 criteria are not exhaustive. A court may regard other factors which it considers significant, for example the interest of a disabled adult: *First National Bank v Achampang* [2004].

Case law influence

The consideration of purpose under s 15 TLATA largely reflects what the court used to consider when receiving applications under s 30 LPA 1925 (prior to TLATA 1996). It would therefore appear that pre-TLATA 1996 case law may provide a useful guide as to how purpose influences a court when deciding whether to order a sale or not.

In circumstances where the purpose for which the property was purchased can still be fulfilled, a court may be inclined not to order a sale as in, for example, *Re Buchanan-Wollaston's Conveyance* [1939].

The purpose of providing a home for a couple may be declared dead upon the relationship breaking down, in which case a court may order a sale: *Jones v Challenger* [1961]. However, the presence of any minors may sustain the purpose for a longer period, as was seen to be the case in *Re Evers' Trust* [1980].

✅ Looking for extra marks?

Remember that pre-TLATA 1996, a court was predisposed towards ordering a sale since under a trust for sale, trustees had a duty to sell. Under a trust of land, trustees have a power to sell, rather than a duty; the emphasis since TLATA 1996 has moved from a duty to a power, thus the presumption for sale has lessened. As such, whilst pre-TLATA 1996 case law may provide a court with some guidance when reaching decisions under s 14 TLATA 1996 applications, it should be treated with caution: *Mortgage Corporation v Shaire* [2001].

Possible outcomes

Remember, that when a court receives an application to resolve a dispute over whether to sell co-owned property, it can make whatever order it sees fit. It could:

- order a sale of the property, for example where the house is excessively large and unsuitable for sole occupation by the co-owner resisting the sale: *Jackson v Jackson* [1971];
- order a sale but postpone it for a short period, for example to enable the co-owners wanting to stay in the property the opportunity to buy out the co-owner wishing to sell:

Ali v Hussein (1974); or because one of the co-owners occupying the property is ill: *Bank of Ireland Home Mortgages Ltd v Bell* [2001]; or to give the husband and wife the opportunity to conclude a private sale and find alternative property: *C Putnam & Sons v Taylor* [2009];

- refuse to order a sale of the property, for example where one co-owner uses the property as a place to work: *Mayes v Mayes* (1969);

- refuse a sale but require the occupying co-owner to pay rent to a co-owner no longer occupying: *Dennis v McDonald* [1981].

Applications for sale by a trustee in bankruptcy

Where a co-owner is declared bankrupt, his beneficial interest in the co-owned property will vest in his trustee in bankruptcy. If he is a joint tenant at the time of becoming bankrupt, the declaration of bankruptcy has the effect of severing his beneficial interest (under an act operating on your own share: *Re Pavlou (A Bankrupt)* [1993] (see 'An act operating on your own share')) so that his now separate beneficial interest in the property can vest in his trustee in bankruptcy.

Remember that only the beneficial interest vests in the trustee in bankruptcy. Where the bankrupt is also a legal title holder, he will continue to remain so upon declaration of bankruptcy.

Example

Gordon, Simone, and Mario hold a property on trust for themselves as beneficial joint tenants.

LAW	Gordon, Simone, Mario	Joint tenants
EQUITY	Gordon, Simone, Mario	Joint tenants

Mario is declared bankrupt. As a joint tenant in equity, bankruptcy will have the effect of severing his interest in equity. His severed share will then vest in his trustee in bankruptcy. There will be no change to the legal title. The position following bankruptcy will thus be:

LAW	Gordon, Simone, Mario		Joint tenants
EQUITY	Gordon, Simone	+	Trustee in Bankruptcy
	Joint tenants		*Tenant in common*
	two thirds		*a third (Goodman v Gallant rule)*

What happens next?

The flowchart in Figure 10.2 illustrates a sale application by a trustee in bankruptcy.

Figure 10.2 Sale application by a trustee in bankruptcy

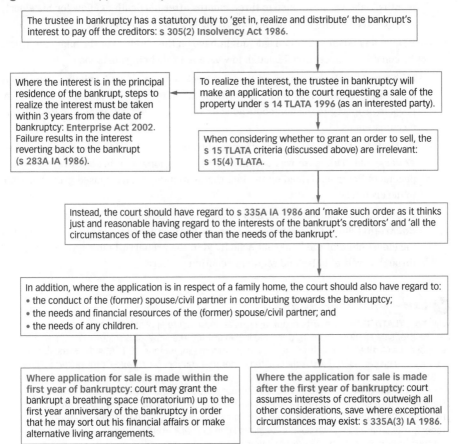

What amounts to exceptional circumstances under s 335A(3) IA 1986?

- Remember, exceptional circumstances cannot include the needs of the bankrupt, this having been expressly excluded by the statute: *Everitt v Budhram* [2009].

- These must be truly extreme and typically involve issues of severe illness or disability.

  - *Nicholls v Lan* [2006]: the spouse of the bankrupt had chronic, long term schizophrenia. The sale order was postponed for 18 months.

  - *Claughton v Charalambous* [1999]: the court agreed to an indefinite postponement of sale where the bankrupt's wife suffered from severe ill health and restricted mobility.

Applications for sale by a trustee in bankruptcy
✳✳✳✳✳✳✳✳✳✳✳

- *Re Bremner* [1999]: the bankrupt had terminal cancer with a life expectancy of six months. Sale was postponed to three months after his death to allow for his elderly wife to care for him in his own home in the final stages of his life.

- Generally, any adverse effect a sale might have on the children of the bankrupt would not be considered exceptional enough to warrant a sale being postponed.

  - *Re Citro* [1991]: disruption of the children's education and eviction from their home, in circumstances where the wife of the bankrupt was unable to buy a comparable property in the neighbourhood or elsewhere, did not amount to exceptional circumstances.

  - *Re Holliday* [1981]: sale was postponed until the second child in the family reached 17 years old. This case was considered an exceptional one in *Re Citro*, with postponement being explained by the fact that it would not have caused great hardship to the creditors.

  - Impact on the health of a child may be considered exceptional. See *Re Haghighat (A Bankrupt)* [2009] where a possession order was postponed for three years in light of the eldest child of the bankrupt, who lived in the property, being severely disabled through cerebral palsy and requiring continuous care.

✅ *Looking for extra marks?*

Whilst pre-**TLATA 1996** the courts adopted a similar approach to applications made by secured creditors for sale as those made by a trustee in bankruptcy, resulting almost inevitably in an order to sell, post-**TLATA 1996** the creditors' needs are not paramount under s **15 TLATA 1996** and are just one factor to be considered with others listed under that section: *Mortgage Corporation v Shaire* [2001]. However, post-**TLATA 1996** case law suggests that the courts still have a tendency to order a sale, not wishing to keep creditors waiting for repayment of debts owed. Issues of ill health or disability are unlikely to do more than postpone a sale, if that: *Bank of Ireland Home Mortgages Ltd v Bell* [2001]. See also *First National Bank plc v Achampong* [2004], where a sale of the property was ordered as it was seen as unfair to keep the bank from its money; this despite the fact that the property was still being used as a home.

Human rights issues

In *Barca v Mears* [2005] and *Donohoe v Ingram* [2006], consideration was given to the courts' strict approach to finding exceptional circumstances and whether such an approach was compatible with **ECHR Art 8** (right to family life and home) and **ECHR Art 1** (right to peaceful enjoyment of possessions).

In both cases, arguments raised to establish exceptional circumstances justifying postponement of a sale, were not successful. Although the courts recognized that a broader interpretation of what is exceptional may be required, so as not to offend Art 8, in both cases, even taking such a broader interpretation, circumstances were not of an exceptional nature. The usual stress and upheaval caused by the sale of a family home (which both cases involved) cannot be relied upon as an *exceptional* circumstance. In *Ford and another v Alexander* [2012] it was further confirmed that s 335A does not infringe Art 8.

Termination of co-ownership of land

Partition

This is where the land is physically divided up between the co-owners so that each becomes absolute owner of his own portion. Powers to partition are given to trustees under s 7 TLATA 1996 (see chapter 9).

Union in sole ownership

This is where the co-owned property falls into the absolute ownership of one of the tenants, for example through the operation of the right of survivorship where the land finally vests in the sole surviving joint tenant.

Conveyance to a single purchaser

Where trust property is sold to a single purchaser, and the mechanics of overreaching are complied with (discussed in chapters 3 and 4), that purchaser will take the property free from the trust.

 ✱ *Key cases*

Case	Facts	Principle
Burgess v Rawnsley [1975] Ch 429	Oral negotiations between co-owners for one to buy the other out, where an agreement had been reached as to the price to be paid, although later revoked with a higher price being demanded, was held effective severance. In reaching the initial agreement, although later revoked, both parties had indicated a common intention to have separate shares in the property and that the right of survivorship should no longer operate between them.	When severing by mutual agreement, the agreement need not be in a specifically enforceable contract. Any agreement must convey an intention to preclude the future operation of the right of survivorship.

Key cases

✳✳✳✳✳✳✳✳✳✳

Case	Facts	Principle
Harris v Goddard [1983] 1 WLR 1203	A divorce petition merely requesting for such orders to be made in respect of the matrimonial home as may be considered just, did not amount to effective written notice. There was insufficient immediacy, as the request related to future court orders that may be made, and insufficient intention to sever, as any future court order may not have involved any severance.	Written notice must convey an irrevocable and unequivocal intention to sever immediately, whether express or implied.
Re 88 Berkley Road [1971] Ch 648	A joint tenant's written notice was deemed effectively served when it was sent by recorded post to the co-owned home, even though it was signed for by the severing joint tenant and had never been read by the intended recipient. The fact remained that it could be proved written notice had arrived at the last known place of abode of the other, non-severing joint tenant and that was sufficient.	Provided written notice has been effectively served, it need not be read by the intended recipient(s) to be effective.
Re Buchanan-Wollaston's Conveyance [1939] Ch 738	The purpose behind a joint purchase of land, to provide four home owners with sea views, was considered to still be continuing when one of the home owners applied to the court under s 14 TLATA 1996 requesting a sale of that land. This, together with the fact that the home owners had covenanted not to sell the land without unanimous or majority vote, led a court to decline ordering a sale of the land.	Upon receiving an application by an interested party under s 14 TLATA 1996 requesting an order to settle a dispute as to whether to sell trust property, a court may decline ordering a sale where the purpose for which trust property was purchased can still be fulfilled (a consideration under s 15 TLATA 1996).
Re Draper's Conveyance [1969] 1 Ch 486	An affidavit in support of a divorce petition, requesting a sale of the matrimonial home and the division of proceeds between spouses amounted to effective severance by written notice. It indicated sufficient immediacy, in wanting a sale to occur as soon as possible, and by requesting her share of sale proceeds, the wife showed that she considered herself to have a distinct and realizable share in the property, separate from that of her husband.	Written notice must convey an irrevocable and unequivocal intention to sever immediately, whether express or implied.
Re Evers' Trust [1980] 1 WLR 1327	A request for the sale of a co-owned family home under s 14 TLATA 1996, was declined by the court since the presence of three children meant that the purpose for which the property had been purchased (to provide a family home) could still be fulfilled (a consideration under s 15 TLATA 1996).	As for *Re Buchanan-Wollaston's Conveyance* [1939].

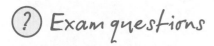
Exam questions

Problem question

Alex, Bobby, Carl, and David are keen surfers and run a surf school business in Cornwall. In 2010, they decided to purchase a large house located near to the surf school with the intention of living there and using it to offer bed and breakfast to the surfers. At this time, Bobby was only 17 years old and could only afford to contribute £5,000 towards the £250,000 purchase price. The remainder was provided by Alex, Carl, and David in equal shares. The house was conveyed to them as beneficial joint tenants.

In 2012, Carl needed to raise some capital to buy himself a car, so he mortgaged his share in the house to Surfs Up Bank plc.

Last year, after a series of heated arguments with Alex, Bobby moved out of the house. He spoke to Alex, Carl, and David and told them that he could no longer live with them. He offered to sell his interest in the house to them. They all agreed that this would be for the best and that steps should be taken as soon as possible to achieve this, although no final agreement was reached as to the price.

Two days later, Bobby was involved in a surfing accident and was killed. His will left all his property to David.

Two weeks ago, having had very few surfers come to their school since it opened in 2010, Alex wrote a letter to Carl and David informing them that he wanted the house sold so that he could get his money out as soon as possible. Carl opened the letter when it arrived at the house, but he became so angry upon reading its contents that he tore the letter up and threw it away. He mentioned nothing about the letter to David.

Alex now wishes to take action to get the house sold.

Advise Alex, Carl, and David as to their interests in the house and how, if at all, Alex could achieve his desire of getting the house sold and his share out.

See the Outline Answers section in the end matter for help with this question.

Essay question

To what extent is it true to say that severance should be final and irrevocable to be effective? Discuss in relation to all modes of severance.

Online Resource Centre

To see an outline answer to this question log onto www.oxfordtextbooks.co.uk/orc/concentrate/

#11

Licences and proprietary estoppel

Licences is a topic that can be tested both in the format of a problem question or an essay question. It can be examined as a self-contained question or be combined with another topic area, typically leases where the focus is often upon how you can distinguish a lease from a licence. Examiners often look to use the topic of licences as a way of testing whether you understand the nature of the distinction between personal and proprietary rights and in what circumstances the distinction is blurred.

Proprietary estoppel can also be examined either by way of an essay or a problem question. Essay questions may focus upon the general nature of estoppel, perhaps questioning when interests may arise through proprietary estoppel. (Remember, that although this topic is discussed in some detail in this chapter in the context of estoppel licences, it may arise elsewhere, such as in the context of land contracts (see chapter 5)). Problem questions typically require you to assess whether an estoppel claim has arisen and this will require a sound knowledge of the relevant estoppel requirements.

Key facts

- A licence is permission given by the licensor to the licensee to allow the latter to enter the land of the former which, without such permission, would otherwise amount to a trespass.

- A licence should be distinguished from a lease (see also chapter 6).

- Different types of licences will have different rules in relation to the original parties and successors in title.

- A bare licence is revocable by the licensor and does not bind a third party.

- A licence coupled with an interest, ie a *profit à prendre*, may be irrevocable and may bind a third party whilst the interest remains.

- Contractual licences are licences that arise under the terms of a contract. Revocation may lead to breach of contract and the intervention of equity to enforce the licence for the benefit of the licensee. Modern orthodoxy suggests such licences cannot bind third parties unless protected by an estoppel or constructive trust.

- An estoppel licence arises as a result of a representation by the licensor and a detrimental reliance by the licensee. It is binding between these two parties but is also capable of binding a third party.

- The key requirements to establishing an estoppel are:
  - assurance
  - reliance
  - detriment
  - unconscionability.

- To satisfy the equity arising by estoppel, the courts have discretion as to the remedy to award but are guided by principles of proportionality and awarding the minimum to do justice.

- The inchoate equity arising by estoppel may be binding upon third parties.

Chapter overview

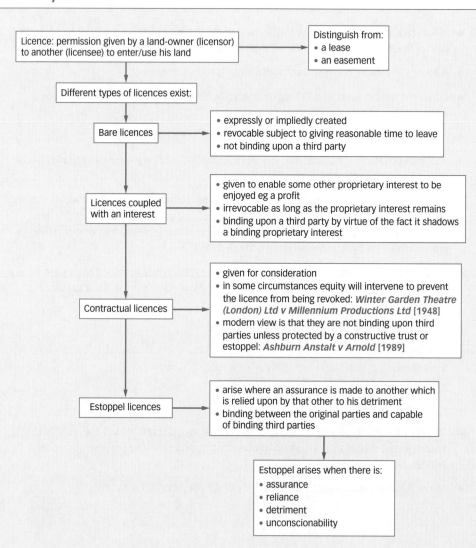

Introduction

A **licence** can be described as permission given by one person (the licensor) to another (the licensee) allowing that other to enter the licensor's land which, without such permission, would amount to a trespass: *Thomas v Sorrell* (1673). It may extend beyond permitting mere entry and give the licensee occupational rights over the land in question.

Revision tip

Remember that a licence is distinguishable from a lease. Any occupational rights granted under a licence will fall short of exclusive possession and/or fail to meet the formalities for the creation of a lease. Examiners often test the distinction between the two so make sure you review material covered in chapter 6.

A licence does not convey a proprietary interest over the land where it is exercised: *Ashburn Anstalt v Arnold* [1989]. Rather it creates a mere personal right between the person giving the permission, the licensor, and the person receiving that permission, the licensee. As a personal right, it is not capable of:

- being transferred to another; or
- being binding upon a third party.

(*Clore v Theatrical Properties* (1936)).

However, the law has developed so that, in some circumstances, a licence can be enforced against both the licensor and a third party purchaser. This, therefore, provides some licences with characteristics of a proprietary nature: see 'Licences coupled with an interest'.

✅ *Looking for extra marks?*

A licence can sometimes appear very similar to an easement giving someone a right of way through the land of another. However, to be an easement, the requirements under *Re Ellenborough Park* [1956] must be met and the right must have been acquired as an easement (discussed in detail in chapter 12). Such requirements do not apply for a licence to exist. The finding of an easement to enter on to the land of another is arguably preferable to the finding of a licence since an easement, as a proprietary interest, is capable of binding third parties. However, do remember that a licence to be, or do something, on the land of another can convert into an easement where (i) it meets the requirements under *Re Ellenborough Park* and (ii) s 62 LPA 1925 has operated (again discussed in more detail in chapter 12).

Categories of licences

Bare licences

When do they arise?

These arise where the licensee is given permission to be, or enter, on the land of the licensor without the need to provide the licensor with any consideration. They may be created:

- expressly, for example by giving an invitation to another to attend your house for dinner; or

- impliedly, for example it is generally accepted that people have an implied licence to walk through your garden gate and along your garden path up to your front door.

By acquiring a bare licence, the licensee is prevented from being a trespasser on the land, so long as he does not exceed the scope of the licence.

Termination

A bare licence may be revoked by simply telling the licensee to leave and then giving him a reasonable time to do so (*Greater London Council v Jenkins* [1975]). What amounts to a reasonable time will vary according to the circumstances but in all cases only if that reasonable time expires and the licensee remains on the land, does he then become a trespasser.

Enforcement against third parties

A successor in title to the licensor is just as capable of revoking a bare licence as the original licensor. Thus, such licences have never been held as binding upon third parties.

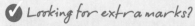 **Looking for extra marks?**

The extent to which an estate owner can give and, more particularly, revoke licences preventing people from being on his land may well be subject to future challenges under the **Human Rights Act 1998**. This may especially be the case where the land in question is privately owned but open to public use. To ensure liberties of citizens are protected, landowners in some circumstances in the future may be allowed to prevent persons from being on their land only where reasonable grounds can be established: *Appleby v UK* (2003).

Licences coupled with an interest

When do they arise?

These arise in circumstances where a proprietary interest has been granted and, in order for that interest to be exercised and enjoyed, access on to land of another must also be given. The licence giving such access arises as a consequence of the proprietary interest that has been granted and thus can be seen as ancillary to that interest. For example, such licences arise with the granting of *profits à prendre* (discussed in more detail in chapter 12). A right to take something from the land of another can only be exercised where it is accompanied by a licence to enter that land.

Although originally the interest did not need to be proprietary, (*Hurst v Picture Theatres Ltd* [1915], where the right was contractual to watch a film), later cases now restrict the interest to be a recognized proprietary interest: *Hounslow LBC v Twickenham Garden Developments Ltd* [1971].

Termination

As long as the proprietary interest remains, the licence that accompanies it is irrevocable.

Enforcement against third parties

As this licence effectively shadows a proprietary interest, it is regarded as having the same enforceability as the proprietary interest to which it is attached, thus binding not only the original licensor but also his successors in title: *Webb v Paternoster* (1619).

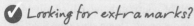

Looking for extra marks?

The fact that this licence may bind a third party has led some to suggest that, albeit indirectly, this type of licence creates a proprietary interest. However, when you consider that its enforceability against a third party is merely a consequence of the fact that it shadows an existing proprietary interest, such as a *profit*, this view may be defeated. Indeed, some have suggested that this category of licence should not exist as a separate category at all. The licence to enter the land of another, in order for an existing proprietary interest to be exercised and enjoyed, is perhaps merely just a component of that proprietary interest and not a separate licence.

Contractual licences

When do they arise?

This is a licence that is given upon the licensee entering into a valid contract and providing some form of consideration. Such licences may arise, for example, when you pay for admission to a cinema or pay for a ticket to a race course.

Termination

Although revocation may equate to a breach of contract, it may be permitted with reasonable notice, with a remedy lying in damages: *Wood v Leadbitter* (1845).

However, as an interest in land is usually seen as unique (see Equity and Trusts for further detail on equitable remedies) it may be that the breach will be remedied by the grant of an injunction. See, for example, *Winter Garden Theatre (London) Ltd v Millennium Productions Ltd* [1948] where the House of Lords recognized that an injunction could be awarded to prevent a premature termination of a contractual licence in circumstances

Categories of licences

✳✳✳✳✳✳✳✳✳✳

where it was intended to be irrevocable until a purpose had been fulfilled or a period of time completed.

In some circumstances, where the licensee has not yet taken possession of the land, an order for specific performance may be awarded where the licensor is refusing entry to a licensee who has a contractual right to enter.

Verrall v Great Yarmouth BC [1981] QB 202

The National Front had contracted to hire a hall for its annual conference. When the Labour council sought to revoke the licence, an order for specific performance was granted. Damages were deemed inadequate as the National Front had not been able to find an alternative venue. With the intervention of equity, the contractual licence was enforced and thus could not be revoked at will.

Despite this intervention of equity, you must appreciate that this does not mean that all contractual licences will now be prevented from being revoked by the licensor when he wishes. Remember that the provision of equitable remedies is subject to discretion and will only be provided in circumstances where damages for breach of contract appear inadequate. The question will be one of construction of the contract and whether, upon true construction of the contract, it was intended to be irrevocable (Megarry J in *Hounslow LBC v Twickenham Garden Developments Ltd* [1971]).

Where equitable remedies are not available, an action for assault may be brought in the event of being forcibly ejected from the land or refused entry on to it.

Enforcement against third parties

Traditionally, it was considered that contractual licences are not enforceable against third parties: *King v David Allen & Sons* [1916].

However, with the intervention of equitable relief making some contractual licences irrevocable in certain circumstances, this view has been subject to challenge. See, for example, *Binions v Evans* [1972], in which Lord Denning declared contractual licences as binding upon third parties by relying upon a constructive trust being triggered in order to prevent a fraud or unconscionable behaviour.

Indeed, some challengers have gone as far as to suggest that the use of equitable remedies, both to prevent premature revocation of contractual licences and to ensure their performance in accordance with the terms of the contract, not only makes contractual licences enforceable against third parties but also confers a proprietary status upon them.

✅ Looking for extra marks?

In *Errington v Errington & Woods* (1952) Denning LJ deemed that the availability of equitable remedies gave rise to an 'equity' in favour of the licensee. This equity would then be enforceable against a third party according to the doctrine of notice, thus conferring proprietary status upon a contractual licence. A comparison was drawn with the development of restrictive covenants. ➡

➡ The willingness of equity to intervene and provide remedies in certain circumstances where restrictive covenants have been breached led to such rights gaining equitable proprietary status and thus the ability to bind third parties (see chapter 13). However, this approach was rejected by the House of Lords in **National Provincial Bank Ltd v Ainsworth** [1965]. The availability of an equitable remedy to enforce a right does not, by itself, make that right proprietary in nature. Other factors must be present, clearly demonstrated in the law of restrictive covenants where several conditions must be met before restrictive covenants can be enforced in equity against third parties.

Final clarification on the issue of enforceability against third parties was found in the case of *Ashburn Anstalt v Arnold* [1989], where the court clearly found that contractual licences cannot bind successors in title. Since enforceability against third parties is an essential characteristic of a proprietary interest, this case also determined that contractual licences do not have proprietary status. This is perhaps a sensible decision, as to rule otherwise might:

- blur the boundaries between licences and proprietary interests such as leases and easements; and

- lead to some land becoming inalienable by a subsequent increase in the number of proprietary interests existing over it.

Ashburn Anstalt v Arnold [1989] declared the true basis for the decision of finding the licence binding in *Errington v Errington & Woods* [1952] was the presence of an estoppel or constructive trust.

✅ Looking for extra marks?

It is worth noting that the decision in the case of **Bruton v London & Quadrant Housing Trust** [2000], as discussed in chapter 6, has led to the existence of a contractual or non-proprietary lease. This lease, whilst having some of the characteristics of a proprietary term of years, such as the granting of exclusive possession, and the protection of Landlord and Tenant legislation, was found, unlike a proprietary term of years, not to be capable of binding a third party. This decision has clearly blurred the distinction between a contractual lease and a contractual licence.

Estoppel Licences

When do they arise?

These are licences used by the courts to protect licensees where it would be contrary to justice to allow strict legal principles to be applied. The licensee must establish that an estoppel has arisen giving rise to an equity in his favour. In effect, the licence is made irrevocable and thus binding upon third parties. This result may be achieved by giving the licensee a recognized legal or equitable proprietary interest (such as freehold title/a tenancy/an easement) or an irrevocable licence under a constructive trust.

Categories of licences

✳✳✳✳✳✳✳✳✳✳✳✳

What are the requirements to establish an estoppel has arisen?

According to *Taylor Fashions Ltd v Liverpool Victoria Trustees Co Ltd* [1982], these are:

1. an assurance/representation by the landowner
   - by words or by conduct;
   - relating to a property right. How precise the nature of the property right, and indeed the land over which it is being claimed, needs to be has been the subject of discussion in two leading cases: *Cobbe v Yeoman's Row Management Ltd* [2008] and *Thorner v Majors* [2009]. In the former commercial case, whilst the identity of the property had been certain, there was complete uncertainty as to the nature of the property right promised to Cobbe. (Furthermore, since the parties had intentionally not entered into a binding contract, it was not deemed unconscionable for the landowner to go back upon its assurance.) Whereas in the latter domestic case, the property right was held to be 'clear enough', despite being drawn from inferences and, although the precise extent of the farmland over which the right was being claimed had not been agreed to in advance, it was understood to be whatever the extent of the farm at the time of the landowner's death.

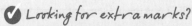 ✅ *Looking for extra marks?*

You should read both of these cases as they provide useful discussion on the elements of proprietary estoppel. The cases show that perhaps the courts are more prepared to use estoppel in domestic cases than they are in commercial ones.

2. Reliance
   - ie that the claimant changed their position as a direct result of the assurance. With no such causal link, no estoppel will arise: *Coombes v Smith* [1986];
   - which must be reasonable and will be presumed unless the party contesting the estoppel can show otherwise: *Greasley v Cooke* [1980].

3. Detriment
   - to be judged at the moment when the person who has given the assurance seeks to go back on it: *Gillet v Holt* [2000];
   - which may include financial expenditure (eg building a bungalow: *Inwards v Baker* [1965]) or a quantifiable financial loss (eg reduction in wages: *Suggitt v Suggitt* [2012]) or a change to circumstances (eg *Crabb v Arun DC* [1976] where land, providing an access route, was sold following assurances that access would be available over alternative property).

4. Unconscionability
   - not enough merely to disappoint the expectations of another-rather it must be unjust for the landowner to deny the assurance(s) made by relying upon his strict legal rights.

- the conduct must 'shock the conscience of the court', Walker LJ in *Cobbe v Yeoman's Row Management Ltd* [2008].

Remember, in *Gillet v Holt* [2000] Walker LJ, in approving these requirements, noted that the court must look at the matter 'in the round' and that unconscionability would be the central factor.

The Remedy?

Establishing an estoppel gives rise to an 'equity' which is an inchoate equitable proprietary right to go to the court to seek a remedy. This inchoate right will crystallize into a specific interest once the court order has been made.

It is up to the court to determine the nature of the remedy to be awarded. Often, this will simply involve giving effect to the assurance, and indeed no award should exceed that assurance: *Orgee v Orgee* [1997]. Sometimes, the court's approach is to compensate for the detriment suffered. With either approach, the basis of the award should be 'the minimum equity to do justice' (*Crabb v Arun DC* [1976]) with the court ensuring that there is proportionality between the detriment and remedy awarded: *Jennings v Rice* [2003]. This might require the court to do nothing at all, as in *Sledmore v Dalby* [1996], or could go as far as entailing the transfer of the fee simple, as in *Dillwynn v Llewellyn* (1862).

✅ Looking for extra marks?

Read Mummery LJ in *Cobbe v Yeoman's Row Management Ltd* [2008] on the difficulties and uncertainty which result from the individually crafted approach taken by the courts.

Example

In *Inwards v Baker* [1965], at A's suggestion, B built a bungalow on A's land under the impression that he would be allowed to live there for as long as he wished. Upon A's death, B was allowed to stay at the bungalow for a number of years, after which A's personal representatives sought possession. This was refused on the grounds that B had acquired, as against A, an irrevocable licence arising by proprietary estoppel, enabling B to remain in the property for his lifetime. This was binding upon A's personal representatives and indeed any purchaser with notice.

Enforcement against third parties

Section 116 Land Registration Act 2002 provides that an equity by estoppel 'has the effect from the time the equity arises as an interest capable of binding successors in title'. Thus, the inchoate and uncrystallized 'equity' can bind a third party where it has been protected in the appropriate way.

1. Where title to land is registered, it will be protected and enforceable against a third party where a notice has been entered on the charges section of the register. It is

also potentially enforceable as an overriding interest under **Sch 3 para 2** should actual occupation and the various conditions under this provision be satisfied (see chapter 3).

2. Where title to land is unregistered, the enforceability of the equity against a third party will be dependent upon the doctrine of notice (see chapters 2 and 4).

What is also clear is that once the court has granted a remedy, any subsequent enforcement against a third party will depend upon the nature of the remedy granted.

 Key cases

Case	Facts	Principle
Ashburn Anstalt v Arnold [1989] Ch 1	A shop was purchased for the purpose of development. It was sold to the purchaser expressly subject to a licence whereby the licensee would retain the shop rent free until the redevelopment took place. It was held that the purported licence was in fact a lease and this was deemed binding upon the purchaser.	Contractual licences are not proprietary interests and cannot bind third parties. However, where the facts are such that a constructive trust or estoppel arises, protecting the licence, the licence may be enforceable against a third party.
Cobbe v Yeoman's Row Management Ltd [2008] UKHL 55	C, a property developer, reached an oral agreement in principle with YRM to buy its property after which C spent considerable sums obtaining planning permission. The owner than refused to proceed on the agreed terms. The House of Lords held that C was not entitled to any remedy based upon proprietary estoppel.	For an estoppel to arise the property right being promised must be sufficiently certain. There must be unconscionability to rely upon an estoppel arising. (Here, the parties having entered into a 'gentleman's agreement' had not shown any intention for the agreement to be binding and thus there was nothing unconscionable about YRM going back on its assurance.)
King v David Allen & Sons [1916] 2 AC 54	A contractual licence was granted to allow the licensee to affix posters to the wall of the licensor's cinema. The right to do so was found not to be binding against a third party.	Contractual licences are not capable of binding a third party.
Pascoe v Turner [1979] 1 WLR 431	A man encouraged his mistress to make improvements to a house on the assurance that it would be hers. When the man tried to evict her, the court found that an estoppel had arisen and ordered that the freehold in the property be transferred to her. The assurance that she had acted upon to her detriment was met.	Where a licence protected by an estoppel has been infringed, the appropriate equitable remedy will be determined in accordance with making sure that justice is achieved for the wronged party.

Case	Facts	Principle
Thorner v Majors [2009] UKHL 18	D had worked on P's farm unpaid for almost 30 years. D was attempting to claim title to the farm through proprietary estoppel. There had been no express statement that D would inherit. Rather D relied upon inferences and the fact that P handed D a bonus notice relating to two policies on P's life saying 'that's for my death duties'. This combination had given rise to an estoppel.	For proprietary estoppel to arise, assurances given must be 'clear enough' and must relate to identified property.
Verrall v Great Yarmouth BC [1981] QB 202	An attempt to revoke a contractual licence granted to the National Front in respect of hiring a hall for its annual conference, was met with an order of specific performance against the licensor to enforce the licence.	An order for specific performance may be awarded where a licensor is refusing entry to a licensee who has a contractual right to enter.
Winter Garden Theatre (London) Ltd v Millennium Productions Ltd [1948] AC 173	A contractual licence to present plays in the licensor's theatre was deemed to be revocable upon giving reasonable notice.	An injunction could be awarded to prevent a premature termination of a contractual licence in circumstances where it was intended to be irrevocable until a purpose had been fulfilled or a period of time completed.

 Exam questions

Problem question-licences

Albert is the registered freehold proprietor of a large estate which includes a wooded area.

In 2004 Albert entered into an oral agreement with Brian. Brian is a sculptor of wood. Albert agreed that Brian could take any fallen wood to use in his sculptures for as long as he wanted. In return Brian gives Albert an occasional sculpture.

Albert's friend Colin is a poet. He finds sitting in the wood inspires some of his best poems. In 2007 Albert tells Colin that he can sit in the wood as much as he likes.

In 2010 Albert enters into an agreement with one of his neighbours, David. The agreement is in writing. Albert agrees that David can store some farm machinery on Albert's land for five years. In return David agrees to pay five hundred pounds a year.

In 2012 Albert decides to sell the whole of the estate including the wooded area to Eric. He conveys the land to Eric who becomes registered freehold proprietor. Before the conveyance he tells Eric about David but does not mention Brian and Colin.

Exam questions

✳✳✳✳✳✳✳✳✳✳

Eric is now refusing access to Brian, Colin, and David.

Advise the parties.

See the Outline Answers section in the end matter for help with this question.

Problem question—proprietary estoppel

Bob owns the registered freehold of 'Groom House'. He persuades his girlfriend, Joan, to come and live with him. He promised Joan that she could stay there for as long as she wished provided she sold her own property and paid for an extension to Groom House to incorporate a new bedroom and ensuite bathroom. She duly sells her own house, moves in, and pays for the extension. After ten years, their relationship breaks down and Bob decides to sell Groom House to Mervyn. Before purchasing the property, Mervyn inspected Groom House when Joan was not present, and saw female clothing in the bedroom. Having asked Bob who it belonged to, Bob replied 'an old girlfriend who has left it behind'. The sale took place but Joan wishes to stay living at Groom House. Advise.

See the Outline Answers section in the end matter for help with this question.

Essay question—licences

Whilst licences are rights connected to the use of land they are unusual since, in theory at least, they do not confer any proprietary interest upon the licensee and thus the protection they afford a licensee is limited.

Discuss.

Online Resource Centre

To see an outline answer to this question log onto www.oxfordtextbooks.co.uk/orc/concentrate/

#12

Easements and profits

The examination

A largely self-contained topic area with the principle focus of a question being on easements, but *profits à prendre* may pop up as a minor element. In addition, aspects of enforcement of easements against third parties may be examined within a question, discussed in this chapter but also link to chapters 3 and 4.

A typical problem question will require you to:

- identify the rights being claimed as easements;
- assess whether such rights have the capacity to be easements by considering the requirements from *Re Ellenborough Park* [1956]. (Where they do not, you may be required to assess what type of right they could be, whether personal, such as a licence (see chapter 11) or proprietary, such as a lease (see chapter 6));
- where capacity is established, assess whether they have been acquired as easements;
- where acquired appropriately, assess whether they are legal or equitable; check they have not been extinguished and consider remedies where there is actual or threatened infringement;
- where the established easement is being denied by a third party, assess whether it is binding upon that third party by applying the appropriate rules, dependent upon whether the easement exists over registered or unregistered land and whether it is legal or equitable in status.

Essay questions may focus upon:

- proposed reform to the acquisition of easements by prescription;

- whether boundaries to determine what can and cannot amount to an easement are sufficiently clear (focus here could include an analysis of the recent proliferation of car parking case law);
- implied acquisition and the Law Commission proposals for reform.

Key facts

- An easement gives either a positive or, less often, a negative right of use over land of another (the servient land), which must be seen to benefit a dominant piece of land.

- For a right to be capable of being an easement, it must satisfy the four requirements under *Re Ellenborough Park* [1956].

- Even where such requirements are satisfied, a right may not be an easement if the exercise of that right requires expenditure by the servient owner, amounts to exclusive possession of the servient land, or is not exercisable as of right.

- A right that is capable of being an easement will only become an easement where it has been acquired by one of the recognized methods of acquisition.

- Where a person claims to have been granted an easement by another over land of that other, this may be substantiated by evidence of an express grant. Alternatively, where there is no such evidence, a court may imply the easement was granted out of necessity, common intention, the operation of s 62 LPA 1925, or the rule in *Wheeldon v Burrows* (1879).

- Where a person claims to have reserved an easement in his favour over land he has transferred to another, this may be substantiated by evidence of an express reservation. Where there is no such evidence, a court may imply the easement was reserved out of necessity or common intention. Acquisition by the operation of s 62 LPA 1925 or the rule in *Wheeldon v Burrows* (1879) is not available.

- Alternatively, an easement may have been acquired out of long use, known as prescription, of which there are three modes: common law, lost modern grant, and the *Prescription Act 1832*.

- An easement can be either legal or equitable in status, depending upon which formalities have been satisfied. The status of an easement will determine the relevant rules governing the enforcement of that interest against a third party. These rules differ depending upon whether the easement exists over registered or unregistered land.

Chapter overview

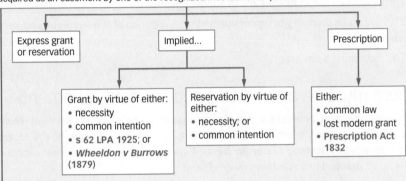

An easement gives either a positive or, less often, a negative right of use over land of another (the servient land), which must be seen to benefit a dominant piece of land.

To be capable of being an easement, the right must satisfy the four requirements under *Re Ellenborough Park* [1956]:

1. there must be a dominant land and a servient land;
2. the right must accommodate the dominant land;
3. there must be diversity of ownership and/or occupation of the dominant and servient lands; and
4. the right must lie in grant.

Even where these requirements are met, the right cannot be an easement if its exercise:

1. requires the servient owner to spend money; or
2. amounts to exclusive possession of the servient land; or
3. is not exercisable as of right.

Once deemed capable of being an easement, it must be established that the right has been acquired as an easement by one of the recognized methods of acquisition:

Express grant or reservation

Implied...

Prescription

Grant by virtue of either:
• necessity
• common intention
• s 62 LPA 1925; or
• *Wheeldon v Burrows* (1879)

Reservation by virtue of either:
• necessity; or
• common intention

Either:
• common law
• lost modern grant
• **Prescription Act 1832**

The easement acquired may be legal or equitable depending upon the formalities that have been satisfied.

Whether the burden of an established easement binds a successor in title to the servient land will depend upon:

1. whether the easement is legal or equitable in status; and
2. whether it exists over registered or unregistered land.

The benefit of an established easement will pass to a successor in title to the dominant land by virtue of **s 62 LPA 1925**

Remedies where an easement has been infringed include:
• abatement
• damages
Where infringement is threatened, an **injunction** may be sought.

Termination of easements is possible by:
• merger
• release

Introduction

What is an **easement**?

- A right over one piece of land for the benefit of another piece of land (for example a right to store, right to light, etc).

- A proprietary interest that has legal capacity (s 1(2) **Law of Property Act 1925**) where created appropriately (see 'Status of the easement acquired').

It gives no right of possession or occupation over the land, save to the extent that is required to enjoy that right.

Capability

To be an easement, a right must satisfy the four requirements laid down in *Re Ellenborough Park* [1956]:

1. There must be a **dominant** and **servient tenement**.
2. The right must accommodate the dominant tenement.
3. There must be diversity of ownership and/or occupation of the dominant and servient tenements.
4. The right must lie in grant.

1. There must be a dominant and servient tenement

The dominant tenement, benefitting from the exercise of the right, and the servient tenement, burdened by its exercise, must be defined at the time of the acquisition of the easement: *London & Blenheim Estates v Ladbroke Retail Parks Ltd* [1994]. An easement cannot exist '*in gross*' ie unattached to a dominant piece of land.

Revision tip

Remember that if a person is given a right to use land of another independently of any land that he may own (ie where there is no dominant tenement), that right is likely to be a mere licence (discussed in chapter 11). Some examiners may link the two topics.

2. The right must accommodate the dominant tenement

The right must make the land a better and more convenient property. Rather than confer a mere personal benefit to the current owner, the enjoyment of the right should be connected to the normal use of the dominant land and thus be seen as a benefit to all future owners.

Remember:

- whether a right accommodates the dominant tenement is a question of fact;

- enhancement to the value of that land may be evidence of accommodation but is not, by itself, conclusive of that fact: *Re Ellenborough Park* [1956]; and

- to accommodate, the dominant and servient tenements must be sufficiently proximate to one another: *Bailey v Stephens* (1862).

✅ *Looking for extra marks?*

A right that conveys a commercial advantage is not necessarily precluded from being one that accommodates the dominant land. Whilst the right to set up a commercial monopoly of putting boats on a canal was rejected in *Hill v Tupper* [1863] (since the right did not accommodate the land; rather it was the land that would facilitate the business being established by the right), the commercial advantage of advertising a business was accepted as a potential easement in *Moody v Steggles* [1879]. The business (operating on the land for many years) had become a normal use of that land. A benefit to the business thus benefitted that land.

---

3. There must be diversity of ownership and/or occupation of the dominant and servient tenements

You cannot enjoy an easement against your own land: *Roe v Siddons* (1888). Such enjoyment amounts to a **quasi easement**, which has the potential to become an easement should diversity of ownership/occupation of the land subsequently arise, for example by selling part of your land to another (see '*Wheeldon v Burrows* (1879)'). A landlord can acquire an easement over his tenant's land, despite being the common freehold owner, since there exists between the lands diversity of occupation.

4. The right must lie in grant

Since an easement is a right capable of existing at law, it must be capable of being granted by deed. This requires:

A capable grantor and grantee

There must be two separate legal personalities, each having legal capacity ie be of sound mind, over 18 years old, etc.

A right that is capable of reasonably exact definition

- Rights of light, water, air, passage, etc should be through defined channels (*Harris v De Pinna* (1886)).

- Rights that require subjective interpretation may be deemed too uncertain: *William Aldred's Case* (1610) (scenic view).

- Rights normally capable of being easements may fail owing to ambiguities within the documentation: *Chaffe v Kingsley* [2000].

Capability

****

A right within the nature of rights traditionally recognized as easements

New easements may arise, since the list of recognized easements is not closed and can be expanded upon: *Dyce v Lady James Hay* (1852).

However, the courts are reluctant to recognize new negative easements: *Phipps v Pears* [1965].

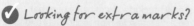 **Looking for extra marks?**

Arguably today with the development of the law of restrictive covenants, any attempts to restrict what a landowner can do over his own land are now better served by establishing restrictive covenants. This may be the motivation for declining to recognize new negative easements. In some cases, decisions have also been influenced by public policy. In *Hunter v Canary Wharf Ltd* [1997], the House of Lords rejected the claim of an easement to receive a television signal. To allow such an easement would have prevented the defendant from being able to build on its land, itself not desirable considering the positive economic impact such building works would have.

Additional factors

Even when the right satisfies the four *Re Ellenborough Park* [1956] requirements, it may still be rejected as an easement where:

The right requires expenditure by the servient owner

- The servient owner should not be obliged to incur expense or other positive obligation so as to enable the dominant owner to enjoy the right: *Regis Property Co Ltd v Redman* [1956].
- Note the spurious easement of fencing, where the servient owner is required to fence his land for the purpose of enclosing livestock: *Crow v Wood* [1971]. (The Law Commission Report No. 327 proposes that such obligations in the future take effect as land obligations.)

Revision tip

Remember, expenditure does not include costing the servient owner by him losing money. The question is rather whether the servient owner has to spend money for the right to be exercised.

The servient owner is under no obligation to maintain and repair so as to enable the right to be enjoyed (*Jones v Pritchard* [1908]), but he is under an obligation to allow the dominant owner access onto the servient land, so that the latter may carry out such repairs and maintenance. Such rights of access have now been incorporated into the **Access of Neighbouring Land Act 1992** and amount to licences, not easements.

Of course, there may be cases where the parties agree, either expressly or impliedly, that the servient owner will bear the cost of repair and maintenance: see *Liverpool City Council v Irwin* [1977].

The right amounts to exclusive possession of the servient land

Revision Tip

This requirement is often used to assess your ability to apply the law to a novel set of facts. Know your case law here; not just the facts and outcomes but the legal reasoning behind the decisions so that this may be applied to your own question's facts. Identify similarities and differences throughout your analysis.

Easements, being mere interests in land, must remain mutually exclusive of possessory rights, such as an estate in land. So, where a dominant owner is granted exclusive possession of the land, it cannot be an easement (although it may be a lease/freehold).

- Easements must not leave the servient owner without any reasonable use of his land: the 'ouster principle': *Copeland v Greenhalf* [1952].
- The question is one of degree and the nature of the right being claimed, and the extent of the physical space being used, may be influential. See, for example, *Miller v Emcer Products* [1956] (where a valid easement arose to use a neighbour's toilet) and contrast with *Grigsby v Melville* [1973] (where the exclusive right to store in a cellar was rejected).
- Being a question of degree, a lack of clarity surrounds the 'ouster principle'; at what point does a dominant owner's use of the land become so extensive that it precludes the servient owner from retaining any reasonable use?

✅ *Looking for extra marks?*

Recent case law development as to the use of the 'ouster principle' has been provided in a number of car parking cases. Whilst the cases of *Hair v Gillman* (2000) and *Batchelor v Marlow* [2003] adopted this test, the House of Lords, in the Scottish decision of *Moncrieff v Jamieson* [2007] was critical of it. Lord Scott preferred to ask whether the exercise of the right would leave the servient owner in 'possession and control' of the servient land. However, *Batchelor* was not overruled and Lord Scott's comments are considered *obiter* since application of either test would have produced the same positive results. In a later first instance decision of *Virdi v Chana* [2008], the judge followed the 'reasonable use' test of *Batchelor*, considering himself not bound by the test advocated in *Moncrieff*.

Revision Tip

As an area which has stimulated much discussion, and where there still exists a lack of clarity as to the test to be adopted and the way in which this area of easements will develop, this could be a focus for an exam question. Read articles on this topic area in preparation.

✅ *Looking for extra marks?*

In the recent case of *Kettel & Ors v Bloomfold Ltd* [2012], the High Court confirmed that it was bound by *Batchelor v Marlow* [2003]. But in doing so, it adopted a 'reasonable use' test that appears to have similarities with that of 'possession and control', thus blurring the lines even further. The Law Commission Report No. 327 has proposed the abolition of the ouster principle. ➡

➡ The effect would be to reverse, for the future, the decision in *Batchelor*, and allow exclusive rights to park arising as valid easements provided the servient owner could still access the land (however limited that might be).

Revision tip

Read the Law Commission Report No. 327 'Making Land Work: Easements, Covenants and Profits à Prendre'. Essay questions on easements may well focus on discussion points and proposals raised within the report.

The right is not exercised as of right

When the exercise of the right is dependent upon constantly seeking permission from the servient owner, it cannot exist as an easement: *Green v Ashco Horticulturalist Ltd* [1966].

Acquisition of easements

Once deemed capable of being an easement, the right must be shown to have been acquired as one. The flowchart in Figure 12.1 illustrates how easements may be acquired.

Figure 12.1 Acquisition of easements

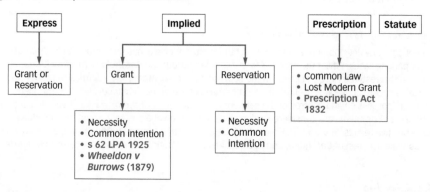

Express

Arises where express words can be found in a document granting or reserving an easement. (The status of the document will help determine the status of the easement—see 'Status of the easement acquired'.)

Implied

Arises where no express words of acquisition are present in a document but a court may be willing to imply their presence. Remember, a court will be less willing to do so in favour of a transferor claiming to have reserved an easement for himself over land that he is transferring to another: *Re Webb's Lease* [1951] (see Figure 12.1).

Implied out of necessity

The easement claimed must be essential to the use of the land, not just merely desirable: *Pryce v McGuiness* [1966]. It can allow for successful claims to rights of way where land would otherwise be landlocked. The existence of alternative, if less convenient, access routes may therefore preclude a right of way arising through necessity: *Manjang v Drammah* [1990]. It may depend upon how realistic the alternative route is: *Adealon International Proprietary Ltd v Merton Borough Council* [2007].

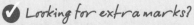

Looking for extra marks?

This mode of acquisition is dependent upon the parties' intentions. In *Nickerson v Barraclough* [1981], no easement of necessity was acquired where the vendor had expressly stated in the document transferring a piece of landlocked land that no right of access was being granted. There was no public policy to grant the right. The purchaser had simply entered into a bad deal. (An approach confirmed in *Adealon*.)

Implied out of common intention

Wong v Beaumont Property Trust Ltd [1965] 1 QB 173

A lease over a cellar was granted specifically to use as a restaurant and contained stipulations to comply with health and safety regulations. To comply, the lessee needed to erect a ventilation system on the landlord's property. An easement to do so was therefore implied.

So consider the questions in Figure 12.2.

Figure 12.2 Acquisition by common intention

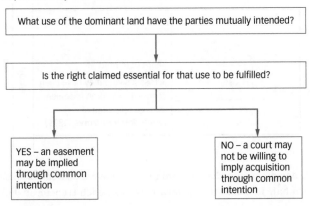

Acquisition of easements
✳✳✳✳✳✳✳✳✳✳

How does this mode of acquisition differ from necessity?

An easement will be implied by way of necessity where it is essential for *any* use of the land to be enjoyed. An easement will be implied out of common intention where it is essential for the land to be enjoyed for the specific *purpose* which the parties have mutually intended.

Wheeldon v Burrows (1879)

> *Revision tip*
>
> Remember, this mode of acquisition cannot be relied upon in a reservation scenario. It can only operate in favour of a grantee (eg a purchaser), not a grantor (eg a vendor).

This rule has the effect of elevating quasi easements ie those rights exercised over, and for the benefit of, your own land, into full easements, whether legal or equitable.

An example of an easement being acquired by virtue of the *Wheeldon v Burrows* rule is illustrated in Figure 12.3.

Figure 12.3 Example acquisition by *Wheeldon v Burrows*

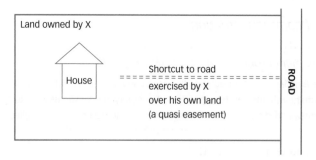

X sells western half of this plot, including house, to Y

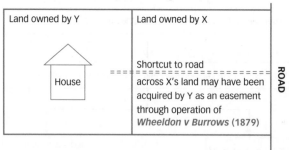

Note, should X decide to split the plot into two and have a contemporaneous sale of both parts (the western half to Y and the eastern half to Z) each transferee will acquire as an easement any quasi easements that were exercised prior to the transfer for the benefit of the land they now own: *Swansborough v Coventry* (1832).

To establish acquisition by this method:

- *The right must be continuous and apparent*

  Continuous will be satisfied by evidence of regular, not necessarily incessant, use sufficient to convey a degree of permanence.

  The right will be apparent where it is discoverable upon careful physical inspection of the property. For example, a worn tarmac road across a field would make a right of way across the field apparent: *Hansford v Jago* [1921].

- *The right must be necessary for the reasonable enjoyment of the dominant land*

  The right need not be something that it absolutely essential for the land to be enjoyed but has to be more than a mere convenience: *Wheeler v JJ Saunders Ltd* [1996]. So in *Goldberg v Edwards* (1950), a right to access an annexe to a house via an indoor passageway, was not acquired under the rule in *Wheeldon v Burrows* (1879), since the annexe could be accessed by an outdoor passage. However, in *Borman v Griffith* [1930], a secondary access route to the dominant land was acquired under the rule in *Wheeldon v Burrows* (1879) since it was the only means by which to access the front door to the house and was the only practical access route for heavy vehicles involved in the claimant's business.

✅ Looking for extra marks?

Whilst there has been some debate as to whether the two tests above have to be met or whether they are alternatives (see, for example, *Ward v Kirkland* [1967]), the dominant view is that both requirements must be met. Perhaps, as was suggested in the case of *Wheeler v JJ Saunders* [1996], this is inevitable since the two requirements tend to interact with one another; if something is found to be necessary for reasonable enjoyment, it is also likely that it will be found to be continuous and apparent.

- *The right must be used by the owner, for the benefit of the piece of land that is to become dominant, immediately before the grant*

  Whilst the right need not be in use at the exact time of transfer, it must have been exercised in the past with an expectation that it would be exercised again sometime in the near future.

  The right must have been in use by the owner of what is to become the dominant land and not, for example, his tenant: *Kent v Kavanagh* [2007]. This suggests that there must be common ownership and occupation of the potential dominant and servient lands prior to the transfer.

- *There must be no contrary intention*

  The parties can exclude acquisition of easements by this method: *Borman v Griffith* [1930]

Acquisition of easements

✳✳✳✳✳✳✳✳✳✳

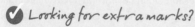

✅ Looking for Extra Marks

The Law Commission recommends replacing the three above methods of implied acquisition with a statutory test based upon what is necessary for the reasonable use of the land bearing in mind additional factors outlined in para 3.45 (Report No. 327).

Section 62 LPA 1925

✅ Looking for extra marks?

The Law Commission regards this as a method of express, rather than implied, acquisition (Report No. 327, para 3.58).

Revision tip

Remember, this mode of acquisition cannot be relied upon in a reservation scenario. It can only operate in favour of a grantee (eg a purchaser), not a grantor (eg a vendor).

Essentially a word-saving provision, s 62 LPA 1925 automatically passes to a successor in title all existing rights, privileges, easements, etc attached to the land without the need for express mention in the conveyance. Not only will it pass existing easements to a successor in title, its operation also appears to create new easements where none existed prior to the conveyance.

. . . .

Wright v Macadam [1949] 2 KB 744

A tenant's revocable licence to store coal in a coal shed converted, upon the granting of a new lease, into a legal easement to store.

. . . .

✅ Looking for extra marks?

The Law Commission recommends that the effect of s 62 LPA 1925 in converting precarious permissions into easements, as demonstrated in *Wright v Macadam* [1949], should be abolished (Report No. 327, para 3.64).

To establish acquisition of a legal easement by virtue of s 62 LPA 1925, you must satisfy all of the following:

- There must be a conveyance

  Defined in s 205 LPA 1925, it includes:

  - a legal sale of a freehold;
  - a grant of a legal lease over three years in duration;
  - a grant of a legal lease less than three years in duration in writing;
  - an assent by personal representatives.

It will not include:

- a contract to purchase/lease land;
- an oral grant of a legal lease less than three years in duration (Rye v Rye [1962]);
- a will.

- The right must exist at the date of the conveyance

  There must be evidence of prior use: Campbell v Banks [2011]. Section 62 cannot be used to revive rights that were used in the far past: Penn v Wilkins (1974).

- There must be prior diversity of occupation between the dominant and servient lands immediately before the conveyance: Sovmots Investments v Secretary of State for the Environment [1979].

  Without such diversity, it would be difficult to identify any 'rights', 'privileges' etc that come under the operation of s 62 LPA 1925.

✅ *Looking for extra marks?*

Does prior diversity need to exist? In cases concerning rights to light (*Payne v Inwood* (1966)), it was deemed not necessary. In the case of *P&S Platt v Crouch* [2004], the Court of Appeal observed that it would not be necessary to establish prior diversity where the right in question was continuous and apparent (requirements identified under the rule in *Wheeldon v Burrows* (1879)): see '*Wheeldon v Burrows (1879)*'. Many academics agree with this approach and, if accepted, this gives the application of s 62 LPA 1925 much greater scope since there is no additional requirement to show that the right claimed is reasonably necessary (as there is under *Wheeldon v Burrows*—see '*Wheeldon v Burrows* (1879)'). Such a position would make reliance upon acquisition by *Wheeldon v Burrows* largely unnecessary, save where acquisition is being implied into a contract, when s 62 LPA 1925 cannot operate. In *Alford v Hannaford* [2011], the *Platt* approach was cited as good law, although s 62 acquisition was not applied since there was no evidence of prior use. Whereas, in *Campbell v Banks* [2011] the Court of Appeal left open the question whether *Platt* is good law.

Revision tip

Since there is still some uncertainty on the issue of diversity, you would be advised in an exam to discuss both approaches and the outcomes that this would produce.

- *There must be no contrary intention*

  It is possible for the parties to exclude the operation of s 62 LPA 1925: s 62(4) LPA 1925.

Key similarities between s 62 LPA and *Wheeldon v Burrows* (1879)

- both require the right to be capable of being an easement; and
- both can be excluded by the parties from operating.

Acquisition of easements

✱✱✱✱✱✱✱✱✱✱

Key distinctions between s 62 LPA 1925 and *Wheeldon v Burrows* (1879)

Table 12.1 explains the key distinctions between s 62 LPA 1925 and *Wheeldon v Burrows* (1879).

Table 12.1 s 62 LPA 1925 and *Wheeldon v Burrows* distinctions

	Section 62 LPA 1925	*Wheeldon v Burrows* (1879)
Situation	Can only apply where, prior to the transfer of the dominant land, there is diversity of occupation between the dominant and servient lands, or, where no such diversity exists, the right is continuous and apparent (assuming the *P&S Platt v Crouch* [2004] approach)	Can only apply where, prior to the transfer of the dominant land, both the servient and dominant lands are under common ownership and occupation
Transaction	Can only operate where there is a conveyance of land (see above)	Can operate upon a conveyance or a valid contract of land
Type of right	The right must be one that exists at the date of the conveyance and, where no prior diversity, must also be continuous and apparent (assuming *P&S Platt v Crouch* [2004] approach)	The right must be one that is continuous and apparent, and reasonably necessary for the enjoyment of the land. It must also be in use by the owner at the date of the grant

Prescription

Easements exercised over the land of another for a long period of time, but where no actual grant of the right can be traced, may be acquired through prescription.

There are three modes of **prescription**:

- Common Law
- Lost Modern Grant
- **Prescription Act 1832**

Regardless of the mode under consideration, you must first satisfy three conditions if you are to be successful in establishing an easement has been acquired.

Table 12.2 explains the three key conditions of acquisition by prescription.

Table 12.2 Acquisition by prescription—three key conditions

The user must be 'as of right'	It must have been exercised: • *nec vi* – without force ie not in a contentious manner. • *nec clam* – without secrecy ie such that a reasonable person would have the opportunity to discover its exercise. • *nec precario* – without permission, whether written or oral. Mere tolerance or acquiescence (knowledge of the user but abstaining to stop it where it is within your power to do so) of the exercise of the right, without any express or implied permission, will not defeat a possible claim to an easement being acquired by prescription: ***Mills v Silver* [1991]**.
The user must be 'continuous'	This may be intermittent provided there is a reasonably uniform quality to the frequency of user and intervals between use are not excessive. Use of a right 3 times in 20 years was deemed insufficiently continuous in ***Hollins v Verney* (1884)**.
The user must be by/on behalf of one fee simple owner against another fee simple owner	The claimant must show that either he is the fee simple owner of the dominant tenement or, if he is the tenant of that land, show that he is claiming the right on behalf of the fee simple owner.

Upon satisfying the three conditions in Table 12.2, you must then establish that the right has been exercised for the requisite time period, which differs depending upon the mode of prescription.

Common law

The user must be shown to have been exercised since time immemorial ie 1189, which is presumed where the claimant can show that the right has been enjoyed for 20 years (not necessarily the 20 years immediately prior to the action). This presumption will be rebutted where there is evidence that the right could not have been enjoyed since 1189, for example a claim to a right of light through a window of a house that had only been built in the 1800s, or evidence that the dominant and servient tenements had been in common ownership sometime after 1189.

Lost modern grant

Recently confirmed in *Orme v Lyons* [2012], where 20 years or more user can be established, the court is willing to presume a valid grant of that right was given some time in the past ie that a deed was executed granting that right in 'modern times' (post 1189), but that that document has since been lost.

It is not possible to rebut this presumption with evidence that in fact no grant was ever made: *Tehidy Minerals v Norman* [1971]. It can only be rebutted if shown that such a grant was legally impossible, perhaps, for example, because there was no legally competent grantor throughout the period of use: *Oakley v Boston* [1976].

Acquisition of easements
✳✳✳✳✳✳✳✳✳✳

Prescription Act 1832

All easements other than right to light

An easement may be acquired upon establishing either 20 or 40 years' uninterrupted use as of right. Unlike under common law, acquisition will not be defeated by showing that the use began some time after 1189.

What is the difference between the two time periods?

When relying upon 20 years' uninterrupted use, a claim will be defeated where it is shown to be based upon either oral or written consent. However, where the use continues for 40 years, the existence of oral permission will not defeat a claim. Only if the use as of right is exercised with written consent will a claim be defeated.

When must the 20 or 40 years period of user occur?

It must be the period immediately before the claim is litigated. The period of user must continue up to the date of the action. Where there is a gap between the period of user and the issuing of the writ, acquisition under the Prescription Act will be of no use, irrespective of the length of user.

What will amount to an 'interruption'?

An interruption in use, that has been submitted to or acquiesced in by the dominant owner for at least a year, will defeat a claim. So interruptions for less than a year will be disregarded. This effectively means that a claim could be established where interruption occurs within the twentieth year ie before 20 years full user can be established. In *Flight v Thomas* (1841), the dominant owner enjoyed the use of an easement as of right for 19 years and 11 months, when the use was then interrupted. A few months passed before the writ was issued. Since, at the date of the issue of the writ, there had been at least 20 years user as of right and the interruption was for less than one year, the right was deemed acquired under the Prescription Act.

Right to light

Twenty years' uninterrupted use of the right immediately prior to an action being taken will result in an 'absolute and indefeasible' easement being acquired, unless it is being enjoyed with written consent (s 3). What amounts to an interruption is the same as above. In addition, under the Rights to Light Act 1959, the servient owner can register a 'light obstruction notice' as a local land charge, thus interrupting user as of right.

Statute

This would cover, for example, the right for an electricity company to put pylons up over land belonging to another.

✅ *Looking for extra marks?*

The Law Commission recognizes pros and cons of acquisition by prescription:

Pros include:

- regularizes long use;
- ensures continuation of facilities essential for use and marketability of land;
- makes good omissions in conveyancing.

Cons include:

- penalizes neighbourliness and generosity;
- lack of written evidence makes it difficult to determine the precise nature and extent of an easement.

Whilst not wishing to abolish prescription, the Commission declared that the co-existence of three methods of prescription was a major defect and proposed that acquisition by prescription would only be possible in circumstances meeting a new statutory definition of 'qualifying use'—requiring 20 years of continuous use, without force, stealth, and permission (see Report No. 327, paras 3.71-3.187).

Status of the easement acquired

Essentially, regardless of whether acquired expressly or by implication, an easement will be:

Legal when:	Equitable when:
<ul><li>created by a competent grantor; and</li><li>created by deed: s 52 LPA 1925 (deed requirements in s 1 Law of Property (Miscellaneous Provisions) Act 1989); and</li><li>equivalent in duration to one of the legal estates in land: s 1(2)(a) LPA 1925; and</li><li>where expressly acquired (by grant or reservation) in respect of registered land, registered in accordance with s 27(2)(d) Land Registration Act 2002.</li></ul>	<ul><li>created merely in compliance with s 53(1)(a) LPA 1925; or</li><li>created merely by an equitable estate owner; or</li><li>an attempt to create a legal easement fails to meet all legal formalities, provided this failed attempt amounts to a valid contract (s 2 LP(MP)A 1989) that is specifically enforceable: *Walsh v Lonsdale* (1882).</li></ul>

Enforcement of the easement against third parties

Figures 12.4 and 12.5 illustrate the enforcement of the easement against third parties over registered and unregistered land.

Enforcement of the easement against third parties

✳✳✳✳✳✳✳✳✳✳

Registered land

Figure 12.4 Enforcement of the easement against third parties: registered land

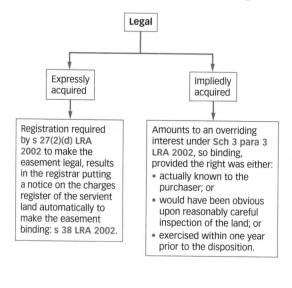

Legal

Expressly acquired

Registration required by s 27(2)(d) LRA 2002 to make the easement legal, results in the registrar putting a notice on the charges register of the servient land automatically to make the easement binding: s 38 LRA 2002.

Impliedly acquired

Amounts to an overriding interest under Sch 3 para 3 LRA 2002, so binding, provided the right was either:
- actually known to the purchaser; or
- would have been obvious upon reasonably careful inspection of the land; or
- exercised within one year prior to the disposition.

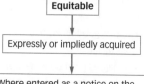

Equitable

Expressly or impliedly acquired

Where entered as a notice on the charges register of the servient land (s 32 LRA 2002) it will be binding. Where no entry is present, the easement will not bind a purchaser for valuable consideration: s 29 LRA 2002.

Is there scope for an equitable easement not entered on the register, to bind as an overriding interest under Sch 3 para 2? In *Holaw Ltd v Stockton Estates Ltd* (2001) a right of way was deemed never to amount to actual occupation, regardless of intensity of use. However, the general possibility of an easement amounting to actual occupation was *obiter* accepted in *Chaudhary v Yavuz* [2011] (although rejected in relation to the right to use a metal staircase in that case).

Unregistered land

Figure 12.5 Enforcement of the easement against third parties: unregistered land

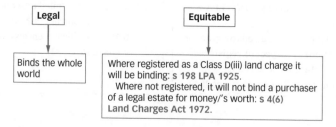

Legal

Binds the whole world

Equitable

Where registered as a Class D(iii) land charge it will be binding: s 198 LPA 1925.
Where not registered, it will not bind a purchaser of a legal estate for money/'s worth: s 4(6) Land Charges Act 1972.

Revision tip

Link your revision here to relevant material discussed in both chapters 3 and 4 on the issue of enforcement of interests against third parties.

Remember that the benefit of an easement appertaining to the dominant land will automatically pass to the successor in title of that land by virtue of **s 62 LPA 1925**.

Termination of easements

Merger

A union of ownership of the fee simple of both the dominant and servient tenements extinguishes, for good, easements that were benefitting what was the dominant land.

A union of occupation extinguishes easements but these could be later revived should occupation of the lands separate again some time in the future.

Release

Express

Where the servient owner acts upon a promise that he has been released from the burden of an easement to his detriment, the dominant owner may be estopped from denying the easement has been extinguished.

Implied

Mere non-user of the easement is not sufficient, although if the easement has not been used for a long period, it could lead to a presumption of abandonment, provided there is some evidence of intention to that effect.

Statute

For example, where a compulsory purchase order is made by a local authority.

Change of character

A change of use to the dominant tenement which leads to a substantial increase in the burden on the servient tenement may lead to the termination of an easement: *Attwood v Bovis Homes Ltd* [2001].

Remedies

Abatement

A self-help remedy allowing the dominant owner to remove any obstruction that prevents him from enjoying the exercise of the easement. He must do so without using any unreasonable force or injuring any person. Its use should be limited to cases of urgency. Preference should be to seek remedy through the courts.

Damages

To be awarded, there must be some substantial interference with the enjoyment of the easement, rather than a mere trivial incident: *Weston v Lawrence Weaver Ltd* [1961].

Injunction

To restrain the interference of the right that the dominant owner complains of, although it will not be justified where the infringement is trivial or temporary.

Profits à prendre

These allow a person to go onto the land of another, the servient land, and take either part of the natural produce of the land, itself capable of ownership (for example crops but not water), or animals. The exercise of the right may or may not be for the benefit of a dominant tenement. Where it is not, the profit exists '*in gross*'. It can be unrestricted as to the amount that can be taken from the land and amounts to a personal right.

Where it is for the benefit of a dominant piece of land, it is known as a profit appurtenant and the conditions necessary for a right to exist as an easement would equally apply. The profit is restricted as to the amount that can be taken from the land and amounts to a proprietary interest.

✅ *Looking for extra marks?*

Look at the Law Commission Report No. 327 on proposals for reform to *profits à prendre*.

 (✱) Key cases

Case	Facts	Principle
Batchelor v Marlow [2003] 1 WLR 764	The right to park a car in a commercial parking space between 8.30am and 6.00pm Monday to Friday was held not to be an easement as it amounted to exclusive possession. The servient owner would only want to use the parking space during business hours and to recognize the right as an easement would have prevented him from doing so.	The exercise of an easement must not exclude the servient owner from having reasonable use of the servient land for himself. The nature of the land in question shall be taken into account when making this assessment.

Case	Facts	Principle
Copeland v Greenhalf [1952] Ch 488	A right to store vehicles on a narrow strip of land was held not to be an easement. The exercise of that right would have amounted to effectively claiming the whole of the beneficial use of that strip, to the exclusion of the servient owner.	The exercise of an easement must not exclude the servient owner from having reasonable use of the servient land for himself. The extent to which the physical space is being used is taken into account when making this assessment.
Hair v Gillman (2000) 80 P&CR 108	The right to park on a forecourt that could accommodate four cars was held to be an easement. There was no exclusive possession as there would always be three other parking spaces for the servient owner to use.	The exercise of an easement must not exclude the servient owner from having reasonable use of the servient land for himself. The extent to which the physical space is being used shall be taken into account when making this assessment.
Hill v Tupper (1863) 2 H&C 121	A claim to an exclusive right to put boats on a canal was rejected as an easement. The exercise of the right was deemed to confer a mere commercial advantage on the claimant, rather than an advantage on the dominant land.	For a right to be capable of being an easement it must accommodate a dominant tenement, rather than confer a mere personal advantage on the current owner.
Moody v Steggles (1879) 12 Ch D 261	The right to put an advertisement on a neighbour's property advertising a pub was held to be an easement. The right would accommodate the land in connection with its normal use as a pub and thus benefit any future occupier of that land, irrespective of who they are.	A right which confers a commercial benefit may not be precluded from being an easement where the commercial activity and the land upon which it is carried out have become interlinked, so that any benefit to the business also benefits the land.
Phipps v Pears [1965] 1 QB 76	A claim of an easement to have a house protected from the weather by another house was rejected as an easement. To allow otherwise would have precluded the owner of the other house from demolishing it.	Negative easements, restricting what a servient owner can do over his own land, can no longer be created.

Exam questions

Case	Facts	Principle
Re Ellenborough Park [1956] Ch 131	A right for residential property owners to use a park adjacent to their houses for recreational use was deemed to be an easement. The right accommodated the land since use of the park was akin to use of a garden; such use being connected to normal enjoyment of a house.	Four requirements must be met for a right to be capable of being an easement. On the issue of accommodating the dominant land, the right should be connected to normal use of the dominant land and thus benefit any occupier of that land.
Regis Property Co Ltd v Redman [1956] 2 QB 612	The claim of a right to hot water as an easement was rejected.	The exercise of an easement should not involve the servient owner spending any money.
Wheeldon v Burrows (1879) 12 Ch D 31	Two plots of land, in common ownership, with one enjoying a quasi easement of light over another. The quasi servient plot was sold to B and a year later the quasi dominant plot was sold to W. When B erected hoardings blocking light to W's land, W was held not to have an easement of light.	Quasi easements may elevate to full easements when the quasi dominant land is transferred to another and three conditions are met.
Wong v Beaumont Property Trust Ltd [1965] 1 QB 173	An easement to fix a ventilation system to the landlord's property was impliedly acquired by the tenant when granted a lease over the landlord's cellar, specifically for use as a restaurant. Without such an easement, the tenant could not comply with health and safety regulations and thus could not use the cellar in the way the lease intended.	Where an easement is essential for the dominant land to be used in accordance with the purpose mutually intended by the parties, that easement may be impliedly acquired by common intention.
Wright v Macadam [1949] 2 KB 744	A tenant's revocable licence to store coal in a coal shed converted, upon the granting of a new lease, into a legal easement to store.	A conveyance in respect of the dominant land may elevate in favour of the transferee any pre-existing licences into easements.

(?) Exam questions

Problem question

In May 2011, Danielle, the registered freehold owner of a large Victorian house, decided to convert the top floor of the building into a flat. She then granted a two-year lease of the top floor flat to Shirley. The lease provided for access to the flat via an outside set of stairs, together with residential parking at the front of the building.

When Shirley moved in, Danielle orally agreed for her to access the flat via the internal stairs. Although she gave no express agreement, Danielle also raised no objection when Shirley set up a flower stall in the residential parking area at the front of the building, which she advertised by fixing a sign to the side of the house.

When Shirley's lease expired, she was granted a new lease by Danielle, containing similar provisions to the original lease. Shirley continued to use the internal stairs and sell flowers from the flower stall advertised by the sign.

At the end of 2013, Danielle sold the freehold to the property to Roger. Roger has since told Shirley that she can no longer use the internal stairs to access the flat and that her flower stall must be removed from the parking area at the front of the house. He has already removed the sign from the house.

Advise Shirley.

See the Outline Answers section in the end matter for help with this question.

Essay question

Whilst the list of rights recognized as easements is not a closed one, are the boundaries which the courts have imposed to limit the expansion of this list appropriate and consistent?

 Online Resource Centre

To see an outline answer to this question log onto www.oxfordtextbooks.co.uk/orc/concentrate/

#13
Freehold covenants

This is typically examined as a self-contained problem question. Such a question frequently involves:

- The sale of part of a freehold estate to another. Covenants are extracted at the time of sale, from the purchaser for the benefit of the vendor. This is so the vendor can retain some control over the land that he is selling for the benefit of the land that he is retaining for himself.
- The purchaser's land then passes to a successor in title who breaches the original covenants and the question then is who can be held liable for that breach: the successor in title who committed the breach or the original purchaser who gave the covenant, or both.
- In addition, the vendor's land may also have passed to a successor in title, so you will need to assess who can enforce that breach: the original vendor who extracted the promise or his successor in title?

Once you have a formula for how to deal with these issues, the good news is that this formula can generally be applied to any problem question set in this topic area.

Essay questions may focus upon a general analysis of the circumstances in which covenants run with the land. Questions may also focus upon areas of controversy such as the decision in *Federated Homes Ltd v Mill Lodge Properties Ltd* [1980] or areas for possible reform. Alternatively, although perhaps less frequently, you may be required to assess the differences between this type of proprietary interest with another, such as an easement for example.

Key facts

- All freehold covenants are enforceable between the original covenanting parties based upon principles of contract law.

- Where successors in title to the original covenanting parties wish to enforce covenants, they must establish the burden and benefit of the covenants passed to them.

- Whilst common law may pass the benefit of a covenant to a successor of the dominant land (express or implied), it will not pass the burden of any covenant to a successor of the servient land.

- Equity will pass the burden of a covenant to a successor of the servient land but only where the four requirements developed from *Tulk v Moxhay* (1848) are met. This is limited to restrictive covenants.

- Where the burden of a covenant has passed to a successor in equity, the benefit must also pass to a successor of the dominant land in equity.

- A benefit of a covenant may pass in equity in one of three ways: annexation, express assignment, or under a scheme of development.

- Following the decision in *Federated Homes Ltd v Mill Lodge Properties Ltd* [1980], the benefit of a covenant will typically pass by statutory annexation, unless expressly excluded by the parties.

- The burden of positive covenants will not pass to a successor of the servient land whether at common law or in equity. Whilst common law has developed ways to circumvent this problem and make positive covenants enforceable against successors, whether directly or indirectly, such methods are of limited application.

Chapter overview

Freehold covenant: a promise extracted by the covenantee from the covenantor, the latter undertaking to do/not to do something over his servient land for the benefit of the covenantee and/or his dominant land

Enforcement between the original covenanting parties: based upon contractual principles

A third party, not named in the document creating the covenant, may enforce a covenant if he satisfies rules under either:
• s 56 LPA 1925; or
• Contracts (Rights of Third Parties) Act 1999

Enforcement between successors in title: must demonstrate the burden and benefit of the covenants have passed

At Common Law

Benefit will pass if either:
• express assignment under s 136 LPA 1925; or
• implied assignment under *P&A Swift Investments v Combined English Stores Group plc* [1989]

The burden of a covenant may be enforceable against a successor in title to the original covenantor:
• indirectly via a chain of indemnity covenants; or
• using the rule in *Halsall v Brizell* [1957]

Burden will not pass: *Rhone v Stephens* [1994]

In Equity

Burden will pass if satisfy requirements from *Tulk v Moxhay* (1848)

Limited to restrictive covenants. Enforcement of positive covenants between successors in title relies upon common law

Where burden has passed in equity, benefit must pass in equity. Benefit will pass either by:
• annexation (express/statutory/implied); or
• express assignment; or
• scheme of development

Equitable remedies available

Covenants no longer enforceable where:
• extinguished; or
• discharged

Introduction

Freehold **covenants** are promises extracted by one freehold owner (the **covenantee**) from another freehold owner (the **covenantor**), whereby the latter promises either to do (positive covenant) or not to do (negative covenant) something over his land. The land burdened by the promise becomes the servient tenement. The land benefiting from the promise becomes the dominant tenement.

Covenants commonly arise when a freehold owner is selling off part of his freehold to another and wishes to maintain some degree of control over the land being sold in order to preserve the value and enjoyment of the land he is retaining. Examples include restricting the ability to build on the land or restricting how the land can be used. Such covenants effectively amount to a form of private planning control. However, despite the development of this area of law, they have not eradicated the need for public planning controls.

Revision tip

Remember not to confuse a question on freehold covenants with one on leasehold covenants, where the promises are extracted between a landlord and his tenant.

Enforcement

This is the key area of focus in an exam problem question.

Between the original parties to the covenant

Privity of contract exists between the original covenantor and covenantee. Should the covenantor breach his covenant, the covenantee could enforce the breach using normal contractual principles.

Generally, only the parties to a deed/contract can enforce the terms of that deed/contract, subject to two exceptions:

* **Section 56 Law of Property Act 1925**

  A person, not a party to a covenant, may sue upon it provided the covenant was purported to be made with him, rather than simply confer a benefit upon an unidentifiable third party: *Re Ecclesiastical Commissioners for England's Conveyance* [1936]. The third party must be identifiable at the time of the creation of the covenant. Consequently, a covenant made with *successors in title* would not benefit those future owners of the land since, at the time the covenant was made, they are not identifiable: *Kelsey v Dodd* (1881).

  Once a benefit of a covenant has been acquired this way by a third party not named in the deed of creation, he is treated in the same way as an original covenantee and may pass the benefit of the covenant to his successor.

Enforcement
✳✳✳✳✳✳✳✳✳✳

- **Contracts (Rights of Third Parties) Act 1999**

  This applies to contracts entered into on/after 11 May 2000. Under s 1(1), a third party may enforce terms of a contract to which he was not a party where:

  - the contract expressly provides that he can; or
  - a term of the contract purports to confer a benefit upon him.

  Thus a party, other than the original covenantee, may be able to enforce the terms of a covenant. To do so, the covenant must have named this person or identified them as a member of a class (here *'successors in title'* would suffice). This person need not have been in existence when the covenant was created.

Between successors in title
The benefit of a covenant

Even after the dominant and servient lands have passed to successors in title, the covenants are still enforceable between the original parties due to their contractual relationship. In reality, however, the original covenantee is unlikely to take action to stop any subsequent breaches of covenant. As he no longer owns the dominant land, he will not suffer any loss as a result of a breach being committed.

Rather his successor in title, the current owner of the dominant land and the person actually being affected by the breach, will wish to take action. However, this will only be possible if he can establish the benefit of the covenant being breached passed to him when he took over the dominant tenement.

The burden of a covenant

Although the original covenantor remains liable for subsequent breaches committed after he has transferred the servient tenement to a successor, he may not be the best person to pursue for the breach since:

- he may be difficult to trace and, if he can be found, any remedy obtained against him would be limited to damages as he no longer owns the servient tenement; and
- pursuing him would provide little motivation for the successor actually committing the breach to stop (unless there exists an indemnity covenant between himself and the original covenantor—see 'Indemnity covenants').

Rather his successor in title, the current owner of the servient tenement and the person actually committing the breach, should be pursued. However, it will only be possible to do so if it can be established that the burden of the covenant passed to him upon the transfer of the servient tenement.

Revision tip

An exam problem question is unlikely to have the original parties staying as owners of the dominant and servient tenements, since there would be insufficient law for you to discuss. You must be prepared to be able to identify the original parties, their respective successors in title and how, if at all, the benefit and/or burden (as appropriate) of the covenant has passed to those successors.

At common law

Passing the benefit of a covenant

Express assignment

Provided it is not purely personal, the benefit of a covenant can be expressly assigned to any third party in accordance with ordinary rules of law. Such assignment must satisfy the requirements under **s 136 LPA 1925**, namely:

- in writing; and

- express notice of the assignment has been given to the covenantor.

Once the benefit has been assigned to a successor in this way, the assignor loses the ability to enforce the covenant. That ability has passed to their assignee.

Implied assignment

The requirements from *P&A Swift Investments v Combined English Stores Group plc* [1989] must be satisfied:

The covenant must touch and concern the dominant land

The covenant must be for the benefit of the land itself, rather than merely a personal benefit for just the original covenantee. A covenant that affects the land as regards mode of occupation or value, in the sense that the owner of that land gets more from his land by reason of the covenant being attached to it, may be deemed to touch and concern that land: *Smith & Snipes Hall Farm Ltd v River Douglas Catchment Board* [1949]. In addition, if the covenant only benefits a party whilst they are the owner of the dominant land, and will be of no benefit to them when they part with that land, it is likely to be seen as a covenant that touches and concerns: *P&A Swift Investments v Combined English Stores Group plc* [1989].

A covenant will not be deemed to touch and concern the land where it has been expressed as personal to the covenantee, even where the tests above are met: *P&A Swift Investments v Combined English Stores Group plc* [1989].

The original parties must have intended for the benefit to pass to successors in title of the dominant tenement

Such intention can be found either:

- in the express wording of the covenant; or
- for all covenants created after 1925, it is implied by virtue of s 78 LPA 1925.

At the time the covenant was created, the covenantee must have held a legal estate in the land to be benefited

The successor in title to the covenantee, who seeks to enforce the covenant, must also hold a legal estate in the dominant land

This need not be the same legal estate as was held by the original covenantee: *Smith & Snipes Hall Farm Ltd v River Douglas Catchment Board* [1949].

Passing the burden of a covenant

At common law, the burden of a covenant will never pass to a successor of the servient land: *Austerberry v Corporation of Oldham* (1885); *Rhone v Stephens* [1994]. Whilst the covenant may remain enforceable against the original covenantor at common law, this will have little practical benefit for the person seeking to enforce the covenant (see 'Between successors in title'.)

> ✅ *Looking for extra marks?*
>
> Why does the common law adopt this position that the burden of a covenant will not pass to a successor in title to the servient land? Arguably, it reflects the common law reluctance to allow restraints to be placed on a piece of land that could affect future generations. To allow this might result in the land becoming so bogged down with obligations that eventually the land becomes inalienable. This could have far reaching negative economic consequences.
>
> There have been attempts to undermine this common law position. For example, it has been suggested that s 79 LPA 1925 allows the burden to pass at common law since it implies into every covenant created after 1925, subject to contrary intention, that the covenant is 'deemed to be made by the covenantor on behalf of himself his successors in title and the persons deriving title under him or them'. This argument has been rejected in *Tophams Ltd v Earl of Sefton* [1967], where it was declared that s 79 is no more than a word-saving provision and does not have the effect of passing the burden of a covenant to successors of the servient land.
>
> The Contracts (Rights of Third Parties) Act 1999 will also provide no assistance in passing the burden of a covenant to a successor. Whilst it allows, in some circumstances, the benefit of a covenant to be enjoyed by persons not a party to its creation, the statute is unwilling to extend this rule to the burden.

In equity

Passing the burden of a covenant

Equity will allow the burden of a covenant to pass from an owner of the servient tenement to his successor in title, where all four conditions, developed from the case of *Tulk v Moxhay* (1848) are met, namely:

1. the covenant must be negative in nature; and

2. the covenant must accommodate the dominant land; and

3. the original parties must have intended for the burden to pass with the servient land; and

4. the purchaser of the servient land must have had notice of the covenant.

The covenant must be negative in nature

Compliance with the covenant should not require action/expenditure of money: *Haywood v Brunswick Permanent Benefit Building Society* (1881). This is a question of substance not form.

For example, a covenant *'not to allow a brick wall to fall into disrepair'*, whilst worded negatively, will require action, ie maintenance work, if it is to be complied with. It is therefore a positive covenant.

✅ Looking for extra marks?

Where a covenant appears to be mixed, with both positive and negative components, either a) the positive element of the covenant may be severed (if this is possible) from the negative component, allowing the latter to pass the first hurdle of *Tulk v Moxhay* (1848) (see *Shepherd Homes v Sandham (No 2)* [1971]), or b) the court will decide which component of the covenant is dominant and this will determine the overall status of the covenant (see *Powell v Hemsley* [1909]).

Revision tip

Unless obvious in an exam question which of the two above approaches should be adopted, you should discuss each approach and then adopt the most appropriate, justifying your reasons for doing so.

The covenant must accommodate the dominant land

This has three components which must all be met:

- There must be identifiable land that can enjoy the benefit of the covenant, both at the time of creation and the date of enforcement of the covenant: *LCC v Allen* [1914].

- The covenant must touch and concern the dominant land. It must not be merely personal to the original covenantor. See the earlier discussion under implied passing of benefit at common law.

Revision tip

Remember that you must establish the covenant benefits the dominant land. Where possible, use the facts given in the question to enhance your arguments here.

In equity

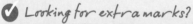

- There must be sufficient proximity between the dominant and servient lands: *Rogers v Hosegood* [1900].

> ✅ **Looking for extra marks?**
>
> Is it possible for a covenant to touch and concern the land when the dominant land is a very large estate? In *Re Ballard's Conveyance* [1937], where the estate was 1,700 acres, it was held that the covenant in question was not effective as it could not be seen to benefit the entire estate. The current view on this point is probably that adopted in *Wrotham Park Estate Co v Parkside Homes Ltd* [1974]: covenants should be seen to touch and concern the whole of the dominant land unless it can be shown that that opinion could not reasonably be held. Here the covenant in question was held to benefit the whole of a plot just less than 4,000 acres in size.

The original parties must have intended for the burden to pass with the servient land

This may be:

- in the express wording of the covenant; for example, '*the covenantor covenants on behalf of himself and his successors in title*'; or
- post 1 January 1926 such words will be implied by virtue of s 79 LPA 1925, subject to contrary intention.

> ✅ **Looking for extra marks?**
>
> Any suggestion that s 79 LPA 1925 by itself will make the burden of a covenant run with the servient land, thus rendering the other three requirements for passing the burden in equity redundant, has been rejected. In *Morrells of Oxford Ltd v Oxford United Football Club* [2001], Robert Walker LJ confirmed that the role of s 79 is merely to simplify the conveyancing process by creating the rebuttable presumption that covenants are made not just with the original covenantor, but also with his successors in title. It will not, by itself, pass the burden of a covenant.

The purchaser of the servient land must have had notice of the covenant

Today, this is essentially a question of registration and the conditions for meeting this requirement therefore differ depending upon whether the covenant affects registered or unregistered land (see chapters 3 and 4). Figures 13.1 and 13.2 illustrate how notice of the covenant may be acquired over registered and unregistered land.

Registered land

Figure 13.1 Notice for Registered Land

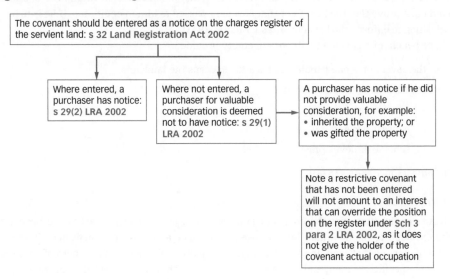

Unregistered land

Figure 13.2 Notice for Unregistered Land

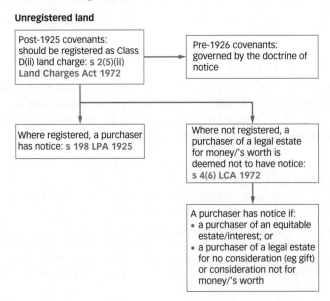

Passing the benefit of a covenant

Where the burden of a covenant has passed in equity, a successor in title to the dominant land must prove that the benefit of that covenant passed to him in equity too, if he is to be in a position to enforce the breach: *Miles v Easter* [1933].

The benefit of a covenant will pass in equity provided:

- the covenant is one which touches and concerns the land; and
- the covenant passed either by:
  - annexation;
  - express assignment; or
  - scheme of development.

(*Renals v Cowlishaw* (1878))

Annexation

Occurs at the time that the covenant is created and permanently attaches the benefit of the covenant to the dominant land. Consequently, once annexed the benefit has effectively become part of that land and will automatically pass to all successive owners of that land without specific mention, and irrespective of whether they know about its existence at the time of transfer.

Express annexation

This is where the wording of the covenant shows that the benefit is being attached to the actual dominant land (and not being entered into merely for the benefit of the covenantee). This can be achieved either by:

- ensuring that the covenant is expressly made '*for the benefit of*' the dominant land: *Rogers v Hosegood* [1900]; or
- ensuring that any reference made to the covenantee is done so *in their capacity as owner of the dominant land*. In *Renals v Cowlishaw* (1878), a covenant entered into expressly for the benefit of the vendor and his assigns was insufficient to result in annexation, since the parties referred to had not been explicitly linked to the dominant land.

✅ *Looking for extra marks?*

Once deemed expressly annexed to the dominant land, the benefit is regarded as annexed to the *whole* of that land. This result has caused problems in the past:

- To be seen as annexed to the whole of the dominant land, you would need to show that the covenant touches and concerns the whole of that land. This may prove problematic where the dominant land is a very large estate (see *Re Ballard's Conveyance* [1937] where a covenant was deemed not to benefit an estate of almost 1,700 acres. Consequently the purported

---

annexation was ineffective and the benefit of the covenant could not pass to successive owners of the dominant land).

- Where the benefited estate is broken up and sold off in parts, it ceases to exist as a whole and any annexation that had existed would cease to be effective, both in respect of the land retained and the land sold off: *Russell v Archdale* [1964].

Today, these problems appear to be surmountable:

- A covenant should be seen to touch and concern the whole of the dominant land unless it can be shown that that opinion could not reasonably be held. Consequently, annexation may be effective irrespective of the size of the dominant land: *Wrotham Park Estate Co Ltd v Parkside Homes Ltd* [1974] (where a covenant was deemed to benefit the whole of the dominant land, despite it being almost 4,000 acres).

- *Marquess of Zetland v Driver* (1939): where a covenant is expressly annexed to *each and every part of the land*, upon sale of part, the benefit will pass. The benefit will also continue for that land retained, thus overcoming the problem with annexation identified in *Russell v Archdale* [1964].

Statutory annexation

In *Federated Homes Ltd v Mill Lodge Properties Ltd* [1980], the Court of Appeal found that s 78 LPA 1925 operates to automatically annexe the benefit of a covenant to a dominant land, without the need for express words. Prior to this decision, s 78 had been interpreted as a mere word-saving provision, operating to pass the benefit of a covenant, only once a valid express annexation had already been established. Brightman LJ rejected this narrow interpretation of the provision. Indeed, he went further and held that automatic annexation by virtue of s 78 LPA 1925 would attach the benefit of the covenant to *each and every part* of the dominant land, thus eliminating the need to do so expressly (as discussed in *Marquess of Zetland v Driver* (1939)—see 'Express annexation'). This has since been confirmed in *Small v Oliver & Saunders (Developments) Ltd* (2006), subject to any contrary intention.

✅ *Looking for extra marks?*

Whilst this fully distributive effect of annexation has been accepted, the decision that annexation can occur automatically without the need for any express words has been criticized:

- Arguably, Parliament only ever intended s 78 LPA 1925 to operate as a word-saving provision. Indeed, the provision itself makes no mention of the word 'annexation'. If this is the case, the decision in *Federated Homes Ltd* goes too far in producing a result that is contrary to Parliament's intention.

- If the interpretation of s 78 LPA 1925 is truly correct, it renders express assignment, as an alternative method of passing the benefit, defunct. If this is true, you have to question why so much case law has arisen surrounding the issue of express assignment if, as is declared to be the case in *Federated Homes Ltd*, the benefit would have automatically passed anyway by virtue of s 78 LPA 1925.

- Section 78 LPA 1925 provides no provision for contrary intention. Arguably, it makes annexation a compulsory consequence of entering into a covenant, irrespective of the parties' intention. This particular criticism has been addressed in *Roake v Chadha* [1984]. Automatic statutory annexation was excluded by virtue of the conveyance stipulating that the benefit of the covenant would not pass to any owner or subsequent purchaser of the dominant land unless expressly assigned. The ability, by way of careful wording, to exclude automatic annexation by virtue of s 78 LPA 1925 has since been confirmed in *Crest Nicholson Residential (South) Ltd v McAllister* [2004]. The case of *89 Holland Park (Management) Ltd v Hicks* [2013] provides an example of an unsuccessful claim to excluding automatic annexation. The court rejected such a conclusion could be drawn from an interpretation of the wording used in the deed.

✅ Looking for extra marks?

Crest Nicholson Residential (South) Ltd v McAllister [2004] indicated that *Federated Homes Ltd v Mill Lodge Properties Ltd* [1980] represents the current law. However, it added that in order for statutory annexation under s 78 LPA 1925 to operate, it would be necessary for the wording of the covenant to actually identify the dominant land. If this is the case, such wording may alone be sufficient to find that the benefit has passed by way of express annexation. This being so, perhaps the decision in *Federated Homes Ltd* is less radical than at first thought. Successful statutory annexation appears to be dependent on the wording used in the relevant documents and is not, therefore, truly 'automatic'.

Revision tip

The decision of *Federated Homes Ltd* and its overall effect, is often the issue for debate in an essay question. Be sure to be aware of criticisms and views surrounding the decision. Those outlined earlier in this section can be explored further.

Implied annexation

Where the court may not find sufficient words of express annexation, it may look at the surrounding circumstances and imply annexation: *Marten v Flight Refuelling Ltd* [1962].

Express assignment

This is where the benefit of a covenant is expressly assigned to the successor to the dominant land. It must occur contemporaneously with the transfer of the dominant land (*Miles v Easter* [1933]), otherwise it will be deemed ineffective: *Re Union of London & Smith's Bank Ltd's Conveyance* [1933].

How does an express assignment of the benefit of a covenant differ from annexation of the benefit?

Table 13.1 explains the differences between express assignment and annexation of the benefit.

Table 13.1 Differences between assignment and annexation

	Annexation	Assignment
Timing	This takes place at the time of the creation of the covenant. When looking for evidence of express annexation, one must look at the conveyance between the original covenanting parties.	This occurs on the transfer of the dominant land from the covenantee to his successor in title. The words of assignment will be found in the conveyance that transfers the dominant land from one owner to the next, and not in the conveyance between the original covenanting parties.
Effect	Annexation permanently attaches the benefit of the covenant to each and every part of the dominant land. From that date onwards, the benefit will automatically pass to successive owners of the whole, or part, of the dominant land, without the need for further words/action.	Since assignment transfers the benefit of the covenant to a successor in title of the dominant land personally, it must be expressly assigned upon every subsequent transfer of that dominant land.

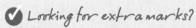 ✔ *Looking for extra marks?*

There has been some attempt to suggest that assignment of the benefit of a covenant will be implied automatically by virtue of **s 62 LPA 1925**. This provision provides that 'a conveyance of land shall be deemed to include ... rights, and advantages whatsoever, appertaining or reputed to appertain to the land ...'. This suggestion was rejected in *Roake v Chadha* [1984], declaring that a covenant that has not been annexed to the land does not appertain to the land. A similar view was held in *Kumar v Dunning* [1989].

Scheme of development

This arises in situations where you have a large estate, owned by a single owner, who subsequently decides to sell the estate off in lots. Upon the sale of each lot, the vendor seeks covenants from the purchasers, with the aim of preserving the overall value and residential amenity of the whole estate. At the time of obtaining these covenants, the dominant land will comprise those unsold lots owned by the vendor. So long as the vendor retains some of these unsold plots, for the benefit of which the covenants were given, he is in a position, as the original covenantee, to enforce any breaches. The difficulty arises when the final lots are sold and the vendor no longer owns any of the estate and indeed, probably no longer cares about whether the covenants are being observed. Those who do care will be the current owners of the lots. Some such owners may be able to claim the benefit of the covenant has passed to them using the rules previously outlined (see 'Passing the benefit of the covenant'). However, those who own lots that were sold before the covenant being breached had been obtained, will not be able to do so. This is because their lots did not form part of the dominant land at the time the covenant was given. To overcome this problem, a scheme was established which essentially allowed for covenants in such a situation to be mutually enforceable between the various owners of the lots.

Following the decision in *Re Dolphin's Conveyance* [1970], there are two key requirements that must be met for such a scheme to operate:

* there must be an identifiable scheme; it must be possible to identify the perimeters of the land to which the scheme relates; and

* of paramount importance, there must be a mutually perceived common intention; that a scheme was clearly intended to be established for the reciprocal enforcement of obligations (see *Small v Oliver & Saunders (Developments) Ltd* (2006)).

For a recent example of a building scheme arising, see *Clarke v Murphy* (2009).

Remedies

Injunction
Damages in lieu of an injunction

Remember, equitable remedies are subject to discretion and exercised in accordance with settled principles.

Positive covenants

In principle, these remain enforceable only against the original covenantor. Neither common law nor equity will pass the burden of a positive covenant to a successor of the servient land. However, ways have been developed to circumvent this position and make positive obligations enforceable against successive owners to the servient land.

Indemnity covenants

The original covenantor remains liable on the covenants, after having disposed of the servient land to a successor in title, due to his original contractual position. Upon disposing of the servient land, he may extract an indemnity covenant from his successor obliging the successor to indemnify him in respect of any damages he pays out as a result of his successor breaching the covenants. It is possible, in situations where the servient land has changed hands many times, that a chain of indemnity covenants will be created. Where a complete chain of indemnities exists (ie upon every disposal of the servient land, the outgoing owner has extracted an indemnity covenant from his successor), ultimately, the party left out of pocket as a result of the breach of covenant, will be the party at the end of the chain ie the person committing the breach in the first place. This, therefore, achieves indirect enforcement of positive obligations against successive owners to the servient land.

There are, however, problems with the efficiency of this system as a means of enforcement of positive obligations:

- Successors in title to the servient land may refuse to give an indemnity covenant to the outgoing owner. Where this is the case, it may create a break in the chain of indemnities. Where such a break exists, the party at the end of the chain committing the breach (ie the current owner of the servient land) will know that he cannot be pursued for the breach either directly or indirectly. He is therefore unlikely to have any motivation to stop committing the breach. The same will also be true where there is a break in the chain through disappearance/insolvency.

- Any remedy obtained using this method of enforcement will be limited to damages against the original covenantor. Since the latter no longer owns the servient land, it would be impossible to obtain an order of specific performance against him, despite this being, in most circumstances, the most appropriate remedy for the breach of a positive covenant.

- After some years, it may not be possible to locate the original covenantor. Thus, even the receipt of damages may not be achievable.

The rule in *Halsall v Brizell* [1957]

A person who wishes to claim the benefit of a deed must also submit to any corresponding burden which is imposed by that deed. There are three conditions which have to be met:

- the benefit and burden must be conferred in or by the same transaction: *Davies v Jones* [2009];

- there must be a correlation between the burden and the benefit ie the benefit must be conditional on, or reciprocal to, the burden: *Rhone v Stephens* [1994]. The benefit need not be explicitly conditional on the burden; it can be implicitly so: *Wilkinson v Kerdene Ltd* [2013]; and

- the successor in title to the covenantor must have had the opportunity to elect whether to take the benefit or, having taken it, elect to renounce it, even if only in theory, and thereby escape the burden: *Thamesmead Town Ltd v Allotey* [1998].

Revision tip

Remember that where a successor to the original covenantee wishes to enforce positive covenants indirectly using indemnity covenants or by using the rule from *Halsall v Brizell* [1957], you must show that he received the benefit of such covenants using common law methods of passing the benefit.

Extinguishment and discharge

Extinguishment

A covenant will no longer be enforceable where the dominant and servient lands cease to be in separate ownership/occupation.

Discharge

By the parties affected

This can be done by deed.

By the court—applicable to restrictive covenants only

In accordance with s 84(1) LPA 1925, as amended by s 28 LPA 1969, any person with an interest in the freehold that is affected by a restriction as to its use, may apply to the Lands Chamber of the Upper Tribunal for an order to wholly or partially discharge or modify the restriction. This may be granted in the following situations:

- where the restriction has become obsolete, due to 'changes in the character of the property or the neighbourhood or other circumstances'; or
- the continued existence of the restriction impedes a reasonable user of the land and either
  - the restriction does not provide any practical benefit to any person; or
  - it is contrary to public interest; or
- those entitled to the benefit have agreed, expressly or impliedly to its discharge/modification; or
- the proposed discharge/modification will not injure persons entitled to the benefit of the restriction.

The power is mainly exercised where the restriction has become obsolete. Where the Lands Chamber agree to discharge/modify the restriction, it has the discretion to require a compensation payment to the owner of the dominant land.

Reform

The Law Commission in its report 'Making Land Work: Easements, Covenants and Profits à Prendre' 2011 (No. 327), recommends the creation of a new legal interest in land called a 'land obligation'. This would incorporate both positive and negative obligations. Various safeguards would be introduced to ensure that land does not become overburdened with the introduction of positive obligations. The benefit and burden of land obligations would transmit in accordance with the same principles applicable to easements and other appurtenant legal interests, thus getting rid of the complex rules of passing the benefit and burden which currently exists. Following the implementation of this proposal, it would no longer be possible to create new freehold covenants whose enforcement is dependent upon *Tulk v Moxhay* (1848), although those already in existence would continue upon that basis.

Revision tip

An essay question may require analysis on the current flaws in the law relating to freehold covenants and proposals to eradicate such flaws. Reading the Law Commission's report will provide you with useful material.

 **⊛ Key cases**

Case	Facts	Principle
Federated Homes Ltd v Mill Lodge Properties Ltd [1980] 1 WLR 594	A restrictive covenant limiting building works referred to 'any adjoining or adjacent property retained by' the covenantee. Upon transfer of part of the covenantee's adjoining land, the benefit of this covenant was deemed annexed to the land and thus passed to the transferee.	Provided the conditions under **s 78 LPA 1925** are satisfied, annexation of the benefit of a covenant to the dominant land is automatic.
Halsall v Brizell [1957] 1 All ER 371	Purchasers of building plots covenanted to contribute towards maintenance costs of roads and sewers in common use of the owners of all the building plots.	Where you wish to take the benefit of a deed, you must also submit to any corresponding burden that deed imposes.
LCC v Allen [1914] 3 KB 642	A successor in title to the servient land started to build on that land in breach of a covenant. The council was refused an injunction to stop the building work.	To enforce a covenant, you must have a dominant land capable of benefiting from that covenant.
P&A Swift Investments v Combined English Stores Group plc [1989] AC 632	Rent obligation between landlord and tenant. Landlord assigned the reversion to the plaintiff. The tenant failed to pay rent and the plaintiff pursued the defendant, who stood as surety for the rent. The benefit of the rent obligation was deemed to have passed at common law to the plaintiff.	Benefit of a covenant may pass at common law where four requirements are met. A covenant is deemed to touch and concern the dominant land where any holder of that land would benefit, not just the original covenantee personally.

Key cases

****

Case	Facts	Principle
Re Ballard's Conveyance [1937] Ch 473	A covenant not to build and extracted for the benefit of a dominant land just less than 1,700 acres, was deemed not to be annexed to that land. Although expressed to benefit the whole of the dominant land, it was deemed to only benefit that part of the dominant land within the immediate vicinity of the servient land, a 16 acre plot. Express annexation had thus been unsuccessful.	For the benefit of a covenant to be annexed to the whole of the dominant land, it must be proven to touch and concern the whole of that land. (But see now *Wrotham Park Estate Co v Parkside Homes Ltd* [1974].)
Rhone v Stephens [1994] 2 AC 310	A covenant to keep a roof in repair was deemed unenforceable against a successor to the original covenantor.	The burden of a positive covenant will not pass at common law to a successor in title to the original covenantor.
Roake v Chadha [1984] Ch 40	A conveyance stipulating that the benefit of a covenant would not pass to any successor of the dominant land unless it had been expressly assigned to him, was deemed to exclude the operation of automatic statutory annexation.	Automatic statutory annexation by virtue of **s 78 LPA 1925** and the decision in *Federated Homes Ltd v Mill Lodge Properties Ltd* [1980] may be expressly excluded from operating.
Smith & Snipes Hall Farm Ltd v River Douglas Catchment Board [1949] 2 KB 500	Defendants entered into a covenant with the freehold owners of land subject to flooding, that they would maintain the banks of a river. An original covenantee conveyed her land to the 1st plaintiff together with the benefit of the covenant. The 2nd plaintiff occupied the dominant land under a tenancy. Both plaintiffs were entitled to enforce a breach of the covenant.	For the benefit of a covenant to pass at common law, the original covenantee and his successor must have held/holds now a legal estate in the dominant land. That legal estate need not be the same.
Tulk v Moxhay (1848) 2 Ph 774	A covenant not to build was deemed enforceable against a successor in title to the original covenantor, since he was aware of the existence of the covenant when purchasing the land affected.	A successor to the original covenantor who has notice of the covenant, takes subject to that covenant. Since extended to incorporate a further three requirements for the burden of a covenant to pass in equity.

Case	Facts	Principle
Wrotham Park Estate Co v Parkside Homes Ltd [1974] 1 WLR 798	A covenant not to build without prior approval of plans, was extracted for the benefit of a dominant land just less than 4,000 acres. When the successor in title to the covenantor breached the covenant, the plaintiff was entitled to enforce the breach. (Note a mandatory injunction was refused. To demolish the 13 houses already built would be 'an unpardonable waste'. Instead, damages in lieu of an injunction were awarded.)	A covenant will be deemed to touch and concern the whole of the dominant land, however large, unless it can be shown that that opinion cannot reasonably be held.

Problem question

David is the registered owner of a 200 acre farm, which includes a house, separate cottage, and a number of outbuildings. The farm benefits from a natural spring which provides the farm with all the water it needs through a system of pipes that David has installed on the property.

In 2011, David sold 15 acres of his farm, which included the cottage and an outbuilding, to John. The purchase was subject to the following covenants:

1. to use the property for residential purposes only;
2. to contribute towards the upkeep of the water pipes;
3. to plant and maintain conifer trees on the boundary between David and John's property.

Two years later, John became seriously ill and was given just a short time to live. He decided that he should travel the world whilst he still could and so gifted his property to his son, Eric.

Eric is an artist and decided that the property was perfect for establishing an art school. So, in 2014, he converted the outbuilding into a large studio for the art students to work in. To ensure that the outbuilding benefits from as much light as possible, he chopped down the conifer trees and replaced them with a picket fence.

David has recently sold his farm to Gillian who is unhappy that Eric is using his property as an art school as it increases the amount of traffic in the local area. She is also annoyed that the conifer trees have been replaced with a picket fence, providing her property with less privacy. In addition, since a recent argument with Eric about these issues, he has refused to make any contributions towards the upkeep of the water pipes.

Exam questions
✳✳✳✳✳✳✳✳✳✳✳

Advise Gillian.

See the Outline Answers section in the end matter for help with this question.

Essay question

What are the circumstances in which the benefit of a freehold covenant will run with the land? Did the decision in the case of *Federated Homes Ltd v Mill Lodge Properties Ltd* [1980] fundamentally alter the law in this area?

 Online Resource Centre

To see an outline answer to this question log onto www.oxfordtextbooks.co.uk/orc/concentrate/

#14
Mortgages

The examination

This is examined largely as a self-contained topic area. To some extent, there are reasonably distinct issues within the topic that can be the focus of an exam question, notably:

- the rights of the mortgagor and, in particular, the role equity plays in intervening to strike out clauses within a mortgage agreement. Such intervention can be seen as restricting freedom of contract and essay questions may require you to consider the extent to which this is true and how the law balances the contractual nature of a mortgage with its proprietary status;
- the concept of undue influence, in particular how it is established and the consequences of finding the borrower has been subjected to it, especially for the lender who often is not the culprit. Essay questions may focus on the relatively recent reworking of the law following the case of *Royal Bank of Scotland plc v Etridge (No 2)* [2002] requiring you to consider whether the law in this area has been clarified/improved;
- the rights of the mortgagee, in particular the remedies available should a mortgagor default on the mortgage payments. These differ slightly depending upon whether the mortgage is legal or equitable in status, so an understanding of how legal and equitable mortgages are created could be required (although it is true to say that most examiners focus upon legal mortgages).

Key facts

- A mortgage is a proprietary interest that can be legal or equitable in status.

- The equity of redemption encapsulates the rights of a mortgagor and includes the equitable right to redeem and the ability to have certain clauses struck out from a mortgage agreement.

- The mortgagor of a dwelling house has special legislative protection.

- Where a mortgage is obtained under undue influence, be it actual or presumed, it may be set aside.

- The mortgagee has various remedies available to it should the mortgagor fail to meet the mortgage payments, dependent upon the status of the mortgage.

- A property may be subject to more than one mortgage and where this is the case and the property is sold, proceeds from the sale will be applied in order of priority.

Chapter overview

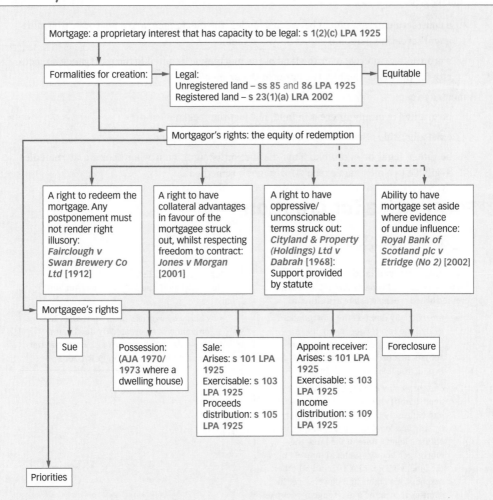

Introduction

A **mortgage** is:

- a contractual arrangement between a lender (the **mortgagee**) and a borrower (the **mortgagor**) creating personal rights between them;
- a proprietary interest over the land of the mortgagor, granted to the mortgagee as security for the money lent by the latter to the former.

A mortgage can:

- be granted over any interest in land, not just the freehold estate;
- exist alongside other mortgages over the same piece of land;
- be either legal or equitable. This distinction is significant when looking at remedies available to a mortgagee (see 'Mortgagee's remedies').

Formalities for creation

Legal mortgages

Over unregistered land

Under s 85 Law of Property Act 1925, mortgages created over a freehold estate are either a:

- *mortgage by demise*: the mortgagor grants the mortgagee a long lease (usually 3,000 years) over his estate subject to a provision that once the debt is paid, the lease will terminate; or

- *charge by way of a legal mortgage*: by deed, identifying the land in question and expressly declaring it to be charged by way of a legal mortgage. Rather than obtain a legal estate in the land, the mortgagee acquires a legal interest in the land: s 1(2)(c) LPA 1925. In all other respects, his rights and powers are the same as if granted a mortgage by demise.

Under s 86 LPA 1925, mortgages created over a leasehold estate will be the same as for a freehold estate save the mortgage by demise will amount to a sub-lease of the leasehold estate out of which it has been granted.

The creation of a mortgage over unregistered land triggers first registration of both the mortgaged estate and the mortgage itself: s 4(1)(g) LRA 2002.

Over registered land

Under s 23(1)(a) Land Registration Act 2002, only

- *charge by way of a legal mortgage*. Not only must it be created by deed, but it must also be registered as a charge at the Land Registry: s 27(2)(f) LRA 2002.

Equitable mortgages

Created where:

- the mortgage is being granted over a mere equitable interest, eg a beneficial interest under a trust of land. The whole of the equitable interest is conveyed to the mortgagee who promises to reconvey it when the debt is paid. The transfer of the equitable interest must satisfy s 53(1)(c) LPA 1925 (see chapter 2); or

- the parties expressly create an equitable mortgage. There must be compliance with s 53(1)(a) LPA 1925 (see chapter 2); or

- the formalities for creating a legal mortgage have not been satisfied ie there is no deed, but the failed attempt amounts to a valid contract (ie complies with s 2 LP(MP)A 1989) that is capable of specific performance; or

- where the land is registered and the mortgage created has not been registered as a charge at the Land Registry: s 27(2)(f) LRA 2002.

Mortgagor's rights

The principle

A mortgage is mere security for a loan. When a mortgagor wishes to redeem the loan, he should be able to do so, recovering his property in an unencumbered state. The mortgagee is only entitled to have the loan monies repaid, together with any interest that might have accrued.

To uphold this principle, equity has created a bundle of rights in favour of the mortgagor: the **equity of redemption**.

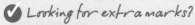 **Looking for extra marks?**

Equity seeks to strike a balance between a desire to ensure borrowers are protected, some of whom may be vulnerable to the sharp practices of lenders, and some recognition of freedom to contract and the need to encourage lending to secure property transactions, itself vital to a healthy economy.

The equitable right to redeem

A mortgage agreement specifies a legal date for redemption, before which a mortgagor cannot repay the loan, without consent from the mortgagee. At common law, if the debt was not paid on this exact date, the property vested in the mortgagee, preventing the mortgagor from ever recovering his property. Since this conflicts with the basic principle of a mortgage (see 'The principle'), equity intervened, giving the mortgagor an equitable right to redeem that commences upon the expiry of the legal date for redemption. Any intervention by the mortgagee which either removes this possibility to redeem or renders the right illusory, will be struck out.

Mortgagor's rights

✳✳✳✳✳✳✳✳✳✳✳

Clauses attempting to remove the right to redeem completely

Equity will not tolerate such clauses. In *Toomes v Consent* (1745), a mortgage term specifying that the property was to become the mortgagee's upon a specified event occurring, was struck out. If the event occurred, the mortgagor would be prevented from ever getting his property back, which clearly goes against the basic principle of what a mortgage is.

Options to purchase the mortgaged property

Table 14.1 explains options to purchase the mortgaged property.

Table 14.1 Options to purchase the mortgaged property

Obtained as part of the mortgage transaction	Obtained in a transaction independent of the mortgage
Option is void, irrespective of whether there was oppression or not: *Samuel v Jarrah Timber and Wood Paving Corporation Ltd* [1904]. Why? If the option was allowed and later exercised, the mortgagor would lose his property. Consequently, he would lose the ability to redeem the loan and recover his property, thus contravening the basic principle.	Option might be upheld: *Reeve v Lisle* [1902]. Depends upon the reality of the situation and whether the granting of the option and the mortgage are truly independent transactions: *Jones v Morgan* [2001]. (Remember, a mere delay between completing the mortgage and creating the option will not necessarily mean that the two are independent of one another. Neither will putting the option into a separate agreement from the mortgage.)

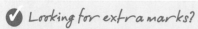 **Looking for extra marks?**

In *Warnborough Ltd v Garmite Ltd* [2004], the vendor was granted a mortgage over property being sold as security for unpaid purchase monies. An option was granted to the vendor to repurchase the property in specified circumstances. The option was upheld. The Court of Appeal declared that it was not part of the mortgage transaction but part of the sale transaction, thus independent of the mortgage. Mortgage rules should not apply when the reality is the transaction in question is of a different commercial character.

Clauses attempting to postpone the right to redeem

A mortgagee may wish to postpone the ability to redeem in order to guarantee for himself a return on his money via interest payments. Whilst acceptable in principle, equity will not allow postponement to be such that it renders the right to redeem illusory. So, in *Fairclough v Swan Brewery Co Ltd* [1912] postponing the ability to redeem until the final six weeks of the mortgaged leasehold estate was held void. If upheld, the mortgagor would recover a virtually worthless estate upon redemption. By contrast, a 40-year postponement clause in *Knightsbridge Estates Trust Ltd v Byrne* [1939] was upheld.

✅ Looking for extra marks?

What facts within *Knightsbridge* allowed the court to reach a different view about the postponement clause?

- The property was freehold so the right to redeem had not been made illusory. Upon redemption, even after 40 years, the mortgagor would recover a property of value.
- The clause had not been obtained through oppression. Both parties were experienced and the bargaining had been an arm's length commercial transaction.
- The terms were the most advantageous available at the time.

The right to have collateral advantages for the mortgagee struck out

Equity has been wary of collateral advantages sought by the mortgagee over and above the repayment of the loan with interest, as these go against the basic principle that a mortgage is mere security for a loan.

Traditionally, the view of equity has been:

- Where the advantage is set to continue after the mortgage is redeemed, it will be deemed void: *Noakes & Co Ltd v Rice* [1902]. The continued existence of the advantage would hinder the mortgagor from recovering his property in an unencumbered state upon redemption.
- Where the collateral advantage is to end upon redemption, provided it is not imposed in an oppressive or unconscionable way, it will be upheld: *Biggs v Hoddinott* [1898].

Today, greater acknowledgement is given to freedom to contract. Unless you can establish that the term was imposed in an oppressive way, the collateral advantage may be upheld as a valid term of a mortgage agreement, whether it is to last beyond the mortgage term or not: *Kreglinger v New Patagonia Meat & Cold Storage Co Ltd* [1914].

This greater respect towards freedom to contract was confirmed in *Jones v Morgan* [2001], which confirmed that no rule in equity precluded collateral advantages being obtained by a mortgagee, provided such terms are not:

- unfair/unconscionable;
- a clog on the equity of redemption;
- inconsistent with the right to redeem.

However, the court added that such advantages should be reached in a transaction truly independent of the mortgage.

✅ Looking for extra marks?

Some collateral advantages may be struck out as void based upon the contractual principle that agreements must not impose unreasonable restrictions on trade; for example, clauses tying ➡️

➡️ the borrower to buy only the lender's products, although validity may depend upon the duration of that tie: see *Esso Petroleum Co Ltd v Harper's Garage (Stourport) Ltd* [1968] and compare with *Alec Lobb (Garages) Ltd v Total Oil GB Ltd* [1985]. Such clauses may also be in breach of EU competition law and especially **Art 101 TFEU**: *Courage Ltd v Crehan* [2002].

The right to have oppressive or unconscionable terms struck out

To be struck out, the term must be more than merely unreasonable. It must have been imposed in a morally reprehensible way: *Multiservice Bookbinding Co Ltd v Marden* [1979]. In making this assessment, have regard to:

- the equality of bargaining power between the parties (see, for example, *Cityland & Property (Holdings) Ltd v Dabrah* [1968]);
- the experience of the mortgagor;
- whether the mortgagor received independent legal advice. If yes, it might be hard to show that the term had been imposed oppressively: *Jones v Morgan* [2001].

Financial Services and Markets Act 2000

First legal mortgages over residential property created on/after 31 October 2004 will be regulated by this Act and may prove useful to mortgagors claiming excessive charges have been imposed upon them. In determining this question, the nature and extent of disclosure of such charges and a comparison with charges for similar products on the market will be considered.

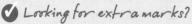 ✅ *Looking for extra marks?*

In 2009, proposals were put forward to extend FSA (now the FCA) regulation to second and buy-to-let mortgages. See *Mortgage Regulation: a consultation*, HM Treasury, December 2009.

Consumer Credit Act 2006

Mortgages regulated under the **Financial Services and Markets Act 2000** are excluded from regulation under this Act, so its application is limited to second and buy-to-let mortgages. The Act provides the court with powers to intervene in 'unfair relationships' between the individual debtor and creditor which, whilst not defined, can be determined by evidence of lack of equality and bad faith.

Undue influence

Evidence that the mortgage transaction was obtained under undue influence (or by any other equitable wrongdoing), may allow for the wronged party to have the transaction set aside.

Is there evidence of undue influence between the parties?

Class 1: actual undue influence

You are looking for actual evidence that a person entered into the mortgage, not out of his own free will, but rather through overt acts of improper pressure exerted upon him by another. Where present, the complainant can have the transaction set aside without having to establish anything further.

Class 2: presumed undue influence

Although traditionally divided into two categories, since the decision of *Royal Bank of Scotland v Etridge (No 2)* [2002], this essentially requires you to establish two things:

* that the relationship between the complainant and the alleged wrongdoer is one of trust and confidence, making it more likely that undue influence has been exerted; and

* that the transaction appears to be one that is disadvantageous to the complainant, to the extent that it requires explanation.

Where these two conditions are met, the presumption is not that undue influence exists, but that it will exist if the alleged wrongdoer cannot explain the nature of the transaction. It is for the alleged wrongdoer to prove that the complainant freely entered into the transaction and that no undue influence was applied.

The effect of finding undue influence

Where undue influence of either class is established, the complainant is entitled to have the transaction set aside against the wrongdoer. Usually, however, the wrongdoer is not the lender. The lender will still want to be able to enforce the mortgage. Has the existence of undue influence affected its right to do so?

The position of the lender

Mortgagee's remedies

✱✱✱✱✱✱✱✱✱✱

→ consider the changes made to the position given in *O'Brien*. It might therefore be useful for you to read the decision of Lord Browne-Wilkinson in that case.

In the key case of *Royal Bank of Scotland v Etridge (No 2)* [2002] it was recognized that a balance must be sought between maintaining the confidence of lenders that mortgages created over family homes will be enforceable and protecting potentially vulnerable parties from agreeing to mortgages out of pressure exerted upon them by another.

To assert the continuing validity of a mortgage between itself and the complainant, despite the existence of undue influence, the lender must establish that it took certain steps to make sure that the complainant received independent legal advice regarding the practical implications of the mortgage transaction, prior to agreeing to the mortgage.

When must the lender take such steps?

- Whenever a wife is standing surety for her husband's debts, either personal or business ie the family home is being mortgaged to provide security for the husband's debts or interests;

- in any non-commercial transaction where the purpose of the loan does not appear to be for the mutual benefit of the parties involved, for example elderly parents guaranteeing their child's debts.

What are the steps the lender should take?

Before the mortgage transaction goes ahead, the lender should:

- take reasonable steps to ensure risks involved in giving the guarantee have been fully explained to the potential complainant;

- ensure the potential complainant takes independent legal advice from a solicitor, in a face-to-face meeting, and in the absence of other parties.

A lender may assume that the solicitor has advised the potential complainant on his own behalf and that the advice given was sufficient and correct: *Bank of Baroda v Rayerel* [1995]. This is so even if the solicitor was also acting for the alleged wrongdoer (*Banco Exterior International v Mann* [1995]) or the lender itself (*Barclays Bank plc v Thomson* [1997]).

What is the effect of having taken these steps?

Once these steps have been taken and the lender has received written confirmation that the potential complainant has been advised appropriately, the mortgage transaction cannot be set aside against the lender.

Mortgagee's remedies

What can a mortgagee do if the mortgagor defaults on a legal mortgage?

Sue on the personal covenant

The mortgagee sues the mortgagor for any sums outstanding. Perhaps preferable in cases of **negative equity** where recovery of the property alone would not satisfy the debt.

Where the mortgage is equitable

As with a legal mortgage.

Possession

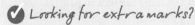 **Looking for extra marks?**

In November 2008, the Government introduced a pre-action protocol in respect of possession claims regarding residential properties, to encourage lenders to seek alternative action and use possession as a last resort.

Why?

To be able to subsequently sell the property with vacant possession. It may also be sought in cases of negative equity. The repossessed property can be let until such time as the market recovers, making a sale more attractive.

When?

Technically, any time after the mortgage has been created, even before any default by the mortgagor: *Four Maids Ltd v Dudley Marshall (Properties) Ltd* [1957]. Typically, such right is expressly or impliedly postponed until such time that a default occurs.

How?

A mortgagee can seek possession of a mortgaged property without a court order (*Ropaigealach v Barclays Bank plc* [1999]), although one may be advisable to avoid any criminal liability under the **Criminal Law Act 1977** (see chapter 6, 'Forfeiture').

Where a court order is sought and the mortgaged property consists of, or includes, a dwelling house, **s 36 Administration of Justice Act 1970**, amended by the **AJA 1973**, gives the court a discretionary power to:

- adjourn the proceedings; or
- suspend an order for possession.

Mortgagee's remedies

✱✱✱✱✱✱✱✱✱✱✱

This power may be exercised where it appears likely that within a 'reasonable period' the mortgagor will be able to pay 'any sums due under the mortgage' or remedy any other breach.

1. What is a 'reasonable period'?

The starting point should be the remaining term of the mortgage: *Cheltenham & Gloucester BS v Norgan* [1996].

2. What are 'any sums due under the mortgage'?

The mortgagor must convince the court that not only can he make a reasonable attempt to pay off the arrears accumulating within a reasonable period, but that he can also meet future payments. Where this is unlikely, a court will not exercise discretion in his favour: *First National Bank v Syed* [1991].

3. What will influence a court in deciding whether to exercise its discretion?

- The mortgagor's current financial position (not speculative windfalls). The mortgagor should provide a detailed financial plan as to how the sums due will be paid (*National & Provincial Building Society v Lloyd* [1996]).

- A more than fanciful prospect of sale of the property by the mortgagor (*Target Home Loans Ltd v Clothier* [1994]), which will enable sums due to be paid.

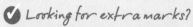

✅ *Looking for extra marks?*

In *Cheltenham & Gloucester plc v Krauz* [1997], the mortgagee had obtained a possession order but had not executed it. The Court of Appeal declined to allow the mortgagor to remain in possession to sell the property himself at a price that would not have cleared the debt, despite that price being better than the one achievable by the mortgagee selling with vacant possession.

Consequences

Having taken possession, the mortgagee can use any income arising from the property in lieu of interest payments due to him under the mortgage. Any surplus may be used to pay off the capital or passed to the next person entitled.

Mortgagee duties when possessing

- Where the mortgagee possesses the property himself, he must pay a fair rent and do reasonable repairs.

- Where receiving an income for the property, the mortgagee must account for that income on the footing of *wilful default* ie account for not only what he receives but also for what he could have received by acting reasonably: *White v City of London Brewery Co* (1889).

Where the mortgage is equitable

The mortgagee may have the right to take possession where he has obtained a court order: *Barclays Bank Ltd v Bird* [1954]. Otherwise, his right is debateable, although few mortgagees risk taking possession without a court order nowadays.

Sale

Why?

To release capital that can be used to pay off the outstanding debt.

When?

The flowchart in Figure 14.1 illustrates when to sell.

Figure 14.1 When to sell.

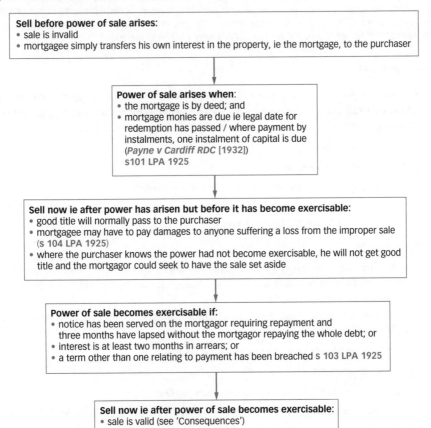

Sell before power of sale arises:
- sale is invalid
- mortgagee simply transfers his own interest in the property, ie the mortgage, to the purchaser

Power of sale arises when:
- the mortgage is by deed; and
- mortgage monies are due ie legal date for redemption has passed / where payment by instalments, one instalment of capital is due (*Payne v Cardiff RDC* [1932]) s101 LPA 1925

Sell now ie after power has arisen but before it has become exercisable:
- good title will normally pass to the purchaser
- mortgagee may have to pay damages to anyone suffering a loss from the improper sale (s 104 LPA 1925)
- where the purchaser knows the power had not become exercisable, he will not get good title and the mortgagor could seek to have the sale set aside

Power of sale becomes exercisable if:
- notice has been served on the mortgagor requiring repayment and three months have lapsed without the mortgagor repaying the whole debt; or
- interest is at least two months in arrears; or
- a term other than one relating to payment has been breached s 103 LPA 1925

Sell now ie after power of sale becomes exercisable:
- sale is valid (see 'Consequences')

Mortgagee's remedies

✱✱✱✱✱✱✱✱✱✱

How?

In theory, the property can be sold without first obtaining a court order (although, in practice, this is exceptional in the case of residential property) and by any method, although expert advice should be sought regarding the method of sale, marketing of the property, and the setting of any reserve prices: *Tse Kwong Lam v Wong Chit Sen* [1983]

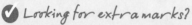 **✓ Looking for extra marks?**

Once a mortgagee has acquired the statutory authority to proceed with a sale (under **ss 101** and **103 LPA 1925**), he may do so without further court sanction. This has been deemed to neither violate **Art 1 of Protocol 1 of the ECHR**, the right to peaceful enjoyment of possessions, (see *Horsham Properties Group Ltd v Clark* [2009]), nor **Art 8 ECHR**, the right to respect for private and family life (*Harrow LBC v Qazi* (2004)). However, recent developments suggest debtors must be allowed the opportunity to contest sales before an independent tribunal on the basis of personal circumstances and the alleged disproportionality of their eviction from home (see, for example, *Manchester CC v Pinnock* (2010)). Note also that the Government put forward proposals (2010) preventing mortgagees of residential owner-occupied properties from exercising their power of sale over such homes without either first obtaining a court order or obtaining the borrower's consent. See *Mortgages: Power of Sale and Residential Property*, consultation paper.

Who can buy?

- The mortgagee cannot buy the property himself or through an agent: *Martinson v Clowes* (1882), unless he is under a direction from the court: *Palk v Mortgage Services Funding* [1993]. Any attempt to do so will result in the sale being set aside.

- The mortgagee can sell to:
  - an associated person; or
  - a company in which he holds a substantial shareholding

    but the burden of proving the transaction was in good faith and without fraud would fall on him: *Tse Kwong Lam v Wong Chit Sen* [1983].

Consequences

The sale transfers the mortgagor's estate to the purchaser free from the mortgagor's equity of redemption and any subsequent mortgages, although it may be subject to any prior mortgages that exist.

The mortgagee is trustee of the proceeds of sale and must distribute them in the order laid down in **s 105 LPA 1925**:

- to discharge total debt owed to any prior mortgagee;
- to discharge any costs of sale;
- to discharge total debt owed to the mortgagee selling;
- any balance remaining, to be paid to any mortgagee next in priority and, if none, the mortgagor.

Where the sale produces insufficient funds to pay off the debt, the mortgagee could then sue on the personal covenant for the remainder.

Duty of the mortgagee when selling

No statutory duties are imposed upon the mortgagee when exercising power of sale.

Duties have arisen through case law and those that exist are owed solely to the mortgagor and not, for example, to a beneficiary where the mortgaged property is held under a trust: *Parker-Tweedale v Dunbar Bank plc* [1991].

- The mortgagee can sell the property whenever he wishes, subject to meeting the statutory requirements discussed earlier. However, when he decides to sell, he must obtain a fair and true market value for the property: *Cuckmere Brick Co Ltd v Mutual Finance Ltd* [1971]. Failure to do so may lead to the mortgagee having to pay the difference or, worse still, the sale being set aside.
- In seeking to obtain a fair and true market value for the property, the mortgagee is not required to incur expense in securing a better price, for example by pursuing planning applications: *Silven Properties Ltd v Royal Bank of Scotland plc* [2004].
- The mortgagee can seek the mortgagor's consent to sell at less than current market value. Where given, the mortgagor would then be estopped from claiming the mortgagee failed to meet his duty, assuming the mortgagor had not been subjected to any undue influence: *Mercantile Credit Co v Clarke* (1996).

Section 91(2) LPA 1925

This gives a court a wide power to order a sale at the instance of any 'person interested'. It is sometimes requested by the mortgagor where the mortgagee refuses to sell.

....

Palk v Mortgage Services Funding plc [1993] Ch 330

The mortgagee wished to lease the mortgaged property, despite the fact that rent acquired would cover no more than a third of the mortgage interest payments. Realizing that the effect of this would be to increase their debt, the mortgagors requested a sale which was granted by the Court of Appeal.

....

Where the mortgage is equitable

Without any deed, power of sale is not possible under s 101 LPA 1925. However, the mortgagee could apply to the court for an order for sale under s 91 LPA 1925.

Appointing a receiver

Why?

Typically appointed where the mortgaged property is generating an income which the mortgagee wishes to intercept to help pay off the debt. It is preferable to the mortgagee taking possession himself, since the duties imposed upon the mortgagee in appointing a receiver are less onerous.

When?

The flowchart in Figure 14.2 illustrates when to appoint a receiver.

Figure 14.2 When to appoint a receiver

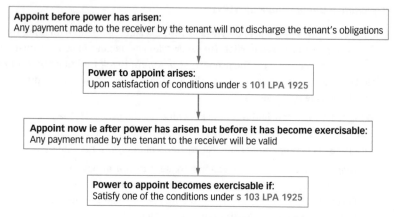

Appoint before power has arisen:
Any payment made to the receiver by the tenant will not discharge the tenant's obligations

Power to appoint arises:
Upon satisfaction of conditions under s 101 LPA 1925

Appoint now ie after power has arisen but before it has become exercisable:
Any payment made by the tenant to the receiver will be valid

Power to appoint becomes exercisable if:
Satisfy one of the conditions under s 103 LPA 1925

How?

The appointment must be in writing.

Who?

The mortgagee may choose whosoever he wishes. The receiver need not be a professional.

Consequences

The primary function of the receiver is to collect income from the mortgaged property (eg rents) and apply that money in accordance with s 109 LPA 1925, essentially paying outgoings on the land including mortgage interest and capital.

Duty of the receiver

The receiver is deemed to be the agent of the mortgagor (although not in the true sense) and, in managing the property, the duty he owes the mortgagor goes beyond acting in good faith. Rather he must manage the property with due diligence subject to trying to achieve a position where the interest payments on the mortgage can be met and the principal sum repaid: *Medforth v Blake* [2000].

Where the mortgage is equitable

Without a deed, the power to appoint does not arise under s 101 LPA 1925. However, the mortgagee could apply to the court under s 37 Supreme Court Act 1981 to request an appointment.

Foreclosure

Rarely sought, this vests the property in the mortgagee free from any rights of the mortgagor; the latter's equity of redemption is extinguished. It has similar application in respect of both legal and equitable mortgages.

Priorities

When a property subject to several mortgages is sold, the proceeds of sale will not be shared amongst the mortgagees equally. Rather, the mortgagees will be paid on the basis of who has priority. The rules to determine this will differ depending upon whether the land is registered or not.

Unregistered land

- Where the mortgagee has the title deeds, he will take priority over all other lenders.
- Where the mortgagee does not have the title deeds, and the mortgage is legal, it should be registered as a *puisne* mortgage; a Class C(i) land charge. Where it is equitable, it should be registered as a general equitable charge; a Class C(iii) land charge. Where no such registration has occurred by the time a subsequent mortgage is created, the subsequent mortgage will take priority over the former. Failure to register the mortgage makes it void against subsequent mortgagees: **s 4 Land Charges Act 1972.**

Registered land

- To create a legal mortgage over registered land, it must be registered: **s 27 LRA 2002.** It will be entered on the charges register of the land over which it exists, with the date of entry being noted on the register. Priority will then be governed by the order in which the mortgages were entered on the register: **s 48 LRA 2002.**
- Where the mortgage is not registered, it will be equitable only. Priority will then be governed by the chronological date of creation, with those created earlier taking priority over those created later. However, once registered, the mortgage will take priority over those still to be registered, but will rank below any charge already entered on the register.

Key cases

Case	Facts	Principle
Cheltenham & Gloucester BS v Norgan [1996] 1 WLR 343	Mrs Norgan had a history of difficulty in paying her mortgage repayments and orders for possession had been made, although postponed. A possession order was finally granted without postponement and Mrs Norgan appealed. Her case was remitted back to the first instance court to determine whether she had the means to pay off the debt and arrears within 13 years, the remaining term of the mortgage.	In assessing what would be a reasonable period to postpone a possession order to allow arrears to be paid, the starting point should be the agreed duration of the mortgage term.
Cityland & Property (Holdings) Ltd v Dabrah [1968] Ch 166	Concerned the sale of a freehold by a landlord to his tenant, with a loan for the purchase being provided by the landlord. The loan repayments amounted to a 57% premium on top of the actual sum advanced for the loan. This was held void.	Clauses in a mortgage that have been obtained unconscionably will be struck out as void.
Fairclough v Swan Brewery Co Ltd [1912] AC 565	A clause in a mortgage over a 20-year leasehold estate postponed redemption until the final six weeks of the lease. Held void.	A clause postponing the ability to redeem must not have the effect of rendering the right illusory.
Jones v Morgan [2001] EWCA Civ 995	A mortgage was created and three years later the parties entered into a second agreement giving the mortgagee the right to purchase some of the mortgaged property. The right was deemed invalid. The second agreement was seen as a reconstruction of the initial mortgage entered into three years previously. The mortgage and the option to purchase were therefore not truly independent transactions.	Where a right to purchase some or all of the mortgaged property can be seen as part of the mortgage transaction, that right will be held void.
Knightsbridge Estates Trust Ltd v Byrne [1939] Ch 441	A clause in a mortgage over freehold property postponed the ability to redeem for 40 years. The clause was held valid.	As per *Fairclough*.

Case	Facts	Principle
Kreglinger v New Patagonia Meat & Cold Storage Co Ltd [1914] AC 25	The mortgage contained a right of first refusal for the benefit of the mortgagee to buy sheepskins produced by the mortgagor at a best price for a period of five years. The loan was repaid after three years but the court upheld the continued exercise of the right of first refusal beyond the mortgage term.	Parties to a mortgage can agree for the mortgage to contain a collateral advantage which is to last beyond the duration of the mortgage itself, provided they have acted freely and the clause itself is reasonable.
Multiservice Bookbinding Co Ltd v Marden [1979] Ch 84	Linking the interest rate to the Swiss franc, leading to large interest payments when currency values fluctuated, was upheld as valid. Equality of bargaining power existed, and since the lender was a private individual anxious to preserve the capital value of his investment, in the circumstances, the hard bargain was a fair one.	A clause will not be struck out of a mortgage agreement for being unreasonable. It must have been imposed in a morally reprehensible way.
Noakes & Co Ltd v Rice [1902] AC 24	Mortgage created over a public house contained a clause tying the mortgagor into selling the mortgagee's liquor for the entire duration of the lease, not just for the duration of the mortgage. The clause was held void.	Upon redemption, the mortgagor should get back his property in virtually the same state as when the mortgage was created, unencumbered by any collateral advantages in favour of the mortgagee.
Palk v Mortgage Services Funding plc [1993] Ch 330	The mortgagee wished to lease the mortgaged property, despite the fact that rent acquired would cover no more than a third of the mortgage interest payments. Realizing that the effect of this would be to increase their debt, the mortgagors requested a sale which was granted by the Court of Appeal.	Under s 91 LPA 1925 the court has a jurisdiction to sell mortgaged property independent of the mortgagee's right to do so.
Reeve v Lisle [1902] AC 461	A mortgage of a ship was created and 12 days later the mortgagee was granted an option to purchase the ship. The option was held valid.	An option created independently of mortgage transaction, even where the option relates to purchasing the mortgaged property, can be upheld as valid.

Exam questions

✷✷✷✷✷✷✷✷✷✷✷

Case	Facts	Principle
Royal Bank of Scotland v Etridge (No 2) [2002] 2 AC 773	Eight conjoined appeals by wives seeking to have mortgages held void as against them on the basis they were obtained by undue influence. In each case, the mortgages appeared to be for the principal benefit of the husbands.	Established key steps a lender must take to avoid being affected by undue influence asserted over the borrower.
Samuel v Jarrah Timber and Wood Paving Corporation Ltd [1904] AC 323	A mortgage of stock gave the mortgagee an option to buy the stock within 12 months of the date of the mortgage. The option was held void.	A mortgage should not include clauses which prevent a mortgagor from ever being able to repay the loan and get his property back.

 Exam questions

Problem question

In January 2012, Karl purchased two pubs. The first pub, the Fox and Hounds, is a freehold property and in order to raise cash to purchase it, Karl mortgaged the premises to Erinsborough Bank plc. The mortgage is a repayment mortgage over a period of 20 years and contains a clause stipulating that the mortgage cannot be redeemed before 1 January 2027. Since Erinsborough Bank plc was uncertain about the commercial viability of the business, it insisted upon an interest rate 10% above current market values. In a separate agreement, completed the day after the mortgage agreement, Karl entered into an option to purchase in favour of Erinsborough Bank plc that stipulated 'the mortgagee reserves for itself the right to purchase the property up to the date of redemption of the mortgage at a price that is equivalent to its then current market value assuming vacant possession at a discount of 4%'.

The second pub that Karl purchased, The White Hart, was a leasehold property. He purchased a 21-year lease from the vendor, King Brewery Ltd. To help raise finance for this purchase, he mortgaged the property to King Brewery Ltd. The mortgage agreement stipulates the earliest date for redemption as 1 January 2029. As part of the agreement, King Brewery Ltd insisted upon the inclusion of a clause that Karl only purchase and retail beer and ale products from the mortgagee for the duration of the lease term.

The pub trade has recently been in decline and Karl now founds himself in three months arrears with his mortgage payments to King Brewery Ltd. King Brewery have recently written to Karl stating that it wishes to seek possession of the property so that it may lease it to another tenant. Karl is unhappy about this; not only has he been living above The White Hart but he is also due to receive a substantial cash inheritance from his Aunt who has just died.

Advise Karl:

1. as to the legality or otherwise of the clauses contained in both mortgage agreements; and

2. as to the likelihood of King Brewery Ltd securing a possession order in respect of The White Hart pub.

See the Outline Answers section in the end matter for help with this question.

Essay question

To what extent does the law strike a fair balance between the interests of the mortgagor and those of the mortgagee in respect of:

1. ascertaining the validity of clauses within a mortgage; and

2. enforcing the mortgagee's remedies of possession and sale?

 *Online Resource Centre*

To see an outline answer to this question log onto www.oxfordtextbooks.co.uk/orc/concentrate/

Outline answers

Chapter 1

Problem answer

1. Determine whether the items are fixtures, and therefore should be returned to Tim (fixtures should convey to the purchaser upon a sale: s 62 LPA 1925), or chattels and therefore have been validly removed.

• Explain the two key tests: degree of annexation and purpose of annexation: *Holland v Hodgson* (1872); *Hamp v Bygrave* (1983).

• Apply the tests to the items and assess their status using case law to support arguments.

• Key cases include *Elitestone Ltd v Morris* [1997]; *Leigh v Taylor* [1902]; *D'Eyncourt v Gregory* (1866); *Botham v TSB Bank plc* [1997].

• Arguments may include looking at whether the items rested on their own weight; if attached, what was the purpose of that attachment; whether any evidence can be produced that the items enhanced the overall architectural design of the property; how much damage, if any, has been caused to the property by the removal of the items etc.

2. Since the true owner of the necklace cannot be found, to determine who can keep it:

• Assess whether it is treasure trove and thus belongs to the Crown. Apply rules in Treasure Act 1996 and Treasure (Designation) Order 2002.

• If not treasure determine whether the object was found embedded in the ground or lying on the surface. Here, under a bush which the postman could see suggests lying on the surface of the ground. Apply rule in *Parker v British Airways Board* [1982].

3. Does this amount to a trespass of Tim's lower airspace?

• Determine what amounts to the lower airspace: *Anchor Brewhouse Developments v Berkley House (Docklands Developments) Ltd* (1987).

• Assess whether overhanging branches invade this space: *Lemon v Webb* (1895).

• If yes, identify whether Tim can keep the branches to make a basket.

Chapter 3

Problem answer

1. Auntie Vera

She has a beneficial interest under a trust.

• Consider whether a restriction has been entered on the proprietorship register (s 40 LRA 2002) which will lead to overreaching (ss 2 and 27 LPA 1925; *City of London Building Society v Flegg* [1988]) and purchaser taking free from the interest.

• If not entered and purchaser deals with one trustee only, as may be the case here, beneficial interest will bind as an overriding interest if conditions under Sch 3 para 2 are met. Key consideration here will be whether Auntie Vera can establish that she is in actual occupation of the land.

2. Malcolm

Appears to have a lease created by deed as required for one over 3 years in duration (s 52 LPA 1925; s 1 LP(MP)A 1989). Consider whether additional formality of registration has been complied with (s 27 LRA 2002):

• if yes, legal lease and notice would have been entered on register to make it binding upon all (s 38 LRA 2002);

• if no, lease could only be equitable

– Would bind all if entered as a notice on charges register (s 32 LRA 2002; s 29(2) LRA 2002).

– If not entered, would not bind purchaser for valuable consideration (s 29(1) LRA 2002) unless binding as an overriding interest under Sch 3 para 2. So would bind Rory as inherited the property but possible enforcement against Natural Farming Ltd would require assessing whether conditions under Sch 3 para 2 are met.

3. Peter

Appears to have an easement of access. Although made by deed it is not equivalent in duration to a legal estate (s 1(2) LPA 1925) and

Outline answers
✳✳✳✳✳✳✳✳✳✳

therefore could only be equitable. Consider if entered as a notice on charges register:

- if yes, binds all (s 29(2) LRA 2002);
- if no, will not bind a purchaser for valuable consideration (s 29(1) and s 132 LRA 2002) unless established as overriding interest under Sch 3 para 2. So would bind Rory as inherited the property but enforcement against Natural Farming Ltd would depend upon whether conditions under Sch 3 para 2 are met.

4. Larry

Appears mere licence as lacks requirements/formalities of lease/easement. Revocable at will.

Chapter 4

Problem answer

Marian

Potential beneficial interest under a trust by virtue of her contribution to the purchase. Identify this as an equitable interest (s 1(3) LPA 1925) incapable of registration as a land charge (s 2(4) LCA 1972), but capable of being overreached. Explain requirements of overreaching under ss 2 and 27 LPA 1925; apply to the facts. Appears not overreached as only one trustee, Guy (*Williams & Glyn's Bank Ltd v Boland* [1981]). Enforcement against Josh thus depends upon the doctrine of notice. Explain and apply. Here the surveyor is likely to have acquired constructive notice of her rights and thus Josh acquired imputed notice: Josh would be bound. Key cases include *Hunt v Luck* [1901]; *Kingsnorth Trust Ltd v Tizard* [1986]. If a giftee, Josh is not a purchaser for value under the doctrine thus bound by the right.

- Potential statutory right to occupy the matrimonial home under Family Law Act 1996, enforceable against Josh if registered as a Class F land charge (s 198 LPA 1925). No information therefore explain whether Josh would be bound if not registered (s 4(5) and 4(8) LCA 1972). If a giftee, Josh would be bound as not a purchaser (s 17 LCA 1972).

Susie

Identify potential easement of access. Consider whether legal or equitable by looking at s 52 LPA 1925, s 1 LP(MP)A 1989. Sold by deed so probably legal. Legal rights bind whole world. No difference if Josh had been a giftee.

Pete

Potential lease. Identify whether legal: s 52 LPA 1925; s 1 LP(MP)A 1989. Whilst signed by grantor other deed requirements not apparent. Assess whether equitable instead: s 2 LP(MP) A 1989; *Walsh v Lonsdale* (1882). Explain enforcement of equitable lease against Josh depends upon whether registered as a Class C(iv) land charge. Discuss s 198 LPA 1925 and s 4(6) LCA 1972; *Midland Bank Trust Co Ltd v Green* [1981]. Explain operation of s 4(6) LCA 1972 means that it would bind Josh if a mere giftee as not a purchaser for money/money's worth.

Chapter 6

Problem answer

Identify the issue: are Raj and Sally tenants or licensees? Explain the significance of the distinction.

Distinguish a lease from a licence. Explain the essential characteristics of a lease. Explain substance not form is important. Key authorities include *Street v Mountford* [1985]; s 205 LPA 1925; *Ashburn Anstalt v Arnold* [1989]. Here, fact called 'licence' agreements is not conclusive.

Assess whether there is certainty of term. Key authorities include *Lace v Chantler* [1944]; *Prudential Assurance v London Residuary Body* [1992]; *Mexfield Housing Co-operative Ltd v Berrisford* [2011].

Assess whether there is exclusive possession. Key points to consider include:

- Landlord reserves right to introduce one other to share. Is this realistic? Look to the number of people that could be introduced to share with Raj and Sally and nature of the accommodation when making this assessment. Look to the relationship between Raj and Sally. Is it feasible others share with them? Has this clause ever been acted upon? Key authorities include *Antoniades v Villiers* [1990]; *AG Securities v Vaughan* [1990]; *Aslan v Murphy* [1990].

- Retention of keys and provision of laundry services. In assessing whether this is real and precludes exclusive possession consider the purpose for which the keys were retained and whether such purpose was ever acted upon. Key authorities include *Aslan v Murphy* [1990]; *Facchini v Bryson* [1952]; *Marchant v Charters* [1977].

Assess whether, if tenants, they occupy as individual or joint tenants. Do they have the four unities to be joint tenants? Key points to consider include the fact they have individual bedrooms, signed separate agreements, and pay £200 each. Key authorities include *AG Securities v Vaughan* [1990]; *Antoniades v Villiers* [1990]; *Mikeover Ltd v Brady* [1989].

Draw appropriate conclusions.

Assess difference if points to consider include:

- whether it is more realistic to introduce others to share if strangers and applied separately;
- whether no unity of title exists if signed on different days.

Chapter 7

Problem answer

This question concerns issues regarding covenants in leases.

First establish whether Patrick is bound by the covenants originally entered into by Miriam. As a new lease, governed by the Landlord and Tenant (Covenants) Act 1995, the burden of the covenants probably passed to Patrick upon assignment of the lease under s 3. (If granted originally in 1994, whether the burden of covenants passed to Patrick upon assignment would depend upon satisfaction of the requirements from *Spencer's Case* (1583).)

Assess whether Patrick is liable for the disrepair. Explain how an express tenant covenant to repair can be overridden by an implied landlord obligation to repair under LTA 1985. As a lease of six years, the LTA 1985 applies. (Had the lease been for 30 years, it would not and liability would fall to Patrick under his express covenant assuming the disrepair falls within the ambit of the covenant. Case law discussion of the boundaries of such express covenants should be analysed including *Lister v Lane* [1893]; *Ravenseft*

Properties Ltd v Davstone (Holdings) Ltd [1980]; *Pembury v Lamdin* [1940]; *Post Office v Aquarius Property Ltd* [1987].)

Assess whether the disrepair in question falls into the LTA 1985. Key authorities include s 11(1) and (2)(a) LTA 1985; *Quick v Taff-Ely BC* [1986]; *Re Irvine's Estate v Moran* (1992); *O'Brien v Robinson* [1973]. Constance may be liable to repair the window but possibly not the damp as Patrick didn't take steps to mitigate his loss.

Identify remedies available for breach of a repair covenant, including forfeiture and damages. (Remember that if a 30-year lease, the Leasehold Property (Repairs) Act 1938 would apply.)

Finally assess whether Constance can withhold consent to the sub-letting to George. Explain s 19(1)(a) LTA 1927 and utilize case law to determine whether she has any grounds upon which consent could be refused. In particular consider *International Drilling Fluids Ltd v Louisville Investments (Uxbridge) Ltd* [1986]; *Ashworth Frazer Ltd v Gloucester CC* [2001].

Chapter 8

Problem answer

Is there adverse possession: *Pye (JA) (Oxford) Ltd v Graham* [2003].

- Is Fred dispossessed of the wooded area? He seems to be given that there is no presence on the property. But not using the property is clearly not enough. It is more arguable that he is dispossessed of the wooded area given that George and Hilly seem to be here on a permanent basis. Remember, Fred need not know of their presence to be dispossessed but they do need to be discoverable.

- Do George and Hilly have factual possession? The test is one which involves a sufficient degree of control (*Powell v McFarlane* (1977)). There are different points when George and Hilly might have factual possession. The tent may be too impermanent, but it could be argued that they are on the land the whole time and the nature of the structure is not relevant. It is certainly not trivial. Fitting the padlock is similar to *Buckinghamshire CC v Moran* [1990] and seems to suggest factual possession.

- Intention to possess. George and Hilly need an intention to possess they do not need to intend to own it. The intention needs to be for the time being not forever: *Buckinghamshire CC v Moran* [1990].

- The possession must be adverse/unauthorized.

You may also mention Sch 1 para 8(4) LA 1980.

Identify registered land and the potential claim is post 2003, so LRA 2002 applies.

Consider the point that Ian and John have only resided since 2002. There must be ten years adverse possession before applying to be registered as proprietor: Sch 6 para 1(1) LRA 2002. However, consider the possibility of establishing continuous adverse possession albeit through different people (George and Hilly) from 1999 (arguably) and certainly from 2000. It is not relevant that the registered proprietor differs at the time adverse possession begins.

Examine procedure under LRA 2002, noting specifically an inability to be registered as proprietor unless one of the exceptions in Sch 6 applies. Explain how, upon notification by the Land Registry, Town and Country Hotels Ltd need to take steps to evict Ian and John within two years and the consequences under Sch 6 if they fail.

Chapter 9
. . . .

Problem answer

The purpose of this question is for you to think about the nature of landholding, TLATA 1996, and overreaching.

Perhaps begin by explaining that Alan holds the property on trust for himself and Bill and Claire as beneficiaries. They are all tenants in common in equity. Alan is the sole trustee under a trust of land.

The starting point is that Alan, as a trustee, has the powers of absolute owner: s 6(1) TLATA 1996.

1. The relevant provision is s 11 TLATA 1996. Apply the wording of this section to the facts, drawing attention to the fact that Bill and Claire are of full age and beneficially entitled to an interest in possession. Alan need only act according to their wishes in so far as it is consistent with the general interest of the trusts. There is a dispute between the parties but Alan seems to be in the majority according

to the value of his interests. There is no provision excluding the right to be consulted: s 11(2) TLATA 1996.

2. The general position is that Bill and Claire have a right to occupy under s 12 TLATA 1996 but the conditions in s 12(1) and (2) must be met.

3. There is no express provision as to consent but Bill and Claire, as persons with an interest in the property, could make an application under s 14 TLATA 1996 given that Alan's power of sale is one of the trustee's functions. They would then need to consider the matters relevant in s 15 TLATA 1996.

4. The question here is whether there is overreaching (ss 2 and 27 LPA 1925). The land is registered but it is unclear if any attempt has been made to protect the beneficial interests, for example as a restriction (s 40 LRA 2002). In any event there is only payment to one trustee and so overreaching cannot occur (*Williams & Glyn's Bank Ltd v Boland* [1981]). The normal rules then apply and in essence Bill and Claire would need to rely on Sch 3 para 2 overriding interests.

Chapter 10
. . . .

Problem answer

Initial purchase

- Identify property held by way of a trust of land and explain how legal and equitable title respectively is held.

- Key authorities regarding legal title include s 1(6) LPA 1925; s 34(2) TA 1925. Remember, Bobby could not hold legal title at this time as only 17 years old.

- Key authorities regarding equitable title include: *AG Securities v Vaughan* [1990]; *Lake v Craddock* (1732); *Bull v Bull* [1955]; *Pink v Lawrence* (1977). Remember, where four unities are present to allow a joint tenancy, an express declaration to this effect will trump presumptions of a tenancy in common based upon business/unequal contributions.

Carl mortgages his share

- Consider possible severance under act operating on your own share, specifically partial alienation.

- Key authorities include *Williams v Hensman* (1861); *First National Securities v Hegarty* [1985]; s 36(2) LPA 1925; *Goodman v Gallant* [1986].
- Here, severance probably effective. Carl remains joint tenant at law but tenant in common as to ¼ in equity. In equity, others remain joint tenants between themselves.

Bobby offers to sell his interest

- Consider possible severance under mutual agreement.
- Key authorities include *Williams v Hensman* (1861); *Burgess v Rawnsley* [1975]; *Hunter v Babbage* [1994]; *Nielson-Jones v Fedden* [1975]; *Gore and Snell v Carpenter* (1990); *Davis v Smith* [2011].
- Here, probably effective based upon all now seeing Bobby as having a distinct share in the property. Lack of agreement regarding price may not be an obstacle. Bobby becomes tenant in common as to ¼ in equity.

Bobby dies

- If effectively severed, Bobby died as tenant in common, so follow instructions in the will.
- Remember, a person (here David) may be both a joint tenant and a tenant in common in equity at the same time.

Alex's letter

- Consider possible severance by notice in writing.
- Key authorities include s 36(2) LPA 1925; *Re Draper's Conveyance* [1969]; *Kinch v Bullard* [1999].
- Remember all intended recipients need not see the notice for it to be effective if it has been effectively delivered.

Alex's desire to sell

- Discuss application under s 14 TLATA 1996 and the s 15 TLATA 1996 criteria.
- Continuing purpose and interests of creditors may be significant.

Chapter 11

Problem answer—licences

This question requires you to think about the consequences of licences and third parties.

Brian

It is suggested that you focus upon considering whether this is a licence coupled with an interest. Explain the circumstance in which such licences arise. Has Brian been granted an 'interest'? What is an interest for the purpose of this licence? Consider key authorities such as *Hurst v Picture Theatres Ltd* [1915] and *Hounslow LBC v Twickenham Garden Developments Ltd* [1971]. It seems this may be unlikely—there appears to be more of an informal arrangement between himself and Albert rather than having been granted a proprietary interest by Albert. A *profit à prendre*, for example, would need to be created by a deed or prescription.

If it is a licence coupled with an interest then it should bind Eric as long as the interest to which it is attached continues.

If not a licence coupled with an interest then it should be considered whether it could be an implied contractual licence with the sculpture acting as consideration. Generally, such licences do not bind third parties (*Ashburn Anstalt v Arnold* [1989]) and since Eric does not know of Brian's existence, it is difficult to see how a constructive trust could arise to make Eric bound by the licence.

Colin

This looks like a bare licence which would not be binding on Eric.

David

This looks like a contractual licence. (You might also consider whether it could be a lease or an easement.) Discuss the issue of whether a contractual licence binds a third party. The starting point would be that they do not automatically bind a third party (*Ashburn Anstalt v Arnold* [1989]) but that they might if there is a constructive trust (*Binions v Evans* [1972]). It would seem, for example, that a mere notice of a contractual licence is not in itself enough; there must be something else to attach to the purchaser's conscience (*Ashburn Anstalt v Arnold* [1989]).

Problem answer—proprietary estoppel

Although Joan never formally acquired an interest in Groom House, can she claim

Outline answers
✳✳✳✳✳✳✳✳✳✳✳✳

to have an equity arising by virtue of proprietary estoppel which may be enforceable against Mervyn, the purchaser of Groom House?

(Note, it would not be incorrect to also consider potential beneficial interest arising under a constructive trust/possible contractual licence; the latter dependent upon establishing a valid contract with provision of some form of consideration.)

Consider whether the facts show satisfaction of the requirements for establishing an estoppel has arisen:

- Sufficient assurance in Bob promising Joan she can live there as long as she likes?
- Sufficient reliance in Joan selling her home and spending money on Groom House? Is there a sufficient causal link or would Joan have done this anyway?
- Detriment incurred?—giving up own home and spending money. How much money does Joan have? Is any detriment outweighed by having lived rent free at Groom House for ten years?
- Unconscionable? Remember not enough if just disappoint Joan's expectations. Look at it in the round. Would arguments be strengthened, for example, if Joan was infirm/old?

Where an equity may have arisen by estoppel, give consideration to the remedy a court may impose and how this decision is made.

Would any inchoate equity Joan has be binding upon Mervyn? Registered land so give consideration to s 116 LRA 2002. Consider the possibility of an overriding interest under Sch 3 para 2. In actual occupation. Was it obvious upon reasonable inspection if not known to Mervyn? Saw her clothes and made enquiries. Bob failed to disclose but as not the actual holder of the interest, will this failure to disclose affect Joan's ability to rely upon Sch 3 para 2?

Chapter 12

Problem answer

Introduction

- Identify issue: does Shirley have a right to use the internal stairs, the parking space for a flower stall and to put a sign on the house? Did she acquire these rights as easements from Danielle? If so, could they now be enforced against Roger?

Main body

- Consider whether rights sought are capable of being easements.
- Identify the requirements under *Re Ellenborough Park* [1956] and assess whether the rights being sought satisfy these requirements. Further, consider whether anything else prevents the rights from being capable of being easements.
- Particular points to discuss here would include whether the placing of an advert on the side of the house actually accommodates the dominant land or rather just the business of the dominant landowner (analyse and apply *Hill v Tupper* (1863) and *Moody v Steggles* (1879), on the facts, it may be the latter); whether the right to use the parking space amounts to exclusive possession (analyse and apply *Copeland v Greenhalf* [1952]; *Hair v Gillman* (2000); *Batchelor v Marlow* [2003]; *Moncrieff v Jamieson* [2007]).

Upon determining those rights claimed that have capability to be easements (possibly all except right to place sign on house), assess whether they have been appropriately acquired:

- Regarding the right to use internal stairs: identify no formal express grant of the right in the lease. Granted a licence which may have elevated into an easement upon lease renewal. Explain and apply acquisition by s 62 LPA 1925.
- Regarding the right to use the parking space: identify formally granted in both leases. However, issue of that right was presumably to park a car, not place a flower stall. How strictly will courts interpret expressly granted easements?

If acquired by Shirley from Danielle, could she now enforce the easements against Roger? Determine the status of the easements ie legal or equitable, and apply appropriate enforcement rules for such easements in registered land.

Conclude

Chapter 13

Problem answer

Introduction

- Identify the issue: can Gillian enforce the covenants breached by Eric against him?
- Identify the original covenantor and covenantee/the dominant and servient land.
- Identify that as successors to the land, enforcement against Eric by Gillian will only be possible if the burden and benefit of the covenants have passed to them respectively.

Has the burden of the covenants passed to Eric?

- Consider common law position that generally burden will not pass: *Austerberry v Corporation of Oldham* (1885).
- Will equity pass the burden to Eric? Identify, explain, and apply the *Tulk v Moxhay* (1848) requirements.
- Particular discussion points here include the fact that only covenant a) is negative (*Haywood v Brunswick Permanent Benefit BS* (1881)); whilst you do not know whether the covenants were appropriately entered on the register to give notice to Eric, as the land was gifted to him he would be deemed to have notice anyway (s 29 LRA 2002).

Has the benefit of covenant a) passed to Gillian in equity?

- Appropriate method to explain and apply on the facts is probably statutory annexation (s 78 LPA 1925; *Federated Homes Ltd v Mill Lodge Properties Ltd* [1980]). Consider whether successful annexation is problematic where the dominant land is a large estate (*Re Ballards Conveyance* [1937]; Brightman LJ in *Federated Homes Ltd*).

What about enforcement of the positive covenants b) and c)?

- Explain ability to enforce against original covenantor: s 79 LPA 1925. Note that John was seriously ill and therefore may be difficult to pursue him/his estate.
- No evidence of indemnity covenant between John and Eric that might exert pressure upon Eric to stop the breaches.

- Explain possibility of using the rule in *Halsall v Brizell* [1957] as regards enforcing covenant b). Identify requirements and apply.
- Remember to show benefit of these covenants passing to Gillian using common law methods; here likely to be implied if satisfy requirements under *P&A Swift Investments v Combined English Stores Group plc* [1989].

Conclude and identify possible remedies.

Chapter 14

Problem answer

1. Mortgagor's Rights–Clauses attempting to postpone ability to redeem.

Consider whether they render right to redeem illusory/imposed in a morally reprehensible manner.

- Key case law to analyse and apply includes *Fairclough v Swan Brewery Co Ltd* [1912]; *Knightsbridge Estates Trust Ltd v Byrne* [1939].
- Relevant points to consider include whether property is leasehold or freehold and the equality of bargaining power between the parties.

High interest rate

Consider whether oppressive/unconscionable.

- Key case law to analyse and apply includes *Multiservice Bookbinding Co Ltd v Marden* [1979]; *Cityland & Property (Holdings) Ltd v Dabrah* [1968]. Consider relevant legislation protecting consumers against unfair terms.
- Relevant points to consider include the equality of bargaining power between the parties; reason for purchase of pub; commercial and not residential property.

Option to purchase

Consider whether truly independent of mortgage transaction.

- Key case law to analyse and apply includes *Samuel v Jarrah Timber and Wood Paving Corporation Ltd* [1904]; *Reeve v Lisle* [1902]; *Jones v Morgan* [2001].
- Relevant points to consider include fact it was a separate agreement and 4% discount.

Outline answers

****

Collateral advantage re purchase of beer and ale

• Key case law to analyse and apply includes *Kreglinger v New Patagonia Meat & Cold Storage Co Ltd* [1914]; *Jones v Morgan* [2001].

• Key points to consider include fact only for duration of mortgage; equality of bargaining power between the parties; no apparent discounts apply.

2. Mortgagee's Rights

This requires detailed analysis of the ability for a mortgagee to repossess the property. Of particular importance will be the fact that Karl resides at the property. Consider the impact of Administration of Justice Act 1970/1973 and how far a court would be influenced by the fact that Karl is expecting to inherit a large sum of money when exercising its discretion under the Act.

Glossary

adverse possession a process by which title to land can be acquired through acts of possessing land of another (i) until such time as the real owner is statute barred from recovering the land (at which point his title to land will be extinguished) or, (ii) until such time as the adverse possessor is registered as owner

assignment a transfer of a proprietary interest (used, for example, in relation to a transfer of a lease or reversionary interest or in relation to the transfer of a benefit of a restrictive covenant)

beneficiary a person who holds a beneficial interest in property held by way of a trust

chattel a thing usually not fixed to the land and not regarded as forming part of the land (as opposed to a fixture)

commonhold a form of freehold estate applicable to blocks of flats where unit holders hold the freehold of their flat (unit) and a commonhold association, of which unit holders are members, holds the freehold of the common parts

conveyance the deed used to transfer the legal estate where title is unregistered

covenant a promise made by deed (either requiring someone to do something ie positive, or not to do something ie negative)

covenantee the person in whose favour a covenant is made and thus who has the benefit of a covenant and may enforce it if breached

covenantor the person from whom a covenant is extracted and thus who has the burden of the obligation

deed a document compliant with s 1 LP(MP)A 1989 and normally required to create a legal estate or interest in land

disposition a dealing with land (for example sale of a freehold estate)

dominant tenement the piece of land that is benefited by a proprietary right

easement a proprietary right exercised over one piece of land (the servient tenement) for the benefit of another piece of land (the dominant tenement); can be positive or negative in nature

equity of redemption the mortgagor's interest in the mortgaged property

estate a type of proprietary right entitling the holder to possess, use, and enjoy land for a period of time, be it unlimited (freehold) or fixed (leasehold) to the exclusion of others

estate contract a contract to grant an estate in land (includes options to purchase and rights of pre-emption)

fee simple absolute in possession the technical title for a freehold estate

fixture a thing that has become fixed to land so that it becomes part of the land (as opposed to a chattel)

freehold estate the largest of the two estates in land that have legal capacity; lasts indefinitely until such time as the owner dies without heirs

headlease the lease out of which the sub-lease has been granted

incorporeal hereditaments inheritable rights that are intangible and which benefit land

in gross where a right exists in gross, it is not for the benefit of a dominant piece of land but merely for the benefit of an individual (for example, *profits à prendre* can exist in gross, easements cannot)

injunction an equitable remedy that forbids someone from doing something (for example erecting a fence that would obstruct a right of way)

interest a type of proprietary right entitling the holder to use and enjoy land of another

inter vivos a disposition which takes place during the lifetime of the grantor (rather than by operation of his will upon his death)

Glossary

✳✳✳✳✳✳✳✳✳✳

joint tenancy a way of holding co-owned property, where co-owners are seen as a single legal entity holding the whole of the property as a single owner (contrast tenant in common). The right of survivorship operates between joint tenants

lease a leasehold estate (also known as 'tenancy')

leasehold estate the second largest of the estates in land that have legal capacity; has a fixed and certain maximum duration

licence permission given by a land owner (the licensor) to another (the licensee) to use his land

mortgage the grant of an interest in property as security for a loan

mortgagee the person to whom a mortgage is granted and who acquires an interest in the property of the mortgagor as security for money lent

mortgagor the person who creates the mortgage and grants an interest in his property to the mortgagee as security for a loan

negative equity where the value of a mortgaged property is worth less than the debt

notice (i) knowledge of an interest: actual (real knowledge); constructive (knowledge of things you could have found out about if you had made reasonable enquiries); imputed (knowledge acquired by an agent acting on your behalf); (ii) a type of entry that appears in the charges section of the register of title protecting certain interests in registered land

overreaching a procedure by which a purchaser of a legal estate can take that estate free from certain equitable interests, notably beneficial interests under a trust, provided purchase monies are paid to at least two trustees or a trust corporation

overriding interest an interest in registered land that binds third parties coming to the land without any need to be protected by being entered on to the register

personal right a right not exercised against the land itself (as opposed to a proprietary right) and (generally) can only be enforced against the person who gave it to you

prescription a method by which easements and profits can be acquired by evidence of long use

privity of contract the existence of a contractual relationship between the parties

privity of estate a direct relationship of landlord and tenant between the parties

profit à prendre a proprietary right that allows a person to go on the land of another and take something from that land, be it natural produce of the land or animals

proprietary right a right governing a person's ability to use and enjoy land that is potentially enforceable against third parties (as opposed to a personal right)

puisne mortgage a legal mortgage of unregistered land that is not secured by the deposit of title deeds. Usually a second or subsequent mortgage

purchaser when used in its technical sense, a person who acquires an estate or interest in land through the action of another, rather than automatically by operation of law

quasi easement a right exercised over, and for the benefit of, your own land which has the potential to develop into a proper easement should that land be divided into two plots that are separately owned and/or occupied

registered land land where title has been registered at the Land Registry

registered proprietor the person registered as owner of a legal estate in registered land

remainder an interest in land granted under a settlement which takes effect after some previous interest has expired

rentcharge similar to rent paid in respect of a lease but rather it relates to a freehold estate

restriction a type of entry that appears in the proprietorship section of the register of title limiting the way in which the registered proprietor can deal with the land

reversion the right remaining in a grantor after he has granted some interest to

Glossary

another that is shorter in duration to his own (for example landlord retains a reversionary interest upon granting a lease)

right of survivorship a process which occurs automatically upon the death of a joint tenant of co-owned property whereby his entitlement to the property extinguishes and the co-owned estate survives to the remaining joint tenants

servient tenement the piece of land that is burdened by a proprietary right

settlement a disposition of land which creates successive interests in that land

severance a procedure whereby a joint tenant becomes a tenant in common

specific performance an equitable remedy that requires someone to do something (for example perform a contract for the transfer of a freehold estate)

sub-let creation of a sub-lease, a lease granted by a landlord who is himself a tenant of another lease (the headlease)

tenancy in common a way of holding co-owned property where each co-owner holds a distinct, individual but as yet undivided

share in the property (contrast joint tenancy). The right of survivorship does not operate between tenants in common

tenure services provided by a tenant in return for holding land from his feudal lord

term of years absolute the technical title for a leasehold estate

title a person's proof of ownership of property

transfer the deed used to transfer the legal estate where title is registered

trust a way of holding property whereby legal title vests in the trustee(s) and the beneficial interest vests in the beneficiaries

trustee a person who holds legal title to property which is held by way of a trust

trust for sale a trust whereby the trustees have a duty to sell. Since TLATA 1996, now takes effect as a trust of land

trust of land a trust whereby trustees have a power to sell. Introduced by TLATA 1996. Any trust with land as trust property will be a trust of land

unregistered land land where title has not been registered at the Land Registry

Index

Index

Index

Index

****

Index

✱✱✱✱✱✱✱✱✱✱